Court Sense

Winning Basketball's Mental Game

John Giannini

Huma

Library of Congress Cataloging-in-Publication Data

Giannini, John, 1962-
  Court sense : winning basketball's mental game / John Giannini.
    p. cm.
  Includes index.
  ISBN-13: 978-0-7360-4423-3 (soft cover)
  ISBN-10: 0-7360-4423-X (soft cover)
  1. Basketball. 2. Basketball--Psychological aspects. I. Title.
  GV889.G53 2009
  796.323--dc22

                              2008026535

ISBN-10: 0-7360-4423-X
ISBN-13: 978-0-7360-4423-3

Developmental Editor: Leigh Keylock; **Assistant Editor:** Laura Podeschi; **Copyeditor:** Patrick Connolly; **Proofreader:** John Wentworth; **Indexer:** Betty Frizzéll; **Permission Manager:** Martha Gullo; **Graphic Designer:** Fred Starbird; **Graphic Artist:** Tara Welsch; **Cover Designer:** Keith Blomberg; **Photographer (cover):** © Greg Carroccio/Sideline Photos; **Photo Asset Manager:** Laura Fitch; **Photo Office Assistant:** Jason Allen; **Art Manager:** Kelly Hendren; **Associate Art Manager:** Alan L. Wilborn; **Illustrator:** Kelly Hendren; **Printer:** United Graphics

Human Kinetics books are available at special discounts for bulk purchase. Special editions or book excerpts can also be created to specification. For details, contact the Special Sales Manager at Human Kinetics.

Printed in the United States of America   10 9 8 7 6 5 4 3 2 1

Human Kinetics
Web site: www.HumanKinetics.com

United States: Human Kinetics
P.O. Box 5076
Champaign, IL 61825-5076
800-747-4457
e-mail: humank@hkusa.com

Canada: Human Kinetics
475 Devonshire Road Unit 100
Windsor, ON N8Y 2L5
800-465-7301 (in Canada only)
e-mail: info@hkcanada.com

Europe: Human Kinetics
107 Bradford Road
Stanningley
Leeds LS28 6AT, United Kingdom
+44 (0) 113 255 5665
e-mail: hk@hkeurope.com

Australia: Human Kinetics
57A Price Avenue
Lower Mitcham, South Australia 5062
08 8372 0999
e-mail: info@hkaustralia.com

New Zealand: Human Kinetics
Division of Sports Distributors NZ Ltd.
P.O. Box 300 226 Albany
North Shore City
Auckland
0064 9 448 1207
e-mail: info@humankinetics.co.nz

For Donna, Brianna, and Jamie—the best parts of my life.

CONTENTS

FOREWORD

It is hard to believe that I have spent more than 20 years in the coaching ranks, and so far it has been one heck of a ride. I have certainly been blessed throughout my career to have been part of four terrific programs, coaching many great players and having the opportunity to be a positive influence on so many young people.

I have been fortunate to work alongside two legends and Hall of Famers in the coaching profession, Morgan Wootten and Mike Krzyzewski. They had a powerful impact and influence on the coach I am today.

Morgan gave me my start in the coaching ranks. After I graduated from George Washington University, he hired me at my alma mater, DeMatha High School, as the junior varsity head coach and varsity assistant. How lucky I was to have had the opportunity to work side by side with him. First as my coach in high school, and then as my mentor along the sidelines, he showed me the importance and value of building relationships with the players you coach. It is something that has stuck with me throughout my years as a head coach. He also taught me the importance of discipline, priorities, fundamentals, teamwork, and enthusiasm in achieving consistently high-level success.

Although I had no prior collegiate coaching experience, Mike Krzyzewski took the chance and hired me at Duke University. While in Durham, North Carolina, we experienced unprecedented success as a coaching staff, winning two national championships and making six Final Four appearances. I had the opportunity to recruit and coach some of the greatest names in the collegiate ranks. A tough disciplinarian, Mike, like Morgan, was passionate and caring about the young men he coached. I continued to learn about building relationships, and I also learned more about the mental components of coaching and the game of basketball.

I will be forever grateful to the University of Delaware for giving me my first head coaching job. I couldn't have asked for a better situation after I left Duke than I had in Newark, Delaware. I had support at every level as we built a great program in the America East Conference.

The University of Notre Dame has been the place my family and I have called home since July of 2000. I am fortunate to coach in arguably the toughest conference in the country, the Big East, and have had the opportunity to recruit and coach many special young men here. Every night, my players and I are tested on the court. As I like to point out to my counterparts, there is no "easy game" in our league. It is, however, a challenge my players and I thrive on. We pride ourselves on working together as a team to meet these challenges. At the same time, I continue to witness how each individual player's work ethic, toughness, and determination can affect the team as a whole.

When La Salle University coach John Giannini explained to me that he had written a book covering all of the player and team "difference-making" qualities that I have discovered during my basketball career, I was very interested. When I was the head coach at Delaware, we had great games against John's teams at the University of Maine. His teams demonstrated the mental toughness and focused effort this book encourages. What intrigued me even more is that John said he wrote the book not only for coaches but also for players who are serious about making themselves as good as they can be. And what pleased me about the work is that it is so readable and practical. John might be a PhD, but he knows how to communicate even complex concepts in a very understandable way.

Court Sense is a good title because the phrase captures all the mental and emotional aspects that truly matter in individual and team performance. The book also addresses off-court influences and behaviors, plus the countless distractions that can sidetrack a player's career or an entire basketball program.

Few are as fortunate as I have been to learn alongside two of the best basketball coaches ever. But great educational opportunities about the game are also available through guys such as John and his outstanding book. Take the time to read it, and see just how much smarter and sharper you will be next season.

Mike Brey
Men's Head Basketball Coach, Notre Dame

ACKNOWLEDGMENTS

I am grateful to Ted Miller of Human Kinetics; he gave me the opportunity to write this book and helped me through the process with great patience. Ted is the main reason I was able to complete this book.

Margie Martin and Jane Bartram were also an enormous help in producing the manuscript. Their patience, commitment, and friendship are greatly valued.

I am deeply appreciative of the contributions made by Mike Brey, Bo Ryan, Steve Donahue, John Beilein, Sean Miller, Joanne P. McCallie, Oliver Purnell, Tubby Smith, Jay Wright, Sharon Versyp, Jamie Dixon, Tom Crean, and Tony Bennett. The ideas they share in the book will be of great help to readers.

My contribution to this book would not be possible without the influence of my mentors in sport psychology, Dan Gould and Bob Weinberg. They have given me the perspective to write this book.

There are far more good coaches than there are coaching jobs. I am grateful to the people who have afforded me these rare opportunities to lead and learn. I want to thank President Brother Michael McGinniss and Dr. Tom Brennan at LaSalle University, Patrick Nero and Dr. Sue Tyler at the University of Maine, and Joy Reign, Ted Kershner, and President Herman James at Rowan University.

I must thank the outstanding coaches I have worked with who have taught me so much. I am forever grateful for the learning opportunities Lou Henson, Tom Cooper, and Tommy Newman gave me. As a young coach I was mentored by Mark Coomes and Dennis Helms, and they, along with David Pauley, continue to be of great help. I deeply appreciate the support of my current staff of Walt Fuller, Horace "Pappy" Owens, and Harris Adler. I have also learned a great deal from working with Ashley Howard, Steve Seymour, Peter Gash, Saul Frankel, Ryan Tozer, Michael Burden, Ed Jones, Michael Mennenga, Andy Bedard, Will Bailey, Jon Hayes, Randy Lee, Dave Lafferty, Bob Pedrick, Chris Martin, Ben Lynch, Art DiPatri, Gary Ruban, and Nick DiCicco. Special thanks go to Ted Woodward and Joe Cassidy, who made great contributions to the ideas in this book as well as to my career.

Most important, I want to thank my players. A few are mentioned in this book to illustrate certain points, but so many more allowed me to try ideas, learn, and have success. I wish I could thank you all by name, but space prohibits a lengthy list here. Ultimately, basketball success is not found on the sidelines but on the court from the hearts and efforts of players. I have never forgotten that and appreciate all of you more than you realize.

PART I

Fundamentals for a Winning Focus

Much of the appeal of basketball is that it permits no shortcuts but also allows for individual shortcomings. Excelling in the sport requires some real basic stuff: dedication, effort, discipline, and unselfishness. Most of us like being around people who have such qualities. But we also appreciate that the game is team oriented and can be played beautifully even when the individual skills of each team member are lacking in some respect. It is the blending of those teammates' respective strengths into a smooth-functioning unit that makes basketball so special. And that can happen in a local rec league facility, on a nearby playground, at a high school gym, or in an NBA arena.

But it doesn't happen by chance. First, individual athletes must ascertain exactly what they bring to the table—er, the court. When doing so, players must be sure to match self-perceptions with reality, which, unfortunately, many otherwise promising players fail to do. Next, players need to direct their energy toward achieving as much as possible with their abilities, both individually and as part of a group. Each player's own aspirations must fit well within his role on the team and within the goals of the team. That's a tall order, and many athletes come up short because they try to take a shortcut.

Part I of *Court Sense* was written to help players and coaches navigate the challenging prerequisites for basketball success. You'll soon see that though I have a PhD in sport psychology, I don't pretend to have any magical mental training tools to make you the next Michael Jordan or Pat Summitt. I've played and coached the game too long to have such delusions. Instead, you'll find very practical suggestions and guidelines that are based mostly on experience and common sense—and that are also supported by research, when applicable. You will, I hope, find this information useful.

CHAPTER

1

Evaluation of Abilities

"Even the greatest players have areas for improvement," stated Naismith Hall of Fame coach Jack Ramsay. Michael Jordan, one of the best players of all time, is proof of this statement.

Recall that Michael Jordan was the third—not the first—selection in the 1984 NBA draft. Though in hindsight it's easy to criticize Houston (who took Hakeem Olajuwon) and Portland (who took Sam Bowie) for bypassing such a spectacular athlete, it is also true that at that point in his career Michael lacked the full array of skills needed to be an all-time great.

As a rookie, Michael's three-point shooting was inconsistent, and his mid-range jumper was only average. Also, he had yet to gain the mass and strength needed in his chest, shoulders, and arms in order to hold defensive position, post up effectively, and finish plays with contact against older, stronger NBA veterans. To his credit, he recognized those shortcomings, and he dedicated many hours on the court and in the weight room to convert those liabilities into assets.

When asked if he was amazed by Michael's phenomenal success, former North Carolina teammate and NBA great James Worthy said that he was surprised only by the tremendous shooter Michael had become. Other NBA players and coaches, who recalled a less muscular Jordan, marveled at his upper-body development and how it allowed him to become a strong post-up player, physical All-NBA defender, and master of "old school" three-point plays.

Like Michael, every player benefits from a mature and objective evaluation of strengths and weaknesses. This helps identify what to work on, defines playing roles based on individual strengths, and moves a player and team closer to full potential.

Daniel Lippitt/AFP/Getty Images

After not making the cut for the Laney High School (Wilmington, NC) varsity team as a sophomore, Michael Jordan developed his basketball skills, physical conditioning, and competitive spirit to become one of the best players of all time.

More recently, we've witnessed transformations of players such as Deron Williams, Dwight Howard, and Brandon Roy as they've expanded and elevated their skill sets. Though all three players already possessed abilities at an all-star level, they sought to improve their games in ways that would most benefit their teams and make them better, more well-rounded players.

You may find it strange that a book focusing on the mental aspects of basketball would begin by emphasizing the assessment and development of physical abilities. But the development of those abilities is often hindered by a player's own overestimation or underestimation of his actual talent. That's just one example of how the mental and physical facets of the game are inseparable.

The first step in accurate self-evaluation and improvement is adopting a humble attitude. Recently, the University of Wisconsin and Washington State University have been among the best basketball programs in the nation. It wasn't always that way. Both programs struggled in tough conferences for years until Coach Dick Bennett began remarkable turnarounds at both schools. He learned that "you can't reach your full potential until you have been humbled." In other words, until a player realizes that he has weaknesses and that there are better players out there, the player will never work as hard as he can to improve. If a player lacks humility—and if overconfidence blinds a player to what he has to work on—then that player will underachieve. If Michael Jordan could see the need to become stronger, a better shooter, and a better passer, then all young players should be able to find things to work on.

BASKETBALL SKILLS

The two physical components required in a basketball player are skill and athleticism. The combination of these two factors dictates the physical potential of a player. The key for today's player—whether highly athletic or not—is to be motivated to learn, practice, and develop skills such as shooting, ballhandling, and post play. Players who gain these skills can often overcome deficits in athleticism.

Take the 2002 World Basketball Championships, for example. The team representing the United States was composed of NBA stars, widely considered to be the best players in the world. Yet that team finished sixth in the competition. Yugoslavia, Argentina, and Germany claimed the first three spots, not because of their physical talent, but because of their skillful play and teamwork. The three teams that emphasized shooting, ballhandling, passing, and teamwork came out on top in the final standings—ahead of a U.S. team that was very athletic but less skilled.

This result not only gave the United States a greater appreciation for international basketball, but it also served as a wake-up call. The lesson was apparent: Even the most abundant physical tools can't overcome a shortage of basketball skills and execution on the court. And yet the United States was reminded of this again in the 2004 Olympics, as its marvelously athletic men's team managed to finish only third to champion Argentina and runner-up Italy.

The outcomes of such competitions are reminders for players and coaches that the game is about much more than running, jumping, and quickness. Those physical abilities are an advantage, but only when combined with skills specific to the game. Therefore, a player's first step toward fulfilling his basketball potential is an accurate evaluation of skill level in each of these areas:

- Shooting
- Inside scoring
- Ballhandling
- Passing
- Rebounding
- Defense

Players should be encouraged to ask critical questions about their skill levels and their level of productivity. Determining whether a player consistently executes fundamentals or reaches statistical performance standards will make that player's strengths and weaknesses clear. Chapter 2 discusses how to use this information to set personal goals for improvement.

Shooting

Putting the ball in the basket is the game's most basic fundamental. Through the years, many great athletes have been cut or relegated to the bench because they lacked essential shooting skills. Good coaches scout their opponents and will tell defenders to "help off" and not guard a poor shooter on the perimeter. All of a sudden, a team with a poor shooter on the perimeter is at a disadvantage, playing four on five offensively. If a player cannot make open jump shots, his defender will help off and make it much more difficult for teammates to drive or post. His defender can clog up the lane so other defenders do not have to help as much; this enables those defenders to stay with and stop the good shooters on the team. Thus, when a player is able to shoot the ball well, this not only helps that player score more, it also helps his teammates score more easily. That is why teams with multiple good shooters have beaten bigger, more athletic teams in recent NCAA tournaments. In 2008, Davidson, Drake, and Butler were teams that had great seasons largely because of outstanding shooting.

Every player won't be a great shooter, but each player should be able to regularly make open mid-range jump shots in order to contribute to the team's offensive attack. Individual players should evaluate their shooting ability based on the following objective and subjective standards:

- A free-throw percentage of 70 percent or higher
- A three-point shooting percentage of approximately 40 percent or higher
- An overall field-goal percentage of approximately 45 percent or higher for guards and 50 percent or higher for post players
- The ability to shoot off screens
- The ability to shoot off the dribble

Shooting is extremely difficult to improve without proper form and technique. As a seventh-grade player, I attended the summer camp of legendary DePaul University coach Ray Meyer. He taught players a mental checklist to help ensure proper shooting form. While players were learning to shoot, Coach Meyer had them practice one-handed shots close to the basket. He had players go through the following mental checklist before and after each shot. Before the shot, the player needed to make sure of these key points:

- The feet and shoulders are square to the basket.
- The ball is off the palm, resting on the pads of the hand and the fingers.
- The ball is over the shooting eye.
- The elbow is in.

- The shooting arm is shaped like a backward "L" and not a "V."
- The guide hand is on the side of the ball, not in front or in back (when shooting with two hands).

After the shot, the player needed to make sure of these key points:

- The feet and shoulders are still square to the basket.
- The legs and feet should be aligned toward the basket, finishing on the toes.
- The thumb of the guide hand is pointed backward (if shooting with two hands).
- The follow-through is held with the wrist snapped down.

Slowing down and meticulously going through a mental checklist before and after each shot can help ensure that the player is learning proper form. I have witnessed NBA-level players slowly shooting one-hand shots from close range and holding their follow-through to maintain proper shooting habits. Mentally repeating and then executing each key will lead to outstanding shooting fundamentals. When players are self-evaluating their shooting form, they may also find it helpful to have a coach observe them or to use videotape. The player and the coach should look for specific flaws before and after the shot that can be addressed through form shooting and practice.

After learning and practicing shooting form, a player can start evaluating his shooting accuracy. To do this, he can practice taking and tracking success on mid-range shots, three-point shots, and free throws. The player should use sets of 50 or 100 shots to obtain shooting percentages from different locations on the court. Keep in mind that shooting percentages in games will be 10 to 20 percent lower than the percentages for practice shots that are done repeatedly and with little pressure. For example, if a player wants to be an 80-percent free-throw shooter in games, he needs to consistently make 9 of 10 or 10 of 10 in practice sets.

Inside Scoring

Offenses are designed to get high-percentage shots, and most good players can score around the basket. This is accomplished either by posting up like Carlos Boozer or by driving to the basket like Dwyane Wade. Players who are effective at these skills are referred to as "finishers" and have the following qualities:

- Post moves that result in consistent baskets and that regularly draw fouls on the defender
- Moves (e.g., pump fakes, spins) and shots (e.g., jump hooks, and for high-level players, "floaters") that allow the player to score against good shot blockers

- The strength to absorb physical contact while shooting and still stay in balance
- The strength to get and keep deep low-post position
- A high field-goal percentage in the post area (approximately 60 percent)
- The ability to shoot with either hand when near the basket

Ballhandling

Dribbling, along with shooting and passing, is one of the three basic skills a player executes with the ball. Good ball handlers have the ability to do the following:

- Dribble well with either hand.
- Change directions while dribbling (e.g., using crossover, "inside-out" [or fake crossover], between-the-legs, and behind-the-back dribbles).
- Change speeds with the ball.
- See the court and see open teammates while handling the ball.
- Push the ball up the court quickly in transition, using few dribbles.
- Bring the ball up the court against quick, aggressive defensive pressure.
- Penetrate past defenders to create offensive advantages.

One guideline commonly used to assess a guard's ballhandling skills is assist-to-turnover ratio. A very good guard should have an assist-to-turnover ratio of 2 to 1 or better. The best guards are closer to 3 to 1.

Passing

Passing is the most important offensive skill because it often leads to high-percentage shots, good team chemistry, and high morale. Unlike shooting and ballhandling, passing is difficult to work on alone. Passing skills are best developed and refined in practice drills involving small groups and in team scrimmages.

A coach can work with players on some techniques, but players will do well to follow two simple rules of passing. One, good passers pass the ball to open teammates when they are open. This rule sounds so simple, yet few players do it consistently. Too often, open players fail to get the ball. Many passes are forced when the passer delivers the ball to a teammate who is tightly covered. The rule for players is simple: If you do not have an immediate shot or an opportunity to penetrate, you should pass the ball to the first open teammate immediately. Don't hesitate. Against a good defensive team, the opportunity won't last long.

One of the more enjoyable teams to watch in the history of the game was the New York Knicks during the golden age of that franchise (1969 to 1973) in which they won two NBA titles. What basketball purists recall most vividly about that team is not any particular individual's play, but how unselfishly and effectively the players performed as a unit. Walt Frazier, Bill Bradley, Dave DeBusschere, and Willis Reed made up the core of that squad, and it was pure pleasure to watch them move the ball on offense. They seemingly hit every open teammate the split second he freed himself from his defender.

Good passers may make some spectacular passes, but most good passes are very simple ones that result in many assists and few turnovers. Thus, the second rule of passing is to pass with two hands, two feet, and two eyes. Passing with two eyes means pivoting into a triple-threat position and looking up the court or at the basket each time the ball is caught. This is called a triple-threat position because it allows a player to shoot, drive, or pass without first having to realign the body. From this position, a player can see the court and spot open teammates.

The player should use a jump stop (i.e., landing on both feet simultaneously) to pass or shoot at the end of all dribble drives. The jump stop helps the player avoid charging as well as jumping in the air with nowhere to go. This results in fewer turnovers and more assists.

Using two hands means not throwing one-handed passes. At times, a quick one-handed pass is advantageous, but as a rule, this is to be avoided. One-handed passing is a bad habit that leads to less precise passes and more turnovers.

A player must continually evaluate himself on this skill in competition. Being a good, consistent passer requires unselfishness, intelligence, and discipline. These qualities involve doing the following:

- Passing to open teammates as soon as they are open
- Passing off jump stops to reduce forced passes, travels, and charges
- Passing with two hands
- Using the triple-threat position
- Having a high assist-to-turnover ratio (at least 1:1 for post players and forwards; at least 1.5:1 for guards but preferably 2:1 or higher)

One final point on passing: Every pass needs a receiver who is intent on and capable of catching the ball. Passers need to know what type of passes each teammate can handle. They must also know where (i.e., what location on the court) they can make use of those passes. For example, it would be unwise to pass the ball to a big man who is an awkward ball handler in the open court or to throw a lob pass to a smaller player against a bigger defender. The passer is responsible for knowing these things and for making decisions accordingly, just as the receiver is responsible for coming to the ball and gaining possession of it.

Rebounding

The skill of rebounding is one of the most important factors in helping a team win a basketball game. Rebounding determines which team has the most chances to score. A player who is an outstanding rebounder (generally 10 or more a game) will almost always earn a key role on a team.

The most important quality for a good rebounder is a strong desire to get to the ball. For example, the odds are 1 in 10 that any specific player in a game will get a given rebound. Thus, to get 10 rebounds, a player should have to go after about 100 missed shots. This leads to two key points. First, a good rebounder never drifts on the perimeter when a shot is taken. The good rebounder attacks the glass—or "crashes"—on every shot. The point is simple: A player cannot get rebounds if he does not go for them. Crashing the boards is a habit of desire. The second point is that the best rebounders do not get only 10 percent (their share) of rebounds. They get more than their share through extreme aggressiveness. A good rebounder does the following:

- Crashes for offensive rebounds.
- Boxes out or "checks" out opponents to be a good defensive rebounder.
- Pursues the ball with great tenacity.
- Does not stop moving when an opponent executes a "box-out" (instead, the player spins or cuts around to get inside position).
- Averages a high number of rebounds per game—8 to 10 rebounds per game for a post player, 6 to 10 for wing players, and 4 to 8 for guards, depending on their size. Anyone averaging over 10 rebounds per game against good competition is an outstanding rebounder.

Defense

A player can improve individual defense simply by working on defensive stance and slides and playing against a tough, competitive one-on-one partner. Like passing, true defensive ability is best evaluated in actual game conditions. Coaches look for players who can do the following:

- Contain dribble penetration. Good defensive players can keep all but the very quickest opponents in front of them.
- Pressure the opponent with the ball, guarding him tightly to make shooting impossible and to make passing and dribbling difficult. The ability to pressure *and* contain opponents separates great defenders from good ones who can only contain (bad defenders do neither).
- Contest every shot without fouling. A good defensive player contains the dribble and then contests each shot with a vertical hand in the

face. Vertical means the arm and hand are straight up and not swinging at the shot. Good defenders do not swing or reach a lot, which also means good defenders do not foul often. They play defense with their foot quickness before using their hands, and they put forth the effort to contest every shot.

- Be a good "help" defender. Good defenders always see the ball and their man when their man does not have the ball. They are ready to leave their man if needed to help stop an easy basket. Easy baskets come from penetration, post play, backdoor passes, and lob passes.

When a good defender sees the ball getting close to the basket for an easy shot, he helps and tries to prevent the shot (by taking a charge or getting a steal) or contest the shot. Then, someone must also "help the helper" by rotating to pick up the opponent left open by the helping teammate. Finally, players must quickly recover back to their original man after helping or rotating.

Coaches have many different philosophies on defensive positioning, help, rotation, and recovery. Most of these philosophies are effective if they are executed well. A player must understand his coach's philosophy on how to play defense off the ball; the player should work on this in every game played year-round in order to build the right habits.

The common teaching point for all man-to-man defenses is a constant awareness of both ball and man (i.e., the person you are defending). Outstanding defenders do this easily. They also do the following:

- Hold opponents below individual scoring averages.
- Pressure opponents into mistakes.
- Get through screens.
- Disrupt offensive plays with steals, charges, and deflections (i.e., "make plays" defensively).

Three of the greatest defenders of all time—center Bill Russell, small forward Scottie Pippen, and two-guard Dennis Johnson—weren't exactly the prototypes for their positions. But what they might have lacked physically they more than made up for on the defensive end with their skills and efforts. None of the three is remembered as an offensive force. But each of them would simply lock up his opponent—almost always the opposition's best offensive player—game after game, season after season, even if that meant guarding someone taller, stronger, or quicker than himself. Little wonder that this trio of defensive greats won a combined 20 NBA titles during their pro careers—further proof that champions are made on the defensive end of the court.

Player Assets

Bo Ryan—University of Wisconsin

When I enlisted in the Army, I was put in the military police. Before we started shooting with a .45 pistol, the instructor asked how many of us were hunters and had fired guns before. Everybody raised a hand but me; I had never held a gun in my hand until the Army. Yet, by the end of the training period, I won the trophy for the best score in shooting. It wasn't even close. The instructor explained that my lack of experience might have actually been a plus. He said he liked to work with novices who had never fired a gun because he could show them right from scratch how to do it properly, and they hadn't already formed bad habits or misconceptions.

In 1997, I recruited a player, Merrill Brunson, from the hills of Richland Center, Wisconsin. In some ways, Merrill's basketball inexperience reminded me of my lack of shooting experience before I joined the military. He had never seen a college basketball game in person and had never played in an AAU game. He played multiple sports in high school and was a good athlete, but he hadn't been immersed in basketball from an early age as so many kids are now. So when he came to us, he listened intently and soaked everything up. By the time he was a junior, he was Division III Player of the Year. That's why I will always say this: The ability and willingness to listen are some of the greatest qualities a player can have.

Evaluating players' ability isn't a science, but there are some guidelines that I've found to be beneficial in assessing potential recruits. For big men, the feet and hands are most important. And a shorter player who has a big wingspan, good hands, and agile footwork is better than a player who might be a few inches taller but lacks those athletic attributes. With perimeter players, I look at how well they see the floor and protect the ball.

Obviously, quickness is hard to teach, and a quicker player has an advantage over a slower opponent. You can improve reaction skills, but only so much.

Young players should work on passing and catching skills because they never know what position their physical development will dictate they play in the future. Joakim Noah is a great example. He is a pretty good passer for his size because at one time, before he had a growth spurt, he was actually a point guard. Also, aspiring players should try to develop good eye-hand coordination. Learning how to juggle and playing baseball, football, or soccer to develop the hands and feet are wise activities. I think kids specialize in one sport too soon, and it hurts them. I've told my big guys that if they had just played baseball when they were younger, they'd have better hands.

In terms of conditioning, I don't want players doing too much powerlifting too soon. They simply need to take care of their bodies and make sure they get the proper nutrition to train and perform to their maximum.

I also really want to see that players enjoy playing the game. I'd much rather have a squad of young men who are passionate about winning than a bunch of guys who are more interested in making great plays every four or five possessions. Point guards need to demonstrate leadership ability, a knack for inspiring teammates to play better.

Hustling for loose balls, running the floor on both offense and defense, wanting the ball at the end of the game, and being able to do something positive with it are additional intangibles that rate highly with me. I believe the most basic question a young player needs to ask himself is this: "Am I playing because I want to play, or because I feel I have to in order to please someone else?" Basketball requires a great amount of time and effort, and that kind of investment can be made only with the right mental approach. That's essential for getting through the long, tough practice sessions, off-season workouts, losses and disappointments, and injuries that can occur.

Looking at film from both practice drills and games gives players a good idea of what areas need improvement. When we point out those weaknesses, we aren't seeking to tear down a player or undermine his confidence; rather, we're giving him an objective assessment of where he's lacking. You can be sure opponents have identified those things in their scouting reports, and there's no hiding such deficiencies on the floor, so it's best to address them and correct them before they hurt the team in a game. And competitive players want to know what they can do better. Although they might not like the criticism, they understand that it's being presented not to discourage them, but rather to allow them to grasp what they need to work on and inspire them to do so.

Some guys, because of their size or speed, can dominate at the high school level, but when they get to college they find out the competition is often bigger and faster. So they can't always leave their feet on defense to block shots, play an opponent from behind, or muscle or outpace their opponents to the basket. That's when they realize the need to move their feet, guard their man honestly and aggressively, and use change of direction and crossover moves.

One of our former players, Devin Harris, really worked to develop his body and skills. He had played both basketball and volleyball in high school and was a very good athlete. But he needed to get stronger to compete in the Big Ten, and he also needed to improve his ballhandling. He did both, gaining a good amount of lean muscle mass and improving his hesitation, head and shoulder fakes, countermoves, and use of his off-hand. He also got better in the post, both offensively and defensively, where he learned to use his quickness to an advantage against bigger, bulkier opponents. Devin was one of those special athletes who could have simply tried to get by with his innate physical gifts, but he was eager to learn and improve. Not surprisingly, his motivation and improvement were noted by pro scouts, and he was scooped up quickly with the fifth overall pick in the 2004 NBA draft.

PHYSICAL TOOLS

Commitment and skill are critical for reaching one's basketball potential. However, players must also realistically assess how their size and athleticism compare to the competition. Size, strength, and athleticism are often the difference between making and not making the step up from high school to college and from college to professional basketball.

Coaches and scouts carefully analyze a player's physical tools when trying to gauge that player's potential upside. This includes size (height and length), strength (muscularity and body thickness), and athleticism (power, speed, flexibility, jumping ability, and, most of all, quickness). Very few players are superior in all three categories, and when they are, they are usually great players. LeBron James and Dwyane Wade are two such unique athletes.

Most highly successful players are above average in two of the three physical areas. They may be big and strong or strong and athletic or big and athletic. An example of a big and strong NBA player is Ben Wallace. Players who are both athletic and big for their positions include Antawn Jamison, Kevin Garnett, and Tracy McGrady. Examples of strong and athletic players include Paul Pierce, Jason Kidd, and Amare Stoudemire.

These physical tools are essential to excel at the highest levels of the sport, but talent alone does not make a winning player. Basketball gyms around the world are filled with superb athletes who don't know how to play the game correctly, outstanding players with off-the-court problems that prevent them from playing at a high level, and great talents who never work hard enough to reach their potential.

The challenge for most players with clear physical advantages is not to rely solely on their size, strength, or athleticism. These advantages can give a player an edge, but for the player to have great competitive success, those physical advantages must be combined with a high level of skill and mental toughness.

Too often, players with physical advantages depend on "outquicking" or outjumping their opponents. When they reach a level with players of similar size, strength, and athleticism, they find they do not have the fundamental skills or mental edge to succeed.

A player who lacks physical superiority in a couple of areas will find it more difficult to succeed, but not impossible. That's why players must consistently evaluate their abilities before they can realistically set goals for their basketball future.

For example, the 2001 Philadelphia 76ers had a trio of small guards in Allen Iverson, Eric Snow, and Speedy Claxton who helped lead the team to the NBA finals. Only Snow would be considered strong by NBA standards. However, they all have one extraordinary asset—blinding quickness. Because of that "burst ability," they are able to penetrate against almost any defender and attack the basket or dish the ball to a teammate. This can be called the "most" quality—whenever a player has the most size (e.g., Yao Ming) or the most quickness on the court, the player can almost always help his team win.

As mentioned before, the other way to succeed with fewer physical assets is to develop extraordinary skills. Mike Bibby, Andrew Bogut, Dirk Nowitzki, and Peja Stojakovic are just some of the NBA players who made it in the league because of their passing, shooting, and overall court sense.

In the late 1980s, three of the best players in college basketball were not big, strong, or overly athletic. These players were Steve Kerr (Arizona), Jeff Lebo (North Carolina), and Jay Burson (Ohio State). All three players were often the smallest, least athletic-looking players on the court. However, they were great shooters and ball handlers, very tough-minded, and exceptionally knowledgeable about how to play the game. Steve Nash earned the 2005 NBA Most Valuable Player Award by developing the exact

Andrew D. Bernstein/NBAE/Getty Images

Steve Nash proves that great effort and skill development through countless hours of practice can make up for deficits in size and athleticism.

same skill set. In fact, Nash is well aware of his physical limitations and how he must overcome them with high levels of skill, conditioning, and determination. He said, "If everyone worked as hard as me, I would not have a job in the NBA." Clearly, few put in as much effort as this perennial all-star.

The point is, any player who is not especially gifted in terms of size, quickness, and strength might be at a disadvantage, but that deficit can be overcome with superior skill development and a winning mental approach. This requires great commitment and many hours of practice. Also, although a player cannot control how big he is, he can improve his strength, speed, jumping ability, and quickness. If a player is below average in one of these areas, a commitment to strength training, plyometrics, and conditioning can produce the improvement needed. In addition, a player can even the playing field—or get an edge—versus physically superior opponents through effective training of peripheral vision, coordination, reaction time, and first-step quickness.

The ways that players can enhance their physical tools and basketball skills are almost limitless. But first, an athlete's strengths and deficiencies need to be accurately gauged.

SELF-EVALUATION OF SKILLS

Players are sometimes reluctant to partake in tests, perhaps thinking that the results might cast them in less favorable light. Therefore, the best method is to use an objective assessment tool that allows players to self-test and examine the results separate from teammates and competitors.

The player self-evaluation form (pages 18-21) can be used to focus on each of the areas that have been discussed. Players should be encouraged to reevaluate themselves before and after each season.

An effective method is to have the player and the coach complete an identical evaluation form and then meet to compare the two. This process can help make sure that differences between player and coach are discussed in a constructive and meaningful way.

A team stat sheet (see table 1.1) can be used in conjunction with player evaluations to provide supporting information. A simple system of symbols (stars for superior performance and circles for poor performance) helps players focus on strengths and weaknesses. Players are sometimes unrealistic about their skill and production levels. This seems to be particularly true regarding the three-pointer, a popular shot that most players like to take. Players with low shooting percentages, poor assist-to-turnover ratios, or poor rebounding statistics should be aware of the statistical facts. These players should work to improve, or they should accept a more limited team role. This same system can be used to track the statistics from each game and for practices.

Table 1.1   Team Stat Sheet

Player	Min	FG	3PT	FT	Off	Reb	Ast	TO	Stl	Blk	PF	Pts
1	27	3-5	0-0	(3-6)	2	8 ★	(0)	1 ★	(0)	0	0	9
2	31	2-5	2-3 ★	2-2 ★	1	(3)	(1)	(6)	3 ★	0	3	12
3	32	3-5	0-0	(6-10)	0	(2)	8 ★	2	(0)	0	4	12
4	33	2-7	2-6	1-2	0	(2)	(1)	2	(0)	0	3	11
5	38	11-20	6-10 ★	8-8 ★	1	7 ★	(1)	3	6 ★	1	1	48
6	21	(1-5)	1-4	2-2 ★	0	(0)	(0)	0 ★	(0)	0	3	7
7	16	2-3 ★	0-0	8-9 ★	1	5	0	2	0	1	1	12
8	2	0-0	0-0	0-0	0	0	0	(1)	0	0	1	0
Totals	**200**	**24-50**	**11-23**	**30-39**	**5**	**27**	**11**	**17**	**9**	**2**	**16**	**111**

Evaluating team statistics in key areas is also beneficial. For example, the 2003 University of Maine team finished with a 14-16 record despite having one of the best field-goal percentages in the country. The team also had a very good defensive field-goal percentage. However, the squad had one of the worst turnover rates in the country and a poor free-throw percentage as a team. These weaknesses contributed to many close losses. With a renewed commitment to improving on turnovers and free-throw shooting, the 2004 team finished with a 20-10 record with almost all the same players. This illustrates how the realistic evaluation of weaknesses can lead to great improvement.

Finally, a coach should have managers and assistants record statistics during practices. The players' performance should be constantly evaluated throughout practice (e.g., stopping to give each player current rebounding or turnover totals during water breaks) and after practice. Research on group performance shows that individuals tend to slack off when they think they are not being evaluated. Common sense suggests that individuals are likely to exert more effort when they believe someone is keeping tabs on their work. Evaluating performance through practice and game statistics is helpful in avoiding the natural "coasting" or "going through the motions" that many players can slip into.

PLAYER SELF-EVALUATION FORM

Ratings: Rate yourself relative to the opponents you will compete against, especially at your position. Base your rating on current and actual play, not on your potential or what you think you can do. Use the following scale:

1	2	3	4	5
Poor	Below average	Average	Above average	Outstanding

Keys for improvement: Many options are provided. Circle or highlight the keys that you think would help you the most. Each evaluation category also has room for your own thoughts for improvement next to the "Other keys" label. Finally, you may also highlight the general areas in which you think it is most critical for you to improve. For example, you might highlight athleticism, shooting, and defense. Younger players should focus on all the areas, whereas more experienced players may have fewer areas for emphasis.

Commitment (time spent on skill and physical development)

Rating: _____

Keys for improvement: Consult with a coach to develop a skill development program; consult with a coach to develop a physical development program; spend more time practicing individual skills; spend more time training to develop strength; spend more time training to develop speed, quickness, and jumping ability; avoid harmful behavior (e.g., alcohol or drug use, not getting sufficient rest).

Other keys: _____

Size (height and width or body thickness)

Rating: _____

Unfortunately, height, length, and width are largely predetermined physical features. Body thickness can be improved by improving strength (the next self-evaluation category).

Strength

Rating: _____

Keys for improvement: Consult with a coach to develop a strength training program; spend more time developing upper-body strength; spend more time developing lower-body strength; gain muscular weight.

Other keys: _____

From J. Giannini, 2009, *Court sense: Winning basketball's mental game* (Champaign, IL: Human Kinetics).

Athleticism (includes quickness, speed, and jumping ability)

Rating: _____

Keys for improvement: Consult with a coach to develop a speed and explosiveness training program; spend more time developing lateral quickness; spend more time developing flexibility; spend more time developing speed and sprinting ability; spend more time developing jumping ability; reduce body fat or weight; spend more time maintaining current programs.

Other keys: _____

Note: Improving strength and athleticism will help all of the following skills.

Shooting Ability (includes all perimeter shots)

Rating: _____

Keys for improvement: Consult with a coach about learning, improving, or changing basic fundamentals of shooting form; consult with a coach to develop a productive shooting routine; spend more time developing a consistent three-point shot; spend more time developing extended three-point range; spend more time developing a mid-range (15 to 17 foot) shot; spend more time developing shooting ability off the dribble; spend more time developing shooting ability off screens; spend more time developing free-throw shooting; put more focus on taking better shots in competition; spend more time maintaining current programs.

Other keys: _____

Inside Scoring (includes all inside shots near the basket area)

Rating: _____

Keys for improvement: Consult with a coach to choose a series of post moves; spend more time developing a series of post moves; spend more time developing the ability to shoot inside shots and layups with weaker hand; put more focus on posting up deeper and stronger in competition; put more focus on using quickness and quick moves to get around defenders; put more focus on using size or pump fakes and jump hooks to score over post defenders; spend more time playing one on one in the post; spend more time maintaining current programs.

Other keys: _____

(continued)

From J. Giannini, 2009, *Court sense: Winning basketball's mental game* (Champaign, IL: Human Kinetics).

Ballhandling

Rating: _____

Keys for improvement: Consult with a coach regarding a program for ball-handling improvement; spend more time using weaker hand; spend more time working on change-of-direction moves (e.g., crossover, between legs, spin, behind back); spend more time working on advanced moves that include change of speed along with combinations of change-of-direction moves; spend more time working on basic ballhandling fundamentals, such as keeping the ball low and head up and pushing the ball up the court faster; put more focus on reducing ballhandling turnovers in competition; put more focus on beating defenders off the dribble in competition; put more focus on cutting down on dribbles to be more efficient; put more focus on using the reverse dribble and change of speed against pressure; spend more time maintaining current programs.

Other keys: _____

Passing

Rating: _____

Keys for improvement: Consult with a coach on passing strengths and weaknesses; use the triple-threat position more; use the jump stop more; pass with two hands more; emphasize precise passing, hitting teammates in the chest with easy-to-catch passes; throw simple passes more often; know teammates better—who should get the ball when and where; hit open people more quickly; pass ahead on the break better; feed the post better; penetrate to create assists more; identify double teams and open teammates better.

Other keys: _____

Rebounding

Rating: _____

Keys for improvement: Consult with a coach on rebounding strengths and weaknesses; crash the offensive boards more consistently; box out more consistently on defense; increase aggressiveness; anticipate rebounds better (act before the release of the shot, study the angle of the shot to see where the ball is going to rebound, anticipate most rebounds going to the weak side).

Other keys: _____

From J. Giannini, 2009, *Court sense: Winning basketball's mental game* (Champaign, IL: Human Kinetics).

Defense

Rating: _____

Keys for improvement: Consult with a coach on defensive strengths and weaknesses; contain the ball better; contest every shot; see ball–you–man better; help and rotate better; close out to recover on own man better; cut down on fouls; cut down on gambles; increase steals and deflections; take greater pride in defensive stops; get through screens better; defend ball screens better; front the post better.

Other keys: _____

Note: Players can copy this form and reevaluate frequently to track how their abilities, role, and level of play change.

From J. Giannini, 2009, *Court sense: Winning basketball's mental game* (Champaign, IL: Human Kinetics).

CHAPTER
2

Commitment to Goals

Goals—what individual players and teams are striving to accomplish—come in all forms and sizes. What drives one player might be quite different from what drives another, and the same is true of coaches. And that's OK, as long as those varied individual aspirations don't conflict with or diminish the importance of the shared objectives of the team.

One tactic used by basketball coaches is to place a large photograph of the site of the national or state championship on the wall in a high-traffic spot such as the locker room. Players passing by each day are reminded of their mission—the destination the program wants to reach that season. For example, Marquette used such a photograph in 2003, when they were a long shot to make it to the NCAA finals, and they claimed that literally keeping their eyes on the prize each day helped them to ultimately earn their trip to New Orleans.

We did the same thing at Rowan University. Before each season, I'd place a picture of the site of the NCAA Division III Final Four near the main entrance (and exit) of the locker room. Our teams reached three Final Fours in four years—winning the national championship in 1996—and we believed that the photo's presence helped us maintain a daily focus on working toward that special goal.

Before you can set a useful goal, you need to know why you would want to do so in the first place. One reason is that goals provide a clear sense of direction. As targets that you're seeking to hit, they help focus attention (as was the case with the photo of the Final Four site). Players and programs without clearly defined goals seldom achieve their potential. They might want to succeed, but they work without a purpose or a plan.

Another potential benefit of a goal is that it can serve as a source of motivation while you are striving to achieve a certain result. As anyone who's been through a tough, long season knows, practices, injuries, travel, and so on can take their toll over several months, and it's easy to get down or distracted. Keeping goals in mind during those tough times can provide that extra spark needed to overcome the inevitable challenges you'll face.

Understanding that goals can be beneficial, what should you consider when trying to identify and set them? Good goals share four basic attributes:

- *Meaningful.* Players and coaches must find value in achieving the goal, and they must be willing to apply the time and effort necessary to do so.
- *Specific.* The criteria for accomplishing the goal must be explicit and concise. Vague or convoluted goals can be misinterpreted and hedged on if players or coaches fail to achieve them.
- *Measurable.* Accomplishment of goals must be based on observable or quantifiable actions, not on subjective standards, "intangibles," or feelings.
- *Consistent with a larger, overall plan.* Individual goals within a basketball team have to fit within and be prioritized according to the primary objectives of the program.

Each year, players and coaches should share in developing the overall plan for the team. This should include setting specific goals and committing to them. The overall plan and the major goals are typically defined in the spring, after evaluation of the previous season has been completed. These goals should be the foundation and focal points of everyone in the program for the season ahead.

TEAM GOALS

Basketball is a team sport. Therefore, team goals should be the first priority for any player. This type of orientation must be instilled and reinforced throughout the program. When players embrace this mind-set—and when it is reflected in how they practice and compete—they earn the label "winners."

The best teams are made up of winners who are positive, tough-minded, smart, unselfish, and dependable in their orientation to the game. A winner does whatever the squad needs him to do for the team to succeed. This could mean being a defensive stopper, dominating on the boards, handling the ball against a press, or getting the ball to a key scorer on the offensive end.

Winners seem to get every critical rebound and loose ball. They step up at crunch time to make the key basket or steal in the decisive moments of a game. They don't fear failure.

Jason Kidd in his prime is an excellent example of a winner. Dating back to his days in high school and college—on teams at St. Joseph of Notre

George Long/Sports Illustrated/Getty Images

Though he received five NBA MVP awards, the Boston Celtics' Bill Russell (6) was much more concerned that everyone associated with that team's 1960s dynasty shared the same mission and goals, and they won an amazing 11 championships during his 13-year playing career.

Dame High School (California) and the University of California—the positive impact of Kidd's presence on a club has been apparent. His arrival in New Jersey in 2001 turned a struggling lottery-level team into an Eastern Conference champion. Why? What makes him special?

Duke and 2008 Olympic team coach Mike Krzyzewski says Kidd's mind is his best talent, and marvels at his "ability to instinctively react to situations on the court," something Kidd himself describes as being able to be creative in a split second. Kidd isn't blessed with the best physical tools or even the greatest basketball skills, yet he consistently does whatever the team needs to be successful—running the point, hitting the open man, pulling down rebounds, shutting down his man defensively, helping out teammates who get beat on the defensive end, diving for loose balls, and so on. Syracuse coach Jim Boeheim reinforced this point when he said,

"Other great point guards have a scoring portion of their game, whereas Jason doesn't need to take a shot" to be the most valuable player on the court. In addition, he fights through fatigue and minor injuries, encourages teammates, and engenders confidence and poise on a team.

Players such as Kidd are inspired by team goals more than their individual stats and celebrity. Coaches must identify the aims that are important to the program and then set standards for the team that spur the winners on the team to take on leadership roles.

Focusing on the team and winning more than his own accomplishments helps an athlete persevere and avoid becoming discouraged when things don't go well personally. This is an essential maturation process that must occur for players to reach their potential—both as athletes on the court and as people off the court. This individual sacrifice might be difficult for some players to accept, but it is truly what's best for both the team and each team member. An undeniable degree of self-centeredness needs to be overcome for players to be willing to sacrifice for team goals. Coaches need to emphasize that winning is the best way to bring attention and respect to individuals. Filling up a stat sheet on a losing team is rarely the way to become known as an outstanding player.

The daily goal sheet on the following page is a good place to begin defining team goals. Start with a team mission. The word *mission* is appropriate here because it is not simply what you are trying to accomplish (goal); instead, the mission is what you think should be accomplished no matter what adversity you face.

A mission is a goal that carries with it an obligation. That sense of commitment gives a program and its players great resolve and resilience through setbacks, and it raises a team above other winning teams that lack such a shared purpose.

Keep that mission statement in a place where every member of the team will see it often, such as the entrance to the locker room or team meeting area. Giving this mission a priority over individual goals reinforces the commitment to team above self.

The mission statement should be powerful; it should include the highest possible team goal the program can achieve. The mission is not necessarily a short-term goal. When rebuilding a program, you can still have a "championship" mission and state that "this is what we work for, and it's only a matter of time until we reach it."

Place the list of team goals near the mission statement to reinforce and specify the actions that will fulfill the purpose of the program. A sample list of team goals might look like the following:

1. Graduate every player.
2. Lead the conference in rebounding.
3. Have a positive team assist-to-turnover ratio.
4. Hold each opponent under 45 percent in field-goal percentage.

DAILY GOAL SHEET

Team Mission

_____

_____

_____

Personal Mission

_____

_____

_____

Today's Goals

Area (list below)   Goals (list below)

_____   _____

_____   _____

_____   _____

_____   _____

_____   _____

From J. Giannini, 2009, _Court sense: Winning basketball's mental game_ (Champaign, IL: Human Kinetics).

5. Win the next game.
6. Win every home game.
7. Win the regular-season conference championship.
8. Win the conference tournament championship.

The importance of the goal to "win the next game" cannot be overstated. This goal creates focus on the present and a beneficial sense of immediacy and urgency. In effect, it is the most important short-term goal for helping to achieve later long-term goals.

Although having a mission statement and specific goals is essential, you also need to have some flexibility when extraordinary circumstances arise. Indeed, goal setting is a dynamic, continual process requiring updates and adjustments when conditions change markedly from when the original goals were set.

For example, our 2002 University of Maine team incurred an unfortunate string of incidents, including a death in a player's family, off-the-court problems for two key players, a serious car accident involving three starters, and a serious knee injury to another starter. The unexpected and unfortunate loss of talent knocked the team out of contention for the regular-season title with six games left. When that goal was no longer achievable, the team set its sights on winning the conference tournament and earning an NCAA bid. However, those goals did not instill a great desire to win in the present. The team went 1-5 the rest of the way, mostly in close games. The mistake of looking ahead and abandoning goals in the here and now will cost you every time. Fortunately, the team regained focus in the conference tournament and made it to the championship game. But the overall season would have been far more positive if we'd had goals to deal with unexpected adversity earlier. For example, we could have set goals for the last six games or for earning a certain seed for the conference tournament.

If a truly challenging goal is set, the team will sometimes come up short (as in the previous example). When that happens, the players and coaching staff must address it immediately and create a new goal to keep the team focused and to keep current motivation high. Such adjustments should be made only if necessary, and they must be made wisely. Never set yourself up for failure with unrealistic goals. And if circumstances preclude achieving the goal, you should identify the next goal and pursue it with equal or greater desire and commitment.

An important distinction separates the team's mission—its ultimate destination—and the important goals that serve that mission. We have already discussed how adverse conditions may lead to resetting goals, but the overall mission of the program does not change. Thus, if a team is in a great situation, achieving goals and progressing more quickly than anticipated, the mission becomes realistic in the short term, thereby keeping the bar raised high.

A mission statement is not a plan for success. It is a contract that binds the team to a shared purpose and set of priorities, thus providing inspiration and a sense of commitment. The plan for success is based on more specific short-term performance goals.

INDIVIDUAL GOALS

The evaluation of skills, covered in chapter 1, serves as a useful tool for determining the strengths and weaknesses of each individual player. Knowledge of present abilities combined with aspirations to improve them sets the stage for individual development and goal setting. These individual goals should push a player to improve in at least one area every day, and they should ultimately produce a better overall player. The following discussion looks at how individual goals can be set throughout the basketball year.

Seasonal Goals

Individual goals must be tailored to each player's attributes and should be adjusted to maximize their relevance and benefits throughout the year. The objectives are different for each phase of the season, and players' goals should reflect that.

Off-season is a great time to work on skill deficiencies and physical shortcomings. Preseason is a period for integrating skills and finding the player's optimal role within the team structure while also reaching a high level of conditioning. In-season requires a high-performance mentality in which each day ultimately is about being prepared for the next game.

Off-Season Goals

Off-season workouts are when champions and great players are born. In fact, many coaches use the motivational phrase "Champions have no off-season." During this six- to eight-month period, an athlete has a great amount of time to accomplish individual goals. Developing the best off-season improvement plan requires careful thought and evaluation. Close consultation between coach and athlete is also essential.

Younger players (especially before high school varsity) should work on their overall skills. At that stage of their career, players should not focus on just a few skills. Although daily performance goals will be very specific, a wide variety of skills should be worked on. Specific goals should be set for shooting, ballhandling, post play, finishing layups, making free throws, and physical conditioning. Having daily performance goals will help players accomplish their goals for the off-season, help them improve in key areas, and ultimately help them reach their individual mission and the team mission. Chapter 4 will describe in detail the types of daily workouts that lead to personal improvement.

Craig "Speedy" Claxton is the epitome of a player improving himself a great deal during the off-season. Speedy attended Hofstra University

Goals for Growth

Steve Donahue–Cornell University

My former mentor at Penn, Fran Dunphy, taught me that outside influence should not influence your goals or how you go about trying to achieve them. No one thought Cornell could win given the program's history and school's location, but I told our players that those things wouldn't determine our success—*we* would determine our success. In all walks of life are people who have overcome all kinds of obstacles and have succeeded, yet other kids have been handed everything and have achieved nothing. What is inside you—not outside influences—is what determines your future.

Think big, act small. That is my philosophy on goal setting. And it's consistent with the approach I encourage our players to take. So, when I focused on the Ivy League Championship as our major goal, I also specified several little things that we needed to do well in order to accomplish that larger objective. And after we won our league, I didn't talk about repeating. Instead, I emphasized what we needed to do in order to get better.

Each day I wanted to see signs of improvement in three or four areas. It could be something as simple as players' punctuality, expecting everybody to be in the locker room 20 minutes before practice and on the court 10 minutes before practice started. Such things may seem or actually be small in the big picture, but they're significant in achieving the ultimate aims. So they're included among the things that I constantly talked about to the team. Doing many little things really is the key to bigger accomplishments.

I am not the type to post quotes all over the locker room, but I do have one from an alumnus that I had painted on the locker room wall: "Create the Future." To me, it says we have to do more than just work hard to win. Producing the results we desire means that each of our players will play extremely hard, be a good teammate, and do all the little things necessary to get a bit better each day.

A coach should motivate players to make progress every single day. This means that a coach also needs to accept the fact that players will make mistakes as they extend themselves beyond their normal performance boundaries. A player needs that freedom to grow, even if the development process might be painful. For example, early last year one of our players tried to do things he could not do off the dribble. Rather than scold him and tell him not to attempt such moves again, I kept quiet, sensing that his effort to improve was a positive move that would ultimately pay off.

No player wants to receive criticism in front of teammates. It's embarrassing and can be counterproductive for some players. It's usually better to discuss the problem one on one, explain the solution, and show the player what he needs to do to correct the problem.

Specify numbers or results you want accomplished in your drills. This focuses players' attention better than if they were to simply go through the drills as a matter of routine with no target performance in mind. Also, when you set goals, do so with an amount of time specified for achieving them. For example, if we do 5 minutes of rapid shooting with three guys and two balls from five spots on the court, not only will we time their shots, but we will also have them compete against one another for the most made baskets. Making it a competitive, high-energy drill simulates game-like shooting much more than a casual, self-paced shooting drill a player might do on his own.

But there is also a point at which a workout produces diminishing returns. If you're in a gym working on your game 60 minutes every day, you might accomplish just as much in that time frame as some other team does practicing twice as long. At a certain point, you don't get as much return on your investment as you think you do.

Each team and player is unique. Ideally, you'd like to see at least 90 minutes of high-level, competitive performance from everyone each day. That's more than double the minutes played in a regulation game, and it trains not only the body but also the mind to stay sharp throughout the session.

One of the few things we chart on the defensive end is the number of times we get three stops in a row. Georgia Tech did this when we played them. We were so impressed by the determination and energy they showed on the defensive end that we try to do the same thing. Now, most defensive drills don't end until one group gets three stops in a row.

We began setting a goal for deflections because I believed we needed to improve in that facet of our defense. So I got hold of a Utah Jazz deflection chart and somehow determined that 35 deflections would be a good goal for our defense. In this case, a deflection includes a variety of things, such as an offensive charge, a tip-out on an offensive rebound, a loose ball, a deflected pass, and a forced turnover. I'm not sure if that was a realistic goal for us, but we made it once or twice. What was important is that by making deflections a priority in players' minds, we increased our defensive movement and intensity, and we had some type of measure by which to gauge their performance.

My philosophy on goals emphasizes quality more than quantity. The degree to which players master a skill or tactic and the level and effort at which they perform it matter more than the resulting stats. So if we do a 10-minute segment on two-on-two closeouts, I want to see successful technique, a high level of conditioning, and physical and mental strength, not just four guys going through the motions. I won't insist on five stops in a row, but rather that the defensive players demonstrate the toughness and positioning necessary for success in game action.

(continued)

Goals also apply to off-court achievement. Sometimes this can be quantified and other times not. Say we have a kid coming in here with a 1400 score on the SAT, and he is doing 2.5 work. That is a disgrace and something that needs to be rectified. Next semester, his goal is a GPA of 3.0 or greater, and we're going to watch his progress report on a weekly basis.

Each of our players also performs 20 to 25 hours of community service every year. We do a lot of it together as a team so that we can share that sense of accomplishment and appreciate one another in a different way. We teach these guys how important it is to give to people who are less fortunate. I try to lead by example so that I don't just dicate that they do the service.

My teams are better in the past few years because they've taken ownership of their improvement. They set goals on their own. They self-correct. They work at it. They demand this of each other. And they've improved. So, while a coach can encourage development through goal setting, the real development happens when players internalize those goals and do their best to achieve those goals together.

and was arguably as quick as any player in America. He could defend, penetrate, create, and pass. He also played tough and smart. However, he relied on his extreme quickness, and he made only 21 percent of his three-point shots in his first three years at Hofstra. Most teams defended Speedy by playing way off him, helping on his penetration, and daring him to shoot, which he would not do.

Then, between his junior and senior years, Speedy set these goals: Become a good shooter, lead his team to the NCAA tournament, and become an NBA player. And that's just what he did. As a senior, he shot 38 percent from three-point range, and he led Hofstra to the NCAA tournament. That June, after impressing scouts with his shooting ability in individual workouts, Speedy was selected in the first round of the NBA draft. His successful pro career includes winning the 2003 NBA Championship with the San Antonio Spurs.

Preseason Goals

Many different types of goals can be set in the fall before official practice begins. This is an especially critical time for final preparation before the season starts. Many coaches set conditioning goals for their team at this time of year. For example, some coaches require players to be able to run a six-minute mile before they are allowed to start practice. Howie Dickenman, the very successful coach at Central Connecticut State, holds an annual 3-mile (4.8 km) race that his players run in. This race takes place the week before practice begins. The race is attended by boosters and is promoted on the team's Web site. The event ends with a social function. Results of the race are posted on the Internet. Thus, the team's preseason conditioning culminates in a traditionally valued, highly public race that emphasizes conditioning goals.

Some NCAA or high school rules prevent or limit the time that coaches can spend with players on the court in the fall. During this time, players should keep their own shooting logs for made shots. They can have goals such as 3,000 made jump shots before the start of practice (100 made shots per day for at least 30 days). Coaches may form a three-on-three league consisting of four or five teams. The league should include a daily schedule and standings, with a champion being determined before the start of practices. By forming this league, the coach knows that his players are competing hard, playing regularly, and learning to play together.

During the period from the start of school to the first practice, NCAA coaches are allowed two hours of instruction per week. Because instruction time is limited, the coach may want to pick just a couple of goals to achieve during this period. Examples could include goals related to individual shooting, one-on-one defense, team defense, man-to-man offense, or zone offense. The first official practice is the beginning of the most important time of the year—the period from the first practice to the week before the first game. This is when the shift to in-season goals takes place.

In-Season Goals

In-season performance goals will hinge on what the coach believes must be emphasized for the team to win. For example, at Rowan we established what were called "the eight commandments":

1. Always sprint the floor.
2. Use two hands, two eyes, and two feet on all passes.
3. Deny one pass away.
4. Take the charge.
5. Crash the boards.
6. Stop middle penetration.
7. No excuses.
8. Avoid being negative.

A set of explicit standards such as this serves as a blueprint for how the team is going to win. When put together correctly, these standards are the perfect meshing of philosophy and goals.

However, when creating in-season goals, you need to be careful not to set too many goals. If too many goals are set, the goals can begin to lose their meaning. Goals are meant to give direction and focus to the team's efforts. Having too many goals makes this impossible. So limit your list to no more than eight goals that players must focus on throughout the competitive season.

The most successful programs win consistently because their coaching staff insists on and preaches certain recurring goals. Rick Pitino's teams at

Kentucky and Louisville have thrived on full-court pressure defense that creates deflections and steals, along with a fast-paced transition offense that emphasizes three-point shots. Bob Knight's teams at Indiana and Texas Tech have won with great mental toughness and a motion offense that focuses on setting and using screens effectively. Princeton University traditionally uses the threat of the backdoor cut along with excellent three-point shooting.

The point is that a team needs *something* to give it an identity and to make the team successful. That something is the core team philosophy, as reflected in the specific, constant goals or commandments that the club lives by each season. And it's up to the coaching staff to insist on excellence in each of those areas.

For some programs, the in-season goals may need to change from year to year in order to find a style of play that best suits the new roster. For example, the eight commandments used at Rowan were changed at Maine, and they have since been modified to fit the situation at La Salle. Goals must be tailored to the strengths and weaknesses of the personnel. If set wisely and carefully, in-season goals or commandments will benefit each team.

Another interesting research finding is very applicable to in-season goal setting—that is, individuals commonly set their own meaningful goals as long as they receive continual feedback about their performance. Thus, coaches should keep practice statistics and should often refer to them during practice (e.g., "Hey, we have been going for an hour, and Jim has no turnovers!" or "Bob only has two rebounds so far, but Terrence has eight!"). This allows players to monitor their performance and spontaneously set their own goals. Similarly, key statistics can be reviewed at halftime or during time-outs on game days. At La Salle, we have often been a good rebounding team, and this may be largely because of the constant feedback our players receive about their rebounding numbers. As mentioned at the end of chapter 1, providing statistical feedback helps self-evaluation, which naturally leads to goal setting.

Short- and Long-Term Goals

Individual goals are secondary but necessary. The team will only improve if the players improve. An individual goal might be to make the high school varsity for the first time, to become a starter, or to compete on the next level. Those are all long-term goals. Such goals are helpful in the following way: They can inspire great effort and perseverance over a long period of time to ultimately reach a special accomplishment. If a player wants something bad enough, it will become a passion that inspires him to work very hard and continually improve. It will become an individual mission.

Short-term goals drive a player to practice and perform up to a certain standard, moving the player toward achieving a long-term goal. For example, a high school guard who wants to play at the college level will need to be a capable (if not excellent) shooter, which we'll define as shooting approximately 40 percent from three-point range.

A player's shooting percentages in drills that involve little pressure, no defense, and a lot of repetition should be 10 to 20 percent higher than in actual game conditions. That means this player must shoot a lot of three-point shots in individual practice and must make about 60 percent of those shots to be able to shoot 40 percent in games. He will also need to shoot this shot off the catch, off the dribble, off screens, and from different areas on the floor.

Based on this knowledge, the player can go

Increasing number of free throws made by a certain percentage is a good example of a specific and measurable goal.

into each workout knowing how many shot attempts, what types of shots, and how many made shots are needed to become a 40-percent three-point shooter in games. For example, he may take 10 three-point shots from five spots each (the two corners, the two wings, and the top of the key) for a total of 50 shots. A minimal goal of 30 makes for 50 attempts would keep the player on track to be a 40-percent game shooter beyond the arc. This is how to set short-term goals in order to achieve long-term success. Following is a more specific look at how to set effective short-term goals.

Specific and Demanding Goals

Effective goals are exact and difficult. Vague goals—such as "to do my best" or "to work hard"—give no direction. It is also impossible to judge when a player has definitely reached these goals.

Examples of specific off-season goals may include gaining 15 pounds (6.8 kg) of muscle, improving free-throw percentage from 55 to 70 percent, shooting at least 200 mid-range jumpers each day, and working on scoring off ball screens (shoot three-point shots off the dribble behind the screen if the defender goes under it, or explode around the corner for pull-up jump shots if the defender goes over the screen). Each of these goals is very specific and can easily be measured and evaluated.

Goals should also be difficult to reach. This creates a need for greater effort and produces greater improvement.

The keys for improvement identified in a player's self-evaluation provide clear areas for focus. Now the player must set specific and challenging goals that can be used every day. These goals must be measurable so that the player knows if and when the goals have been reached. After achieving certain goals, the player should then set more difficult goals.

Two samples of such goals are found in tables 2.1 and 2.2. These are examples of players who have identified areas of focus (based on the keys for improvement from their self-evaluation) and then set specific goals to help them improve on a given day. Notice that the goals are both difficult and measurable. These examples show how to complete the daily goal sheet (page 27).

These two examples include goals for both skill development and competitive play. Each player used a day in the off-season to work toward his individual and team missions through short-term performance goals. Once again, these examples are only used to illustrate how to set specific goals. Any drill or skill can be used as long as the goal is specific and challenging.

Academic Goals

Many very talented players have lost the privilege to compete because they've failed to meet their responsibilities in the classroom. In the United States, the student-athlete concept is emphasized from grade school to high school to college. This concept has two components.

First is the belief that sport provides lifelong lessons of discipline, teamwork, leadership, and perseverance that are part of a young person's education. These values are ones that all students should learn, and school-sponsored sports can help in this area of personal development.

Second is the belief that playing a sport—getting to compete and represent a school—is a privilege. That privilege is taken away if a player is not learning in the classroom and is not showing an interest in his own education. Eligibility rules enforce academic standards and make a number of talented athletes ineligible to play.

Education is far more important than just a way to stay eligible to play basketball. The knowledge gained and experiences available through coursework provide a basis for informed judgment and successful career opportunities in the future.

Although many talented young players may aspire to play in the NBA, few actually realize that dream. Approximately 1 out of every 10,000 high

Table 2.1 Goal Example 1

Area	Goals
Post moves	*Moves from 2 spots (right block and left block)* Make 5 of each of the following shots from each spot: 1. Slide dribble to middle for jump hook. 2. Slide dribble to middle, then counter with drop step back to baseline for power layup. 3. Slide dribble to baseline for power layup. 4. Slide dribble to baseline, then counter with drop step back to middle for jump hook.
Shooting	*15- to 17-foot jump shots from the high post* Make 100 jump shots.
Conditioning	*Rim touches* Perform 5 sets of 30 seconds. Touch rim 30 times each set.
Play pickup	*Physical post defense (don't give deep position)* Crash for rebounds. Use slide dribble to attack basket and defender.

Table 2.2 Goal Example 2

Area	Goals
Shooting	Make a set of 30 to 50 three-point shots (10 shots each from 5 spots). Make 20 free throws in a row.
Shooting and ballhandling	Crossover move into 50 made pull-ups. Inside-out move into 50 made pull-ups. Up and down court 10 times using change of pace and using behind-the-back and between-the-legs dribbles for change of direction.
Using screens	Set chair for ball screen (4 spots): left wing going middle, top of key going right, top of key going left, and right wing going middle. Complete the following at each spot: 1. Make 5 pull-ups (turn corner hard and tight). 2. Make 5 three-pointers (string dribble out behind screen). 3. Make 5 driving layups (fake using screen, drive opposite the screen). Set chair on block for down screen (2 spots): right block and left block. Starting under the basket, complete the following at each spot: 1. Make 10 three-pointers popping out to wings (catch, pivot, shoot). 2. Make 10 short jumpers in paint (curl around screen).
Play pickup	Use two hands, two eyes, and two feet for passing. Reduce turnovers. Contain and contest on defense.

school varsity basketball players will ever play at that level. Therefore, any responsible junior high, high school, or college coach will specify academic goals for players that will help those athletes prepare for life after their playing days are over—which is likely to be sooner than they think.

Jeff Ruland was a standout player at Iona College and was talented enough to jump to the NBA after his junior year. Jeff used his massive body (six feet, nine inches tall and 280 pounds), effective post moves, and a soft shooting touch to enjoy a lot of success early in his NBA career. He was named to the all-star team twice, and he signed a lucrative long-term contract with the Philadelphia 76ers. Then Jeff suffered a career-ending knee injury.

With his playing days over, Jeff wanted to coach at the college level, but he could not do so without a college degree. His experience, leadership, and knowledge of the game—along with his fame and wealth—were not enough to get him the job he wanted unless he completed his educational requirements. So Jeff went back to school, committed to earning his degree. He did so, and he has gone on to lead his alma mater to the NCAA tournament.

Young players must understand that their education will determine the type of job they will someday have. Setting educational goals is the mature and realistic thing to do.

Statistics show that the average college graduate earns approximately $40,000 a year more than the average high school graduate. Since most people work about 40 years, this means the average college graduate earns over $1,000,000 more during his work career than the average high school graduate. That's just one of the payoffs of furthering one's education.

Ben Franklin said, "Every time you speak, you show your education." This is a powerful statement. It means that a person's vocabulary, logic, creativity, and understanding are obvious to all. These things make up who a person is. Most young people do not realize that academic work is not only about absorbing information; it is also about interpreting information and communicating it. It is about developing intellectual ability.

And it's no coincidence that intelligence is one of the most important factors in leadership. People are more willing to listen to others who have a lot of knowledge. Knowledge brings respect. If a young person wants to be a leader, earn respect, and become a knowledgeable person, that young person should make academic goals a priority.

Examples of specific academic goals may include earning a 3.0 GPA, making the honor roll, earning a college degree in four years, and being accepted into a graduate or professional school. Mid-semester is a good time to look at current grades in each class and set specific goals to improve each grade by the end of the semester. Just as there are winners on the court who play the game with great effort and intelligence, there are winners in life. These winners use basketball to further their education.

They are able to succeed at many things during their basketball career—and especially afterward.

Examine the form on page 40. This form presents an opportunity to list academic goals. Succeeding or failing at such goals will likely influence future success more than basketball ability will. Every young player should be encouraged to want to learn, grow as a person, build a future after basketball, and earn the respect of others by developing knowledge and mature values.

A number of strategies can be used to encourage academic goals. Some of them are described in the following sections:

Weekly Academic Check-Ins   Each player provides a weekly update on his academic progress to the coach. A form such as the one shown on page 41 can be used. This is equivalent to setting short-term academic goals and making plans for time management each week. Coaches can schedule a weekly academic check-in appointment to meet with each player and discuss this form. Individual players could also use such a form to plan for themselves.

Study Halls   Study halls are the most common strategy used by coaches, but they are only effective when a productive study environment can be created (e.g., quiet, access to computers, strong supervision). This in effect sets goals for the time spent studying weekly.

Academic Recognition   When I was the head coach at Maine, the first goal posted for the team in the locker room was "Graduate every player." Next to the goal board was a Wall of Pride. The Wall of Pride included the names and graduation dates of all the basketball program's graduates. A coach could also have an area for photos of recent graduates as a way to honor these alumni and make current players aware of their successful peers. This honors the graduates and is a constant reminder to current players that they are expected to follow these past examples of academic success. Another good idea is to hang a plaque that recognizes every student-athlete with at least a 3.0 GPA over the last year. The intent of all of these practices is to encourage and recognize academic achievement.

Most teams have some sort of rules for academic performance and conduct. These rules often involve goals for class attendance, requirements for maintaining a certain GPA, and discipline for academic dishonesty. Although serious or consistent academic problems can lead to player suspensions or dismissal, many of these problems can be prevented by addressing failures in reaching short-term goals (i.e., class attendance, late or missing assignments). Many coaches favor consequences that help individuals academically, do not penalize innocent team members, and do not hurt the team on the court. One effective consequence is requiring extra early-morning study halls for players with academic violations. The individuals don't like getting up early, so they experience a negative consequence. They also get quality work done, which is a positive outcome.

LIFE AND ACADEMIC GOAL SHEET

Life Mission

_____

_____

_____

Life Goals

_____

_____

_____

Today's Life and Academic Goals

_____

_____

_____

From J. Giannini, 2009, *Court sense: Winning basketball's mental game* (Champaign, IL: Human Kinetics).

Name _____ Date _____

1. Follow up on any issues from last week (if any): Have they been resolved?

   _____

   _____

2. Attendance update: Past week results (date and class, comments).

   _____

   _____

3. Academic results from last week: Show syllabus, homework, notes, papers, quizzes, and tests.

   _____

   _____

4. Plans for this week: What is due and when (homework, tests, quizzes, assignments, papers)? What is your plan for completion? Do you need help from a tutor? Whom are you working with?

   _____

   _____

5. Recommendations: Strategies for assignment completion (tutors, references, time management, schedule; topics, ideas).

   _____

   _____

6. Present grade in classes: 1._____   4._____

   2._____   5._____

   3._____   6._____

7. Final comments, concerns, or problems:

   _____

   _____

8. Check-in attitude:

   _____

   _____

From J. Giannini, 2009, *Court sense: Winning basketball's mental game* (Champaign, IL: Human Kinetics).

Character and Behavioral Goals

Poor academic performance is not the only way talented young athletes can fail to reach their potential in life. Headlines appear every day about athletes and a wide range of problems, including violence, theft, and the use of drugs and alcohol.

These problems aren't unique to athletes, much less basketball players; they occur in all parts of our society. But athletes' digressions are more highly publicized and can lead to a loss of playing privileges in addition to possible criminal penalties.

An athlete must learn lessons such as responsibility and pride. Athletes have responsibilities to many people: themselves, teammates, family, and others who may be harmed by poor decisions. When a grave mistake is made, many people are affected. As an athlete, the public nature of problem situations is especially embarrassing. Most important, mistakes may victimize others. Consider the many innocent deaths caused by drinking and driving or drug use.

One player had a father who was a prison warden. One day his father took him through the prison. The young man met many people who did not look as bad or act as bad as he had expected. In fact, he remembered liking many of the prisoners he met. During the tour, the father reminded his son that he was the warden and that the prisoners had lost their freedom. Then he asked his son, "Do you know the difference between me and the prisoners?" The father gave his son the answer: "One mistake."

Players should be encouraged to build their lives on principles of honesty, nonviolence, caring for others, and abstinence from alcohol and drugs. By doing this, a person is training to avoid that one mistake that can cost a life, an education, one's freedom, or a basketball career. A team can set a goal that will help players live life in an ethical manner. Examples of this type of goal are to seek to give, not to take; to say no to drugs and alcohol; and to faithfully live the commandments of one's religious faith. On the form on page 40, players should include a commitment to being a wise, caring person as part of their life mission. Players need to set a goal or standard for life off the court.

The La Salle team has embraced the following quote: "Those who are first will be last, and those last will be first." The team has emphasized putting personal desires last and putting family and team first. A lot of negative behavior is selfish (e.g., drug use, alcohol use, neglecting academics). Individuals choose those behaviors selfishly without thinking of their parents, teammates, or coaches. I know of one highly talented player who was a legitimate NBA prospect but continually failed drug tests for marijuana. He was on the verge of dismissal from the team if he tested positive again, which would have destroyed his NBA chances. However, by thinking of his financially poor family and how they were counting on him, he placed others before himself, stopped using marijuana, and enjoyed a professional career. This player's success enabled him to help many people. By placing himself last, he finished first. If a young player puts the values taught by parents and coaches first in his life, that individual is ultimately going to be very successful. Young players who place themselves first and always do whatever they feel like doing often finish last—both on and off the court.

To address on-court behavior, the list of eight commandments presented earlier included two behavioral goals. That season we insisted that no complaining or criticism between players was allowed (avoid being negative). We also specified that no excuses were permitted when a player failed to adhere to one of the commandments. Together, these two behavioral goals produced a more focused, more positive, and tougher team.

Recently, a very close game between two outstanding programs was marred by the conduct of one of the players. The player dove for a loose ball but lost it out of bounds, and the opposing team was awarded possession. Frustrated by not being able to secure possession, the player picked the ball back up and slammed it to the floor. This emotional outburst garnered a technical foul, which gave the opponent free throws and the ball, and was a big factor in the guilty player's team losing the game.

A goal that specifically stated that negative emotional outbursts of this sort are not permitted might have precluded such behavior. Goals of this nature encourage players to conduct themselves in a way that both increases the chances of winning and diminishes unfavorable conduct. The key is that this code of conduct must be enforced consistently in practices and games for both the star player and the deepest reserve. And it sure helps if the coaching staff conducts itself according to the same behavioral guidelines that players are expected to follow.

Strength and Conditioning Goals

Off-season strength and conditioning goals are critical for physical development and playing at the highest level possible. As competition increases, so does the average size, strength, and athleticism of the opponents. Increased strength means better rebounding, post play, defense, shooting range, ability to score on drives, and ability to get loose balls. It also increases mental toughness and confidence. As a player gets stronger and accomplishes goals in the weight room, physical toughness, mental toughness, and confidence usually follow.

Strength and conditioning workouts should be included in daily goals. Because a workout will have many exercises, sets, repetitions, and weights to record, you may need to use or develop your own workout form. This will allow you to keep daily conditioning details separate from the daily basketball goal sheet.

An effective strength and conditioning program—specifically tailored to a developing athlete's needs and rate of maturation—can pay big dividends. Ed Biedenbach, head coach at the University of North Carolina at Asheville, has seen it happen firsthand. Coach Biedenbach is also a former assistant under Jim Valvano at North Carolina State (including when the Wolfpack won the national championship in 1983).

In 1988, the North Carolina State coaching staff debated whether to offer a final scholarship to a gangly prep player from Huntington Station, New York. Few other big-time programs were recruiting this player. Coach Valvano liked his shooting touch and court sense, but the kid lacked the muscularity and strength of most ACC recruits. North Carolina State eventually did offer him a scholarship, but the meager 171 minutes he played his freshman season made it clear that his physique was inadequate for ACC competition. So the coaching staff, who loved the player personally, told him that he could remain on the team but would likely play more if he transferred to another school.

With this challenge, Tom Gugliotta said he was staying, and he hit the weight room with a passion. During the course of his Wolfpack career, he

Noah Graham/NBAE/Getty Images

Once a gangly recruit at North Carolina State, Tom Gugliotta developed his body strength to become an NBA all-star.

gained some 40 pounds (18 kg) of muscle, worked tirelessly on all aspects of his conditioning, and honed his skills on the court. Tom blossomed into an All-American by his senior year, and he is one of only three North Carolina State players to have scored more than 1,500 points and claimed more than 800 rebounds. He was also an Academic All-American, and North Carolina State now annually honors its most improved men's basketball player with the Tom Gugliotta Award. Coach Biedenbach still marvels at how "Googs"—through countless hours in the weight room and on the court—transformed himself from a marginal recruit in 1988 to the sixth player selected in the 1992 NBA draft. Tom eventually became an all-star at the professional level.

It is not uncommon for players to gain 30 to 40 pounds (14 to 18 kg) of muscle over four to five years as their body matures and benefits from effective strength training. Players should consult someone who is very knowledgeable and experienced in basketball conditioning. They should follow the prescribed program and track their improvement. Every day should be viewed as an investment—one in which the work put in will pay off in terms of developing a stronger, better player.

RECOGNITION AND REINFORCEMENT

Let's face it, all the effort applied toward achieving goals must, in the end, produce some type of reward if it is to be sustained. The formal term for this is *positive reinforcement,* which is defined as any consequence that increases a desired behavior.

Praise is a great reinforcer. Another great reinforcer is increased playing time. Recognition as "practice player of the day" and other such acknowledgments also encourage behaviors that bring individual athletes and the team closer to their goals.

Coaches need to be creative in recognizing and reinforcing both effort toward and achievement of goals. As mentioned, at the University of Maine, we had a Wall of Pride in the locker room to recognize academic success. We also had an honorary "M" board to acknowledge achievement of important basketball goals. A player earned an "M" for being named team captain, participating on a winning team, being selected to an all-conference team, contributing to a 20-win team, or being on a conference championship team roster. Thus, it was possible to earn up to 5 Ms a season, or 20 during a career. This system rewarded accomplishments that the program valued most: excellent leadership, outstanding individual play, and team success.

Half of the board was used to recognize the career leaders for honorary Ms in the program so current players could see what others had accomplished. The other half of the board was used for current players. Therefore, the current group of players was often comparing its success to its predecessors'. This served as a great motivator, especially to upperclassmen who suffered losing seasons early in their careers. They were even more dedicated to winning and earning their spot on the "M" board their junior and senior years.

Coaches should also be sure to reward goal achievements with playing time. For example, if a coach believes rebounding is a measure of effort, he could make sure the leading rebounder in the last practice, week, or game is automatically a starter for the next game. The 1996 national championship team at Rowan had a turning point in our season when effort was rewarded. This team was immensely talented but underachieving. Assistant coach Dave Lafferty said, "Coach, you can talk about playing hard all you want, but until you start Osco Williams [our hardest worker], no one will listen." Osco was talented, but not as talented as our first five. However, his effort and heart were extraordinary. Once we rewarded Osco (we started him the rest of the year), our whole team worked harder because they knew this was the criteria for playing time. It was a turning point.

COMMITMENT

At the college level, most highly committed athletes spend two to six hours per day working to become better players. For example, a morning weight training session followed by afternoon individual skill work and pick-up games in the evening is a common summer routine for dedicated players. High school players who aspire to play at the college level would do well to adopt this level of commitment early. Almost all players like to play basketball, but great players also like to work at basketball. They find great satisfaction in honing certain skills and building up their physical tools. This means countless sets and reps in the weight room. This requires practicing skills such as explosive dribble moves to the basket, pull-up jump shots, three-point shots, post moves, and shots off screens at a gamelike intensity over many repetitions.

A wise coach once said, "Repetition is the mother of all learning." In other words, skills must be practiced repeatedly to become automatic.

Great players do something every day to make themselves better, as reflected in the book *Heaven Is a Playground* by Rick Telander. This book is about a summer spent on the playgrounds of New York City. It followed the area's best players, including Ernie DiGregorio, who was a great point guard at Providence College and had a successful NBA career.

Ernie D. expressed his love for playing and his commitment to the game by being the first to the park and the last to leave—and playing as much as possible in between. One day the temperature soared to over 100 degrees, and he was the only player on the hot asphalt. He said that he knew then that no one else had the will to outwork him or would ever stop him from achieving his goals.

All great players work on their basketball skills at times when others don't. They work when no one makes them. They work when there are no coaches or teammates around. It is this type of commitment and work ethic that separates the great achievers from those who simply do less.

Every player who believes he wants to reach his basketball potential must ask himself the following questions: Am I putting in the necessary time and effort? Am I outworking my competition? Do I love playing the game enough to sacrifice other things and to be dedicated every day?

No coach, parent, or teammate can make an athlete want to improve; that must come from within. But the goal-setting concepts and processes presented in this chapter will help manifest that athlete's ambition to its fullest potential.

CHAPTER

3

Expectations of Success

Once labeled a "mid-major," Gonzaga University's men's basketball program emerged in the mid-1990s as a national power that has become a perennial presence in the NCAA tournament. Not only have the Bulldogs compiled a very impressive win–loss record; they've also earned respect by competing and faring well against the country's top teams.

What's unique about Gonzaga is that they play in a good conference, but not one that is ranked among the nation's best. The eastern edge of Washington is a nice place, but recruiting young players to this area on a national basis can be a challenge. The basketball program now has a new gym, but the previous facilities didn't compare to the mega-arenas and practice-training-office complexes available at the big-budget, high-profile schools. So, how did Gonzaga attain and maintain such a high level of performance?

Sorry to disappoint you, but Gonzaga-like success doesn't happen with a flick of a confidence switch. Enduring confidence doesn't come about nearly so quickly or easily. In the early 1990s, Coach Dan Fitzgerald assembled an excellent staff at Gonzaga, including young assistant coaches Dan Monson and Mark Few. That staff upgraded recruiting significantly, and they also conveyed their confidence in achieving a higher level of success to the players they brought on campus. So, when Monson became head coach following the 1997 season, he was hardly starting from scratch. The home-court advantage at "The Kennel" was already working to the program's advantage; the team's record in Spokane was 61-5 from 1993 to 1997. Monson—and then his successor, Few—were able to ramp up recruiting even further and substantiate their high expectations through winning at home, on the road, and most notably, in the NCAA tournament.

Now Gonzaga's coaches and players clearly have the confidence—even deep conviction—that they can challenge and, on a given night, beat teams at the top 25 level. They have used their success over the years to build on that confidence to the point that they now consider themselves among the nation's best programs. And they have the resume to support that claim. So, when recruits arrive on the Spokane-based campus, they bring with them that same mind-set—an expectation of success.

The same kind of confidence-building process has resulted in Davidson University reaching the 2008 Elite Eight and George Mason University reaching the 2006 Final Four. In both cases, the teams had the confidence and ability to beat elite programs with a lot of advantages.

Such underlying confidence is the key to building psychological momentum. That term was coined by renowned sport psychologist Dr. Rainer Martens to describe the increasingly positive mental and emotional state that leads to high performance. A more familiar slang term for the same phenomenon is "mojo."

Psychological momentum, or mojo, is often associated with emotions—both the highs and lows encountered during the course of a competition and season. And basketball is definitely an emotion-provoking sport.

Although outward expressions of emotions by a player might not always be reflected by his actual performance on the court, a player's internal

AP Photo/Michael Conroy

Gonzaga has continued to build upon the plan for success first conceived and implemented during Dan Monson's time with the team in the 1990s.

state (i.e., energy and drive) certainly affects how he plays. Teams with players who question their abilities tend to be more tense. They begin thinking negatively and worrying, which creates additional tension. And, when an athlete or a team is tight, we know what happens. Apprehension grows, actions become hesitant, and emotions are negatively charged.

Dr. Martens' concept of psychological momentum states that peak performance most often occurs when confidence and energy levels are high. Individual players and teams as a whole set the stage for success when they believe in their ability to perform well—and when they combine that belief with a burning desire to outcompete the opponent. When channeled appropriately, the emotional excitement in the gym and the intense competitive atmosphere in a game can further contribute to this positive motivational state.

BUILDING CONFIDENCE

The truism "Nothing predicts future success better than past success" could easily be reworded to "What best enhances confidence in a task is previous success in that task." Clearly, athletes—like everyone else—gain the greatest confidence in their ability to perform through successful experiences in that sport. Legendary football coach Bill Parcells summed it up well when he said, "Confidence comes from demonstrated skill."

Albert Bandura, a renowned psychologist, developed a well-supported social theory about self-efficacy that explains and describes the phenomenon that Parcells and others have observed. Bandura's theory, supported by many experiments, explains how higher self-expectations lead to higher performance.

Research on the relationship between confidence and performance confirms the following: The more a player expects to achieve, the more he actually will achieve. The confident player expects to shoot a high percentage, pass consistently well without turnovers, defend successfully, and get a lot of rebounds.

Bandura made another point that may seem obvious: Confidence is mostly based on past performance. In other words, the better players have performed in the past, the more confidence they'll have in the future, and the better they'll actually perform. This leads to the most obvious way to build confidence—that is, to play well consistently and expect to play well in the future. Thus, a very skilled and proven player should be confident. A player with weak skills and without a successful background is likely to be diffident—the opposite of confident. Confidence without ability is a false or unrealistic confidence. Following are some tangible ways to develop skills and competitive success in an effort to *begin* building confidence.

Skill Confidence

In high school and college, coaches usually meet with players individually in early September, and teams play their first game in late November. This means there is a period of approximately 80 days from the first meeting with each player until the first game, ample time for the athletes to work on and improve specific skills—and to gain confidence in those skills.

As we all know, the three-point shot has become an important part of most teams' offenses. The early portion of the school year—before the first official team practice—is a golden opportunity for players to sharpen their shooting eye from the arc. When practicing, a repetitive shooting drill can be used to time how long it takes a player to make 100 three-point shots (working with a rebounder who passes the ball back). Perimeter players should be able to do this easily within 10 minutes. Bryce Drew, the former Valparaiso University guard who hit the famous buzzer beater to upset the University of Mississippi in the 1998 NCAA tournament, once sank 100 three-pointers in only 7 minutes 30 seconds when performing this drill.

Rules limit how much contact and oversight coaches can have with players in the preseason. Therefore, for shooting or any other skill improvement to occur, players must commit to performing drills on their own, without a coach monitoring them. Players who make that commitment can make great strides. A perimeter player, for example, can easily make more than 10,000 three-point shots during preseason workouts (i.e., a little more than 100 makes per day). And, based on what we know about the experience of success, that player should be more confident shooting from the arc when the season begins.

Physical Confidence

Proper conditioning of the body is also important, not only for the strength and stamina needed to compete at a top level throughout a game, but also for performing skills proficiently. As discussed in chapter 1, increased physical strength can enhance inside scoring, rebounding, and defensive abilities.

Strength gained in the weight room also tends to elevate a player's personal and athletic confidence. Belief in oneself blooms as a result of consistently fulfilled daily goals in the weight room, increased strength evident in greater maximum lifts, and visible changes seen in a more muscular physique (everyone likes to look strong!). A hard worker and achiever in both the weight room and gym is often a more confident athlete.

Richard "Rip" Hamilton is one player who has benefited significantly during his career because of his dedication to off-season workouts. His outside and mid-range shooting prowess was developed through countless hours alone on the court. And when Rip decided to apply that same dedication to his physical conditioning in the midst of his NBA career, it resulted in improvement to his shooting, movement without the ball, and defense. These improvements came about not only because he was in better shape, but also because he had greater confidence in his abilities as a result of his tireless training regimen.

Competitive Confidence

The best way to build true, realistic confidence is for players to use the strength and skills they've acquired in workouts and practices to achieve greater success in games. The more game success players experience, the stronger their confidence becomes.

But coaches and players have to answer some critical questions to determine the best nature of those competitive experiences. What level of competition is most appropriate for the player to be challenged but not frustrated by the size, skill, and maturity of opposing players? What age, talent level, and types of personalities of teammates will make for the best fit? What kind of structure would be most beneficial to expand yet not clash with the style that seems most suitable? The answers will differ based on each player's background and attributes.

Two Stages of Competitive Confidence

Remember that the underlying key is building true, long-term confidence. But achieving that is a process that some athletes complete more readily than others.

The "Potential" Player Potential players are those who can be successful but have not yet had a high level of success. There can be many reasons why the player has not had success yet: youthful immaturity, inexperience, lack of coaching, lack of confidence, or lack of mental toughness. However, the player has the physical ability and skill he needs in order to be successful.

One basketball club (Pussihukat) in Helsinki seeks out the best young players and is committed to developing them, whereas many other clubs search for older, more proven players who seem ready to win. Still, Pussihukat has been very successful in the Finnish League and has set the stage for many players to move on to NCAA and European competition.

One year, former coach Pekka Salminen organized a tour of the United States to play against a number of top NCAA Division I teams. He believed that the tour would be a great educational and team-bonding experience. He also thought the tough competition would help get Pussihukat ready for their season. However, the team was younger and had less experience than the competition. The players were also unaccustomed to such travel and worn down from playing night after night with no rest. They were talented, but they were overmatched. After the team suffered repeated defeats by large margins, Coach Salminen saw the confidence drain from his club, and he found that it took a very long time to restore it. Instead of starting their regular season strong because of improvement from playing against strong competition, they started poorly because of low confidence.

The point is that potentially good players must build competitive success through the proper challenges. The competition should be at a level that enables players to earn playing time, match up to some degree against opponents, and win with some consistency when they perform well individually and as a unit.

Once competitive success becomes consistent, the team should seek out greater competitive challenges. For example, it makes sense for a proven team—such as a defending conference champion—to select a more difficult schedule the next year. It makes equal sense for an unproven team to select a schedule that will help the team build experience and confidence.

The implication for individual players is that they should seek out the competitive level that will enable them to build a pattern of game success. Seeking out the highest level of competition is not wise for the potential player because this player has not yet established a pattern of success nor a high level of confidence.

Seeking out the highest level of competition has destroyed the confidence of many potential players. These players need to establish a history of success and build confidence before they can succeed at the highest level possible. They have talent. They just need to find a situation that enables them to develop confidence first.

The Player Who Has "It"   The second type of player to discuss is the player who grasps what is needed to be successful and knows how to go about achieving it. "It" is the focus, commitment, maturity, attitude, character, and toughness that characterizes special players and key contributors to winning teams. In many ways, this book is intended to help players reach this level of functioning.

Occasionally, talented young players possess unusual maturity and have great success early in basketball. They seem to have it at a young age. These unique individuals can rise to the challenge and play at the highest level available, even though their age would suggest that they might not be quite ready.

The best recent example of this is LeBron James. The native of Akron, Ohio, became one of the most ballyhooed high school players ever, drawing extensive national media attention during his junior year and having his games broadcast on ESPN networks several times during his senior season. Drafted by the Cleveland Cavaliers in 2003 as an 18-year-old (before the NBA raised the age requirement for eligibility), LeBron had many lessons to learn during his rookie season. No longer could he dominate opponents simply because of his great physical size, strength, and power. At times, his decision making was poor, his turnovers multiplied, and his shots were forced. However, these early failures could not shake his belief in himself. The miscues and media criticism only drove him harder. He was confident that experience and dedicated learning of the NBA game's nuances would lead him to improve and become a truly great player. He

Gregory Shamus/Getty Images Sport

LeBron James' self-confidence combined with his physique, skills, and knowledge of the game make him nearly impossible to guard.

was right! By the end of his first NBA season, he was named Rookie of the Year and was on his way to a tremendous NBA career. Some players, like LeBron, possess that magical combination of superior ability and self-confidence that allows them to elevate their game to play at the highest level possible.

Players who step up to the challenge in this way become leaders through their actions, if not through their words. We'll delve deeply into what is required to be a leader in chapter 10. For now, I'll just point out that the two most important facets of leadership are these: being confident in oneself and inspiring confidence in others.

Signs of Confidence

The best way to breed confidence in others is to demonstrate it yourself. This should be done with enthusiasm at every practice and in every game. That's easy to do when things are going well, but it's a real challenge when the chips are down. Offenses and defenses may struggle, turnovers and mental errors may multiply, shooting percentages and rebound totals may plummet, and losses may mount. Leaders withstand such adversity, acknowledge what corrections are needed, and continue to perform with confidence. They stay calm, poised, and confident in the face of adversity. Their demeanor does not change when things are going against them. From Jerry West to Tim Duncan, such players have been the beacon of light to guide their teammates through the storm. The apparent confidence of these players spreads the message to everyone on the team that they can withstand the present challenge and prevail in the end.

Andy Bedard, a great former point guard at Maine, would often renourish his teammates' confidence when the team was losing. In time-outs, he would take charge and say, "We're all right, guys. We're okay. It's still early. Let's get some stops and good shots. Don't worry." Players who are confident and also show leadership are a blessing to a coach and a team.

If you believe that facial expressions and body posture are unimportant, think again. We perceive others' psychological and emotional states by how they look. A leader—player or coach—who appears tense, confused, or dejected is hardly going to inspire the kind of actions needed to be successful. And, when you give the appearance of being in control, it may actually help you feel more confident and in command—researchers have found that making certain facial expressions can initiate corresponding emotions. So, if you want to lead, try to channel your negative emotions positively, at least for others to see.

Some players and many coaches—including me—let frustration take over and let it show instead of keeping a poised and confident demeanor. Emotional control is a challenging area of leadership that many coaches need to improve, and we'll cover this topic in more detail later in the book. There just might be something to that saying, "Never let 'em see you sweat!" So be confident and look confident, not only for yourself, but also for your team.

MATURING CONFIDENCE

Fine wines result from a very good variety of grape passing through a successful aging process in the right conditions. The best confidence in sports is developed in a similar way. Players need a solid grasp of their abilities (see chapter 1) and potential, they need to be properly challenged in practice and training, and they need to experience success over time. Any attempted shortcuts or faulty steps along the way will result in an inferior product.

Immature Confidence

In some cases, a player will have a history of success and will have gained substantial confidence. However, because the sense of mastery was obtained from questionable data or unreliable sources, that player's confidence is fragile and often detrimental to both personal and athletic development.

This type of player is often a physically gifted young player who has matured early and has dominated opponents who are less physically mature. It could also be a player who has been outstanding in a smaller school or area but has not been regularly tested against tough competition. Such highly touted young players often have an entourage and family members who inflate their ego far beyond any proven degree of merit. This type of player might appear confident, but he's not. He's arrogant, and feelings of superiority prevent him from challenging himself and risking the chance of failing a time or two along the way. Actually, this individual avoids challenges because he lacks true confidence. Commonly, this type of player wants to be promised that he'll be a starter, receive a lot of playing time, and get plenty of shots. A mature player with true confidence believes he will earn playing time and success and never feels a need for star treatment.

Falsely labeled prodigies are very prone to becoming bigheaded and often lack respect for coaches, teammates, opponents, and the game itself. They project a great belief in themselves but not in others. When they lose and are outplayed, they find a scapegoat—a coach's bad strategy, an official's call, the team's failure to get them the ball, or bad luck. They never examine themselves or take responsibility. As a result, these players can continue to fool themselves and act far more confident than they have a right to be.

Immature behaviors and the resulting penalties (technical fouls and benchings) are common. In short, players with immature confidence detract significantly from a team and can ruin it. Exaggerated, immature confidence rests on the belief that success will happen simply because of superior talent. The most obvious problem is that the player who has this exaggerated sense of how good he is can never live up to the hype—especially his own. But in trying to do so, he brings everyone around him down and disrupts team chemistry.

A player with immature confidence is not strong enough to admit when something is his fault. Such a player can be very frustrating to play with or coach. The player may exhibit cockiness, a habit of blaming others, and a sense of already being good enough (or great) without having to change or improve. This type of attitude does not help anyone in any way, and it can be very harmful to the team. Unless the coach or team leaders step in and correct the situation, the problem can build and spread to the point that it pulls members of the squad in all different directions.

The challenge is for that player to develop a more realistic and healthier perspective. The new perspective should still include a mostly positive self-perception, but also an awareness of the weaker areas that need attention. This positive–negative approach allows a player to keep his ego mostly intact while admitting that improvement is needed (through hard work) to fulfill his potential. The first chapter of this book stresses the need for realistic self-evaluation, and that is exactly what the immaturely confident player needs to progress to a mature level of confidence.

At the postgame press conference after winning the 2006 national championship, Florida coach Billy Donovan spoke on this very topic: "So much of it now has nothing to do with talent level. If you have a guy who is talented but is totally into himself, it's really hard to change that mentality. [Whereas] if you have a player who has a great level of unselfishness and work ethic, he's going to overachieve."

Mature Confidence

As stated in chapter 1, mature confidence includes humility. The mature player knows he is good. He knows there are other good players. He knows those other players are always working somewhere to beat him. He knows that if he also works hard to keep improving, his skills and strength will be as good or better than the competition. Finally, he knows that if someone else is just as strong and skilled as he is, then he will outplay the opposition with great heart and toughness. This way of thinking is extremely confident, but not arrogant. It is the mind-set of ultimate achievement.

Indeed, this mentality has helped produce some of the most memorable wins in basketball. In 1983, North Carolina State—with veteran players who had mature confidence—dismissed the prevailing notion that they had no chance against an awesomely talented and successful Houston team. The Wolfpack's belief didn't waiver as they won the game and the NCAA championship at the wire in thrilling come-from-behind fashion. Perhaps no example of unwavering confidence is more storied than tiny Milan High School's run to the Indiana state high school championship in 1954, made famous by the movie *Hoosiers.* And, far less publicized but more immediate to my experience while coaching at the University of Maine were our memorable victories over outstanding programs such as Marquette and Providence. In all of these cases, less physically gifted teams benefited from their mature confidence in their ability to play harder and smarter on the way to victory.

Mature confidence doesn't automatically guarantee winning, however. During the 1999 to 2000 season, our very mature Maine club believed strongly that they could beat a far more talented UCLA team. That Bears squad respected all opponents and acknowledged their own deficiencies, but they always believed that they could win each game. That particular day, however, the Bruins played very well and beat us by 20. But that outcome didn't shake our players' underlying confidence. They simply took stock of the deficiencies in that day's performance, gave the opponent credit, and moved on to the next challenge. The mature confidence of the players made the team very tough and successful. A better example may be the experienced and mature Davidson team that advanced to the 2008 Elite Eight. Early losses to powerhouse programs such as North Carolina, Duke, and UCLA did not shake their confidence on the way to an undefeated conference season and a memorable NCAA tournament run.

Players and teams who always believe they can win—whether that belief is realistic or not—will play more aggressively as a result of this confidence. This does not mean a coach should refrain from making strategic adjustments against a more talented opponent (e.g., slowing the pace or protecting the basket defensively). Sometimes players view such adjustments as the coach not having confidence against a strong opponent. Any adjustments, along with respect for the opposition, should be conveyed as part of the winning game plan. This information should be communicated with firm confidence.

Initial confidence comes from players developing a high level of physical ability and skills, followed by winning and playing well consistently. This history of success makes a player or a team good even if the confidence is immature. Mature confidence makes a player or a team move from good to great.

To summarize, mature confidence is developed as follows:

1. Repetitive skill work increases ability and confidence in those abilities.

2. The right competitive challenges along with great toughness and effort provide game success that produces a history of success and higher confidence.

3. Players desire greater success, and they are mature enough (e.g., humble enough) and confident enough to acknowledge personal weaknesses and areas that need the most improvement.

4. Players are mature enough (e.g., humble enough) and confident enough to acknowledge the strength of the competition, which provides motivation to continue to work and improve.

5. Players can be self-critical, can experience failure, and can take coaching criticism without losing confidence. They know that future success is certain because of their commitment to personal improvement.

6. Players *always* believe they will outcompete the next opponent with great effort and toughness—and they are able to win.

Individual Motivation

John Beilein–University of Michigan

As a father of four children, I realize how different each child is. Similarly, as a coach, I find that each player has a unique motivational makeup. And because each of them is different, they should be treated as individuals, not all the same.

We try to measure each of our players' self-esteem to get a better sense of who can lead, who needs a push, who would benefit from a hug, and perhaps who needs to be motivated by extra sprints. A combination of those individualized motivational methods builds the collective effort of the team.

In attempting to develop a team, try to blend players' assets so that they fit together and function as a unit while playing different roles on the court. Some players have more responsibility to rebound, others to distribute the ball, others to be defensive stoppers, and so on. The aim is to get players to understand, embrace, and execute their respective duties for the good of the team.

In the process of motivating individually and molding players into a team, be careful not to tear down someone the teammates know and love. That can backfire because the player loses what little confidence he has left and his teammates perceive that he is being treated too harshly. So treat everyone fairly and let each team member know you respect him.

At the same time, you want players to feel a certain sense of urgency, a need to prove themselves in practices every day and in games. My own son, Patrick, felt he had to prove that he merited playing time because of his contribution to the team, not because he was my son. Johannes Herber sought to show everyone that he could come to the United States from Germany and be successful against great competition. J.D. Collins, a point guard, received just a few scholarship offers from so-called high majors, so he tried to prove that he could be successful against top-rated opponents. None of those players felt they were entitled to anything. They strove to prove their abilities and value to the team each time they stepped on the court, and they proved every day that they could play at the highest levels of collegiate basketball. Their backgrounds led them to play with a competitive edge that made them special.

At the high school level, players need more assistance and direction, someone telling them what they can and can't do. As a coach of high school players, emphasize their strengths, encourage them to work on them as much as possible, and reinforce how valuable they can be to the team when they apply themselves. Do not dwell on players' weaknesses. If a player is not doing the job on defense, however, point it out and correct it. At the same time, that remark about poor defensive play might be stated as, "If you would play defense as well as you shoot, you'd really be a hell of a player."

As a younger coach, I too often failed to combine compliments on one facet of a player's game with criticism of another aspect of his play. That oversight defeats the purpose of trying to get the player to feel good about his game while he continues to work at it.

Players who don't get into many games need to be just as involved in practices and film sessions as the starters are. We film every practice and usually watch about 30 cuts of every practice the next day. In those sessions, we show individual positive highlights of the previous practice. It might be just diving on a ball or taking a charge, but I want the bench players to get a sense that they are improving and are an important part of the team. Whether a walk-on who's on the scout team in practice or the top scorer, every player should know that the coaching staff admires him and that he is a key part of the team.

As a coach, I can help shape players' attitudes about winning and try to see to it that they stay hungry even when success comes their way. As a high school coach, you don't have as much control over what players are available. But with the help of parents in the kids' maturation and development process, you can help them establish a strong work ethic and appreciate the fact that no significant accomplishment comes easily.

Handling success is really hard for some players. As their coach, you have to make sure they stay grounded and understand that there is always more work to be done and improvements to be made. Usually a "good" loss somewhere along the line can straighten that out very quickly.

MAINTAINING CONFIDENCE

At some point during a season and many times during the course of a career, basketball players and teams will encounter difficulties. Players and teams lacking confidence or possessing immature confidence are going to struggle and likely succumb to such adversity. Those with mature confidence have a much better chance of withstanding setbacks. However, their resilience still depends on how effectively they respond to the rough patches.

The most important advice for dealing with difficult times is this: Don't overreact. As upsetting as the situation might be, an immediate, emotion-driven response to try to correct a problem will likely only make matters worse. Instead, step back and address the circumstances rationally after the disappointment and hurt subside. Reflect on why the problem arose, not to dwell on the negative or to assign blame, but rather to take all contributing factors into account and determine the best and quickest solution.

Following are several of the more common areas in basketball in which a player's individual confidence or a team's collective confidence can be shaken. The recommended responses should serve as general guidelines rather than specific measures to be taken in any particular situation. So tailor your exact response to best address each situation.

Poor Team Performance and Losing Streaks

If there was any one thing that our coaches and players did especially well while rebuilding the La Salle University basketball program from 2004 to 2008, it was dealing with poor team performance and losing streaks in a positive manner.

The first coaching point for dealing with a struggling team is completely counterintuitive—that is, when the team is doing well, the coach can and should be very critical in order to help the players stay grounded and identify areas for improvement. Criticism does not usually shake the confidence gained from success. However, criticism can kill all remnants of confidence during a losing streak. The more a team loses, the more positivity is needed. Over those years, we had losing streaks of 5 to 7 games a few times. In each instance, we responded with significant winning streaks and our best basketball of the year. The key was simply not beating our players up emotionally. The point is that a coach can be more negative when the team is playing well and must try to be positive when the team is losing.

The second key is to not dwell on losses. In the locker room after a loss, the coach should review the game but then immediately discuss the next opponent. At that point, the coach should not bring up the loss or anything about that game. This also ties in with the constant goal of trying to win the next game and not looking behind or ahead too far.

The third key is to not make wholesale strategic changes during losing streaks (i.e., overreact). Making one or two key changes is usually the best strategy, and those changes almost always include more simple and more aggressive play. For example, after a losing streak during the 2004 to 2005 season, our team simply set continuous ball screens in our offense and became very aggressive off the drive. We went from a 7-game losing streak to quality wins over Xavier, UMass, Rhode Island, Fordham, and Richmond in our last 10 games. In the 2007 to 2008 season, after a 5-game losing streak, we ran less flex (the pattern we were using at the time) and fewer set plays. We really emphasized running the floor and a motion offense with few rules. With these adjustments, we scored a lot more points, and after going 6-8 in our moderately difficult nonconference schedule, we went 9-9 against Atlantic 10 competition that saw 8 of 14 teams go to the postseason. Simplifying and increasing aggressiveness seemed to enhance confidence and performance for a team dealing with poor results. Note that we did not do a lot of new things with the adjustments we made. We already had ball screens, running, and simple motion in our offensive package. We just chose to use fewer sets and patterns and to focus on the most simple and aggressive things that the players had been taught.

Poor Individual Performance

Every player has bad games. When subpar performances occur, it's natural for frustration to set in. So it's okay to be upset, as long as the player's reaction to that displeasure is positive.

Struggling players need to focus on individual strengths. Past success didn't just happen by accident. So evaluate and emphasize those things that you do especially well—the things that contributed to successful performances before the downturn. A good example of this is an outstanding defender I coached. In his freshman year, he played with a couple of great scorers, and his tremendous defense was a key ingredient in the team having a very successful season. Naturally, as a sophomore, he wanted to expand his role. He tried to do more offensively and, as a result, lost some defensive focus. Things did not go well for the player or our team. However, by refocusing on being a great defender, he played better, got more playing time, and made more shots (because he wasn't forcing them). As a result, our team won more.

Sometimes writing down performance affirmations that focus on strengths can help players stay focused on the positives. The more detailed and positive the analysis, the better. For example, a player whose rebound totals have dropped might reflect on his previous success on the boards. This player could write the following: "I go after each rebound like an animal. I crash hard and quick. No one denies me the ball. Each missed shot is mine. Defensively, I box out hard every time." To deal with a stretch of ballhandling miscues, a player who has had a high assist-to-turnover ratio in the past might write the following: "I keep control of the ball and make the good pass no matter what. I play smart and help my team score. I make the easy, fundamental passes, first spotting the open teammate, and then delivering the pass on the money. I handle pressure using my reverse dribble, strong pivots, and strong drives. I'll take a five-second call before losing the ball or forcing a pass."

This activity can also help players to go to a quiet place and clearly imagine themselves playing the way their affirmation states. They can use their written statement as a guide for positive imagery. After each sentence, they can close their eyes and imagine performing as written. It is a good exercise for any player to think about how he wants to play, describe it in writing, imagine it, and, finally, do it. Another good way to maintain confidence is to show edited personal highlight tapes of the player performing successfully. The purpose here is to center players' thoughts positively on their strengths—what they are confident in—and to prevent negative thoughts from intervening.

Playing Time

Most basketball teams have 12 to 15 players, but only 5 can compete on the court at one time. And, typically, of those 7 to 10 players on the bench, only 3 to 5 of them will garner significant playing time. Thus, nearly every team has 3 to 7 players who do not play regularly.

This situation is difficult for most players. But if they are going to earn more playing time, they need to be both individually motivated (to improve and play more) and team oriented (unselfish)—as opposed to being negative and disruptive about their lack of minutes.

Coaches should have great empathy for committed players who get little playing time in games. The coach must make each player feel important and feel like a contributing team member. This requires communication (i.e., telling them why they are not playing more), encouragement (i.e., telling them what is needed and how they can do it), and acknowledgment of positives (e.g., effort, attitude, potential, progress).

Players should not be resigned to their situation on the bench; instead, they should strive to earn more opportunities to play and help their team. However, players must also understand and accept their respective roles for the welfare of the team.

When players are outwardly negative about their personal playing time, their attitudes and actions suggest that they believe their teammates on the court are not deserving. That can destroy team unity. They must also realize that the key to getting more playing time is not being as good as teammates, because the coach has to make tough choices between similar players, and someone is sure to be disappointed. To truly earn playing time, a player must make the coach's decision easy by consistently being better and more deserving than others.

Players should channel their thoughts and energy toward proving to the coach each day in practice that more playing time is warranted. Any player who makes a convincing case and earns playing time through outstanding practices will be welcome to more minutes by the coach and teammates. A player must prove that he is clearly a better contributor. In this way, a player learns how to handle adversity, grow as a person, develop as a player, gain the respect of teammates, and become a leader.

Players should focus on what they can control. Every player should act as if he has a game every day in practice. The player should work hard in every practice to build up his confidence, his role on the team, and the team itself.

Players should not let playing time dictate their belief in how well they can play. Remember, mature confidence cannot be broken! Coaches want players to be loyal, unselfish, and inwardly driven to prove that the team will benefit from them getting more playing time. And, when players demonstrate that they deserve more minutes in games by their effort and performance on the practice court, the coach needs to reward them accordingly.

A reserve who isn't getting much playing time can maintain confidence by doing the following:

- Communicate to the coach a desire to play more, but understand that the coach has tough decisions.
- Ask what you can do better and what will increase your chances of playing more.
- Dedicate yourself to improving in the ways the coach suggests by doing the extra work.
- Perform better and consistently in practices.
- Stay respectful of teammates.

Substitutions

We've all seen or experienced this scenario: A player makes a mistake, and the coach removes him from the game immediately. Many people may infer from the coach's action that he lacks confidence in the player and doesn't believe the player will avoid similar errors as the game progresses. But that might not be the case.

Perhaps the coach has been resting an outstanding player who plays the same position, and the coach wants to get that player back into the game. Or maybe the player who committed the miscue had been playing for an extended period and needed a rest. Or maybe the opposing coach has made a substitution that created an unfavorable matchup for the player, and a player on the bench is more capable of dealing with that particular opponent. And yes, it might be the case that in a very close game the coach has little patience for errors. All of these explanations are viable and rational decisions based on the coach's responsibility to do what is best for the team.

Another common coaching dilemma is dealing with a player who works extremely hard in practice and earns a chance to play, but then gets so nervous when put into a game that his performance diminishes. Such players want so badly to play well that they think and worry too much; they tighten up and make costly mistakes. This is sometimes referred to as "paralysis by analysis." Their anxiety is clearly visible. In short, they lack game confidence. The coach senses it and gives such players fewer minutes, which causes the players to lose even more confidence.

Is there a better way to handle this to produce a more positive outcome? A relaxation technique presented later in this book (see page 223) can help players deal with such anxiety. This technique may help these players perform as well in games as they do in practice.

I once had a player who was completely dedicated to the program. He was always great in practice, but he had two personal obstacles. First, he had excellent teammates who were playing well in front of him. Second, he tried so hard in games that he tightened up and lost confidence. It was clear to everyone that he was not as confident in games as he was in practice.

In his senior year, we really needed this player when we lost several players to injuries. He was good enough and had earned the chance. We just needed him to be confident. We were playing a conference game on the road. I spoke to this player before the game. I told him he was a good player and that all he had to do was play like he did in practice every day in "The Pit" (our practice facility). I emphasized, "Play like you do in The Pit, where you play great," but I also tried to bring out an angry, aggressive emotion that would become his focus as opposed to any worrisome thoughts. To do this, I told him, "Let it loose. You're too old and too good not to play well. You have sacrificed for this way too long."

© Greg Carroccio/Sideline Photos

Many factors are considered before making substitutions, so players being taken out of the game should not assume such moves are prompted by their poor performance.

The player knew that if he didn't play well immediately, I would take him out, but that no longer concerned him. He felt challenged. He believed that he deserved this and that no one should stop him from getting the success he deserved—not himself or any opponent. He was finally aware that he could play well anywhere, whether in The Pit or any other gym. For the first time, it all became the same for him. Playing became playing whether it was a practice day or a game day. Any gym felt the same to him. His confidence matured. This player, Todd Tibbetts, played great in his first start, scoring a career high of 21 points, and we won convincingly. He started the rest of that injury-plagued year and was a key contributor as the 2002 Maine team advanced to the America East championship game.

For players who get taken out of games quickly and lose confidence, the lesson here is that they need to bring the same emotion to games as they do to practice. The more similar their approach is to the two settings, the more similar their level of play will be on the practice floor and the competitive court. The key is to replace worry with aggressiveness. Players need to adopt an assertive form of confidence, as in, "I am going to play tremendously hard and better than I have shown so far." As that mind-set takes over, the player will become even more confident and capable of translating those thoughts to actions.

Shooting

Rare is the player who is never affected by a shooting slump. Cliches start to fill the player's mind: "Good shooters keep shooting." "Shoot your way out of it." "Believe the next one is going in."

And yes, good shooters should keep shooting, because they have proven their skill in this area. If a player has developed proper shooting technique through thousands of made practice shots over the years and has also shot well in games, then the player's confidence should be high. If a player is deeply confident and realizes that even the best shooters have bad streaks, he will break out with a good game soon and be back on track. The next shot will go in (or at least it will very soon). Keep shooting. That is what Peja Stojakovic, Ray Allen, and Jason Richardson do. They've developed mature, unshakeable confidence in their shot through a great deal of practice and success, and they aren't going to be deterred by a temporary decline in shooting percentage.

Other players—although they still seem to be confident in the midst of a shooting slump—become very worried, frustrated, and tense. These players need to find a way to confidently relax. Rather than trying to shoot their way out of a slump, the best way for these players to get back on track is to be more selective and look to score off high-percentage shots: layups, post-up moves, and free throws. To restore their confidence and relieve their tension, these players simply need to see the ball go through the hoop after they release it. Coaches can modify the offense or run special sets to help players create these scoring opportunities. The sooner the player can get to the basket or the free-throw line, the better. It is amazing how any made shot helps a player get the old confidence back.

Another—and perhaps the worst—scenario is that the slumping player also has immature confidence and thinks he is a better shooter than he actually is. Even when the shooting percentage drops below 40 percent (and less than 30 percent from three-point range), such players refuse to get the message that shooting is not a strong suit. So, what they call a slump is really a reflection of their true ineptitude as shooters.

Within this same category of player is the athlete who thinks shooting is part and parcel of playing a certain position, regardless of how poorly he shoots. I recall one very good but undersized post player who thought he had to take perimeter shots to prove he was a "small forward." He had convinced himself that he was a better shooter than he was. This was another case of immature confidence hurting him and his team.

In stark contrast to this is the story of Errick Greene, a former outstanding player at the University of Maine. Errick was a powerful, quick guard who could drive, post, and defend with the best of them. He once held a future NBA player to 0 points from the field while guarding him for 40 minutes. He played unselfishly and was a winner. The only problem was that he was a poor outside shooter.

In his first season, Errick did not take three-pointers because he knew he was not likely to make them. In the off-season, Errick took a mature approach to this weakness. He worked with the coaches to correct his faulty form, and he practiced shooting for countless hours trying to develop a consistent, accurate shot. His next year, Errick made 35 percent of his three-point shots, including a couple of key shots late in games. He didn't take a lot of three-pointers (51 all season) or become an outstanding shooter, but he did score 45 points in one game, and he played to his strengths (posting and driving).

Similarly, at La Salle, our talented six-foot-five point guard Rodney Green was 0 for 3 on three-point attempts in the 2006 to 2007 season. He wisely did not attempt shots he could not make. He dedicated himself to improving in the off-season, and he shot a respectable 16 of 47 three-pointers (34 percent) in the 2007 to 2008 season. He also made 78 percent of his free throws.

The lesson here is that sometimes a slump is not a slump. Poor shooting might reflect a lack of skill that must be developed or be properly counterbalanced with mature decision making and contributions in other facets of the game.

Ben Wallace, former center for the 2004 NBA champion Detroit Pistons and currently with the Cleveland Cavaliers, knows he's not the best shooter in the world, yet he's valued highly as an NBA player. Instead of trying to be something he's not, Ben takes only very high-percentage shots and does all the dirty work: defending, rebounding, setting picks, and so on. Similarly, ESPN analyst Doug Gottlieb was a superb player for Oklahoma State, but he rarely shot the ball. Instead, he focused on getting the ball to better scorers (in 2000, his senior year, he was second in the nation in assists). By doing so, Gottlieb led OSU to consecutive NCAA tournament appearances and outstanding records his junior and senior seasons.

Wallace and Gottlieb found ways to be "winners" for winning programs even though shooting wasn't one of their skills. Such players can focus on their passing ability, defense, and leadership. Confidence comes easily when you do what you do best.

Outside Criticism

In this age of unrealistic fan expectations, intense media coverage, Internet message boards, and overzealous parents, athletes and coaches alike have never received so much criticism. Even winning teams and good players are criticized, because in the eyes of a vocal minority, any level of success is never enough. So how do players and coaches maintain confidence in the face of ever-growing criticism? The first step is to acknowledge that outside criticism exists—and then choose to ignore it. A growing number of coaches do not read newspapers during the season. They ignore Internet message boards completely, and they politely listen to personal critics. They do not deny external criticism. They simply choose to ignore it in order to focus on the team. This is not to imply that a coach or player should not be self-critical. Being self-critical is part of the necessary humbling process in building mature confidence. However, it is difficult to remain enthusiastic and positive when being hard on oneself and simultaneously being open to outside criticism.

Remember, as performance decreases, positivity in the face of criticism is more necessary than ever to turn things around. In addition, players and coaches need to be educated about today's highly critical environment. They must be taught to expect criticism, because it exists for every school and team. They must not feel persecuted or hurt, because every other player and coach goes through it. Outside criticism must be expected, acknowledged, and minimized so that a player or coach can make focused, confident efforts toward improvement.

CHAPTER
4

Off-Season
Work Ethic

The phrase, "What really matters is what you do when no one is looking" is especially true when it comes to basketball players. An athlete's level of self-motivation is revealed during the off-season.

Joe Cassidy, the very successful head coach at Rowan University, gives players a simple way to test their self-motivation. His idea is that players should do the same things on and off the court whether a coach is present or not. Committed players should drill the same way, play with the same intensity, and be just as focused in pick-up games and off-season workouts as in practices with coaches pushing them.

From spring to early fall, a player must be willing to devote the time and expend the energy required to improve—outside the watchful eye and daily encouragement of a coach. From April through September, players demonstrate their level of maturity and desire to develop themselves both fundamentally and physically.

Current ESPN analyst Tim Legler was one player who certainly was prepared to do what it took to fulfill his basketball potential. Following a fine career at La Salle University, Tim soon learned it would be a challenge to make an NBA roster when his name was not called in that year's player draft. Tim went to work on his game and his conditioning. His intense off-season practice sessions paid off. Tim made the CBA all-star team with a 27-point scoring average in the 1992 to 1993 season, and he was signed by the Dallas Mavericks. By 1996, Tim shot an amazing 52 percent from beyond the arc, and he was the NBA's three-point champion that season.

Off-season options available to basketball players are so plentiful now that it's easy for players to get sidetracked. Many AAU tournaments and summer camps are now for exposure. The goal is to be seen by college coaches and to impress. The following sections provide some simple ideas that will allow players to improve their fundamental play in these environments and in individual workouts. Ultimately, playing fundamentally sound and playing with great effort and energy will win more games and impress more coaches. AAU tournaments, all-star camps, three-on-three competitions, and other summer events are still no substitute for serious time in the gym and weight room. The following sections discuss how to get the most benefit out of summer competition and what kind of off-season workouts best enhance skills.

PICKUP GAMES AND SUMMER BASKETBALL

Few things are more fun for the serious player than getting together with a group of talented players on a playground or in a gym and competing for time on the court. The code in these informal pickup games is as follows: Winners stay and play, and losers wait for "next." Most great players were made in these places. Confidence, pride, techniques, instincts, and competitiveness are cultivated on such courts—that is, if the competition is approached with the right frame of mind.

Because summer ball is often less structured, players are prone to abuse that additional freedom. Fundamentals are often abandoned in pickup and summer-league games, and players waste a great opportunity to develop their individual skills and understanding of team tactics.

That's not surprising, given that today's players have grown up in an era when nightly TV highlights showcase slam dunks, buzzer-beating three-pointers, and no-look passes. Meanwhile, crucial defensive stops, box-outs for key rebounds, and passes that lead directly to game-winning assists garner no media attention. As the saying goes, "Out of sight, out of mind." And it's only natural for players to seek to reproduce the types of plays that get the publicity rather than the basic plays that go unnoticed. So, unfortunately, what the typical off-season game amounts to is an inordinate number of missed dunks, errant alley-oop passes, askew three-pointers, silly turnovers, and matador defenses.

If you're the exceptional player who makes the most of the off-season by stressing offensive and defensive fundamentals, improving specific individual weaknesses, and playing unselfish team basketball, you can skip the next several pages. And, if you're that rare coach whose players always dutifully work on the techniques and tactics you've specified for the off-season, then you can fast-forward to the next chapter as well. But for the 99 percent of players and coaches who are trying to make the off-season more productive, the rest of this chapter is for you.

GUIDELINES FOR OFF-SEASON GAMES

Players who are seeking to maximize improvement in their skills but who also have an unselfish team-directed attitude should consider how to best apply that approach in off-season competition. To help with this, the following sections identify specific facets of the game and how such players should approach them on the court.

Transition Game

Players should always sprint the court. They should never "basket-hang"; this habit is lazy, leads to losing, and hurts conditioning. A player should be involved with every possession. If a player always runs the court hard and plays regular pickup ball, he will be in excellent condition and have little need for a cardiorespiratory conditioning program.

Two rules can be used in off-season games in order to encourage all players—offensive and defensive—to be involved in the transition game: (1) If a defensive player has not made it past half court by the time the offense scores, the basket counts and the offense gets the ball back again. (2) If an offensive player has not made it past half court by the time a teammate scores, the basket does not count and the defense gets the ball. Such rules will get players in the habit of running full court, something that happens far too infrequently in off-season play.

Andrew D. Bernstein/NBAE/Getty Images

Two of the best point guards in the world, Deron Williams and Jason Kidd, demonstrate the serious attitude and great effort needed for players to improve their skills and make a habit of playing at a high pace against good competition during the off-season.

Defense

A defender should always be in a stance. Lazy, ineffective defenders stand around on defense. A defender must be low and quick, and he must always work to contain the ball. Defenders should not let people drive to the basket. Being able to defend the player with the ball is essential to being a good defender. The one-on-one style of many offenses in pickup ball presents a great opportunity for players to practice guarding good players with the ball. To get better, a player should always volunteer to guard the best player possible on the other team.

Defenders should also contest every shot. They should never let a shot be attempted without a hand up in the shooter's face. If a player sprints back on defense, picks up a man, stays low and quick in a stance, contains the ball, and contests shots, that player is playing sound defense and preparing to win.

If team members have a chance to play together in a summer camp or summer league—or even if a few teammates find themselves on the same side in a pickup game—they should try to execute the offensive and defensive tactics taught by coaches during the season. Once again, this will help them prepare to win.

Offense

The skills required to become a good offensive player are developed in individual workouts, but the poise, instincts, and decision-making ability needed to use those skills come through competition. Most of all, players must be efficient and fundamental.

This is especially true regarding the use of the dribble. A player should not need more than two dribbles to make an explosive move. Players must not get into the playground habit of using five or six dribbles to set up a defender while everyone else just watches. This habit reflects selfishness, because the ball is being dominated by one person (unfortunately, this is modeled after watching the large number of isolation plays in the NBA).

When playing with teammates, a player should try to execute the offensive system and fundamentals his coach has already taught. The best examples of executing a style of play can be found at places such as Princeton, Georgetown, and Richmond, where they practice the Princeton offense. These players run their unique brand of offense—which is focused on screening, cutting, reading, and passing—throughout the year in pickup games. This extra repetition in the off-season gives them great preparation before fall practice.

Also, the following principles are straightforward and will result in smart offensive play: If a player is open, he should shoot; if a teammate is open, the player with the ball should pass the ball when that teammate is open—the player should not hesitate and then pass after the teammate is no longer open. Excellent shooters should shoot whenever the defender's hands are down and should drive whenever the defender's hands are raised. And players should jump-stop at the end of drives to reduce charges and turnovers.

To review, good offensive players need only a few explosive dribbles to penetrate a defense. They hit open people when they are open. They take open shots and take what the defense gives them. They are aggressive but under control, using jump stops on penetration.

In the post, offensive players should always try to maintain legal physical contact with defenders. This is achieved by getting the deepest position possible (i.e., closest to the basket) and by seeking out contact with the defender. Once contact is made, the offensive player should use the body to hold position without illegally pushing backward. After getting the ball deep, scoring with post moves and shots becomes much easier. In other words, post up strong!

At the same time, post players must not get into bad habits of fouling and pushing. Posting up strong means seeking out the defender and using one's body and strength to hold position and stop the defender from getting around to deny the pass. Post players may extend the elbows, but they may not swing the elbows or extend the forearms. Players should learn to post strong, deep, and legal.

Rebounding

Offensive rebounding is primarily a matter of desire: Who is most determined to pursue and claim missed shots? To be the quickest to the ball, a player must anticipate the shot and get inside rebounding position before the defense starts to box out. If boxed out, the player should spin or cut around the person. A rebounder must not relent until the ball is securely in the possession of an opponent.

Although he played many years ago, Paul Silas still remains one of the best examples when it comes to rebounding. In his three-year career (81 games) at Creighton University, Silas accumulated an astounding 1,751 rebounds. And, even as a relatively small (six-foot-seven) baseline player and part-time starter in the pros, he averaged 10 rebounds a game. Silas was also a winner—an integral part of two NBA championship teams in Boston and one in Seattle. Here's how the Celtics' site on NBA.com described him: "Paul Silas epitomized effort and diligence . . . [H]e succeeded with relentless work on the boards and unparalleled tenacity on defense." Recently, Paul Millsap of Louisiana Tech—also six-foot-seven—led the NCAA in rebounding for an incredible four straight seasons. He became a key contributor to the Utah Jazz because of his great overall effort, which makes him a truly outstanding rebounder.

Frontline players should develop the habit of crashing the boards on every shot. Guards must read floor balance. If a guard is above the top of the key when the shot is taken, he must be back on defense to prevent an easy score. This is also the case when another guard penetrates.

Blocking out is the first priority in defensive rebounding. Defenders usually have inside position when a shot is taken, and they will get the majority of rebounds if they keep inside position.

An effective box-out is achieved by seeking out the nearest offensive player, pivoting into him, and keeping him on one's back to prevent him from getting inside. This is one of the easiest basketball fundamentals to neglect, and not boxing out has cost many teams wins. A player who makes boxing out a habit is a disciplined, fundamental player. The toughest part about boxing out is that the defensive player usually thinks that he is already in good inside rebounding position, and it sometimes feels unnatural to go away from the basket to execute a box-out. Defenders must always remember that aggressive offensive rebounders are crashing for good position and will often succeed unless they are boxed out. Also, long rebounds go to the offense more often when no box-out occurs.

Some coaches are now teaching their players to use a "check-out" instead of a box-out when on the perimeter. Crafty offensive rebounders are likely to change directions as soon as their defender turns his back to box out. This often enables the offensive player to successfully maneuver around the box-out. To combat this, a check-out involves facing the offensive rebounder and momentarily blocking his path with a forearm. The forearm is not extended to push, strike, or foul; the forearm simply blocks the opponent just as the back does in a box-out. After impeding progress with a quick check-out (the defender has prevented the opponent from going around him), the defender turns to pursue the rebound as opposed to holding the box-out. In general, it makes sense to box out in the post area and to check out on the perimeter.

Pickup games are a perfect opportunity to get into the winning habits of crashing the offensive boards and boxing or checking out defensively. Another point to remember is that getting a loose ball is as good as getting a rebound. Players should get in the habit of grabbing loose balls (not dribbling them) and diving on them if necessary. This is a tough play that has been the deciding factor in winning and losing many games. Rebounding may be the best objective statistical measure of individual effort. To get a lot of rebounds, a player must demonstrate effort and toughness. This is a great identity for any player or team. La Salle has consistently been one of the top rebounding teams in the Atlantic 10 because we keep track of rebounds in practice, drill on rebounding, emphasize rebounding, and reward top rebounders with playing time. Rebounding creates an identity of effort and toughness, and it helps win games.

SUCCESSFUL PRACTICE HABITS

Some players work very hard on their shooting but never improve. They fail to improve because they are practicing mistakes. This phenomenon has given rise to many cliches, such as, "Practice does not make perfect;

perfect practice makes perfect." When it comes to basketball skills, old habits are indeed difficult to break. That's why players need to learn the proper fundamentals at an early age and practice the techniques correctly until they become habitual. Once the basic skills are mastered, players must apply those fundamentals in competitive conditions. This is far easier said than done. Besides being motivated to practice, a player must know how to practice.

High-Speed, Gamelike Conditions

Other than physical traits (size, strength, and athleticism), the most obvious difference between middle school and high school players—and between high school and college players—is the speed with which they perform skills. As the level of competition increases, so does the pace of every facet of the game, except perhaps free throws. So any athlete aspiring to compete at the next level must be constantly striving to do things quicker.

Former NBA coach Doug Moe employed a successful fast break and an unusually fast-paced motion offense. He said the execution of his system was simple, but that passing, catching, and shooting at high speed were difficult skills that needed to be practiced. Moe's practices never lasted that long—typically less than two hours—but they were intense, designed to develop the pace, style, and stamina that players needed to excel in his system. Those who were capable of executing at the desired speed through the course of a game earned roster spots and playing time. Those who couldn't adjust to the quicker pace were usually cut or traded.

Now consider what most players do when they shoot on their own. They usually go about it at a very relaxed, comfortable pace. And how many times do they have the luxury of shooting under such conditions in their games? Never, or at least seldom.

So, once proper shooting form and consistency are developed, players need to develop the fast footwork and quick moves necessary to get the shot off. The pace of their shot mechanics will need to be much quicker to avoid blocks. This disparity between the leisurely pace of practice shooting and the explosive movement required to get open and quickly release a shot in games is why so many shot attempts appear to be (and are) rushed in competition. And when that occurs, we know what happens to a player's shooting percentage.

This principle applies not only to shooting but to all skills and tactics. Therefore, for off-season workouts to be truly beneficial, they must be performed at full speed or game pace. Slides, pivots, jumps, dribble moves to the basket, and breakouts for a catch should all be executed with maximal effort.

The need for players to amp up their off-season work is all too evident at the start of preseason practices. Bad passes and turnovers, blocked and errant shots, and defenders whose feet appear to be in cement are,

Off-Season Development

Sean Miller—Xavier University

Off-season skill development is analogous to making a chain. Each week you add another link, and the strength of each link hinges on the quality and variety of work you do every day. Any individual link might be slightly stronger in one respect than another (say you concentrated more on shooting one week, ball handling the next), but together they form a complete chain that has no weak link.

Too often players try to master skills and moves through a series of crash courses, working very hard on one skill for a week or two, then dropping it and focusing on another skill, and so on. They develop no continuity and foster inconsistency, which result in little or no progression.

Working on your game too many hours every day isn't good, either. Eventually you reach a point of diminishing returns, and performance sags as mental and physical fatigue set in. Some players lose their enthusiasm, having essentially burned out their interest in the game. So, instead, it's better for players to get into the gym or training room for a very focused 45-minute workout, doing things the right way, several days a week.

It's best to get into a Monday-to-Friday routine, then add time on the weekends as the schedule allows. Basketball players improve inch by inch, not by leaps and bounds. Players should work on a variety of things daily during the off-season. Consistent work each day on several areas will produce the most gains over a long period. Say you're a big man and work on low post moves, a jump hook, free throws, and your conditioning from May through August. After four months, you should notice significant improvement in those areas.

Forcing yourself to do in an individual workout what you would do in a game, such as using screens from trash cans and catching the ball on the move off a tossback machine, is the kind of quality work that's needed in the gym. Also, incorporate conditioning into technique-development activities whenever possible. Perform dribbling skills while running, pivoting, and changing direction. Simulate situations and the physical effort required in competition, even if it is just you or you and one other person in the gym.

If you have a plan, are precise at what you are trying to improve, invest yourself over a longer period of time, and don't waste time, progress will be evident. A good individual workout plan should be as specific as possible. With some input from your coaches, identify the areas in your game that need extra attention, and build time for that into the plan.

It really helps to put the plan in writing or type so that when you step on the court you have a preplanned workout to follow and you have a place to record what was accomplished each day. How many shots did you shoot? How many shots did you make? How has your shooting percentage improved over time? After a while, the results start to reinforce your efforts and you develop more pride and confidence in your shot. Repetitions start taking hold and you develop consistency over a long period. The same type of thing is true in weightlifting and other areas that will be included in your workout plan.

Derrick Brown entered our program a year younger than everyone else. He was very talented athletically and had a great mind, but we decided to red-shirt him his freshman year to allow him to mature and be on equal ground, age-wise, with the first-year class starting the next season.

So Derrick did nothing but practice, lift weights, and work on his game for an entire year. In that time, he went from 187 pounds to 215 pounds, yet his percentage of body fat remained the same. He was very disciplined, never missed a summer workout in the weight room, ate properly, and followed our plan to a tee. He stayed equally invested in improving during our fall program. Although not playing in games that season was difficult, he stayed on track with lifting weights and practicing, building up his body and adding new dimensions to his game.

After another great off-season of work, Derrick was really ready to play and has continued to improve throughout his career. He's currently 234 pounds and stronger and more fit than ever. I don't think he has missed a lift in his three years here, and he's obviously benefited for his dedication.

In addition to on-court practice and conditioning, players need to compete in the off-season. The right type of competition helps players stay sharp, keep in some semblance of game shape, and test the skills they've been developing in workouts.

When you get better, you play to win. One problem now is that players take part in so many games and tournaments during the off-season that the scores and results of most games aren't very meaningful. There is too much of it. I recommend that players get on an AAU team that is structured, has a good coach, is composed of good players and people, and competes in the right tournaments. Players don't impress anyone by showing up for 20 tournaments during a summer and playing subpar in several of them or incurring an injury. It's far better to choose the right five or six tournaments that are spaced out at reasonable intervals, and play your best and hardest in each of them. Plus, not taking part in so many tournaments allows more time to work on things in between and stick to a conditioning regimen.

A player, his high school coach, and parents really need to make responsible decisions about off-season competitions. Don't just say, "Hey, I'm going to play in whatever tournaments this AAU team can enter." Really think about what's best for your overall physical development and progression as a player.

(continued)

Since I was young, I've spent countless hours on the basketball court in an effort to improve as a player and a coach. Perhaps having a dad who is a very successful high school coach encouraged such practice habits and a love for the game. After all these years, I'm convinced there's no easy way to get better and compete in this sport, and I don't expect that will ever change.

unfortunately, the norm. What is the reason for this? Players have spent the summer playing at a more relaxed pace without intense defense. Then, when more quickness and speed are required, skills and decision making are too slow and deficient.

Should every activity in an off-season workout be intense and full speed? No. Gradual warm-up is important in preventing injuries. Also, if a player is trying to improve basic shooting mechanics, the player should first master the proper technique before worrying about quick moves for getting open and releasing the shot against defenders. And, when a player is learning a new move, it's fine to start slowly in order to make sure that posture, footwork, and fakes are correct. The player can then build up speed and explosiveness.

Those exceptions aside, most practice activities and drills should be performed at a gamelike tempo. If not, the off-season work a player has put in will all be for naught, and the player will find himself behind teammates when it comes to competing for a roster spot.

Shooting and Strength

NBA scout Steve Rosenberry once said that when he evaluates players over time, he always looks for improvement in shooting and strength. He believes that these two areas respond the most to effort. In other words, if a player improves his shooting and strength from year to year, Steve knows that the player has a strong work ethic. If a player has the same shot (i.e., same flaws and skill level) and the same body (i.e., no added muscle) from year to year, this player most likely has a poor work ethic.

At La Salle University, our first recruiting class (in 2006) was very athletic but did not contain a good outside shooter. We had great success helping the players improve their shooting using progressive goals in the off-season.

Each player had a personal shooting coach. That player worked only with that coach to make sure the player was never getting mixed opinions and ideas. First, we had the player work on form shooting from 1 to 14 feet. The player focused on having the ball rest on the fingers and pads of the hand (not on the palm), having square feet and shoulders, bringing the ball above the shooting eye, having the shooting arm begin in an

"L" position (not in a "V"), having the elbow in, following through, and having the guide hand not push the shot (i.e., keeping the thumb of the guide hand back).

We would not allow a player to shoot free throws until we thought he had mastered good form and technique. After numerous successful repetitions—with the player striving only for perfect form and habits—the player began to work on free throws. Free throws were practiced with an emphasis on applying the proper techniques learned in form shooting. We would not allow a player to shoot a 15- to 17-foot jump shot until we thought he had an accurate free throw. After the player demonstrated (over hundreds of repetitions) that he could make a minimum of 75 percent of his free throws—with consistent streaks of 7 to 50 makes—we would then let him move on to practicing 15- to 17-foot jump shots.

The next step was to start workouts by reviewing form shooting and free throws, and then practice 15- to 17-foot jump shots. The player would pick a spot and stay there until he made at least 5 in a row and then move to another spot. We would not allow a player to shoot off the move until he could accurately catch and shoot without moving. Once a player could easily and routinely make 5 to 10 stationary jump shots in a row from any spot at 15 to 17 feet, we let that player shoot off the move.

Next, the player progressed to starting workouts with form shooting, free throws, and stationary jump shots. Then we worked on shooting off the move. Players shot sets of 15- to 17-foot shots while moving after each shot. The player would shoot and then sprint to another spot, and the rebounder would pass the ball to the shooter on the move. At this point, catching, squaring, and shooting on balance were emphasized. We would not let a player take a three-point shot until he could routinely make 30 to 40 out of 50 shots off the move from 15 to 17 feet. Once a player mastered shooting off the move, we had him start working on catching and shooting stationary three-point shots.

The next step was to start workouts with form shooting, free throws, stationary jump shots, and shooting off the move. Players would then shoot sets of 25 three-point shots (5 each from the two corners, two wings, and top of the key). Players had a goal of making 15 to 20 shots per set, depending on the player.

After progressively teaching shooting skills and setting goals, we enjoyed significant shooting improvement the next season and led the Atlantic 10 in three-point shooting percentage. Certainly, having our weaker shooters improve was important, but all the extra shooting work turned our one good shooter, Darnell Harris, into a great shooter. Darnell was a 37-percent career three-point shooter in his first three seasons, and he shot 48 percent beyond the arc his senior year. He was one of the top shooters in the nation and proved it by winning the annual NCAA three-point shooting contest during the 2008 Final Four weekend in San Antonio. The lesson is that even good shooters can improve significantly.

The biggest key to this progression was teaching about form. This involved helping players initially change their shooting form (this was actually the most difficult phase because many players had to overcome years of bad habits). The next key was making sure a player demonstrated mastery of one skill level before moving on to the next. The last key was quickly reviewing form shooting and free-throw shooting every day before moving on to more advanced shots.

Ballhandling

One of the beautiful things about basketball is that all a player needs in order to improve is himself and a ball. It is difficult to realistically practice football tackling, blocking, passing, or receiving by yourself. It is difficult to realistically practice baseball skills such as hitting, pitching, and fielding by yourself. However, all a basketball player needs to become a better shooter is a ball and a basket at which to shoot. To become a better ball handler, only a ball is required; a basket is not necessary.

Another wonderful concept is that a young player can develop a high level of skill simply because of his desire to learn and practice hour after hour. Matt Brady, the current head coach at James Madison University, was a record-setting point guard at Siena College who had tremendous ballhandling skills. He did three simple things as a young player to become a highly skilled ball handler. First, he would dribble with his left hand at every opportunity (Matt is right-handed). He would do this to begin every drill, whenever he dribbled his ball home on the sidewalk, or whenever he brought the ball up the court in a game with no pressure on him. By using his "weak" hand first in drills and whenever else he could, he soon had no weak hand but was equally strong going right or left.

Second, he emphasized speed (as mentioned in the preceding section). Matt would practice figure eights, crossovers, spin dribbles, behind-the-back dribbles, between-the-legs dribbles, inside-out dribbles (i.e., fake crossovers), and speed dribbles (sprinting all out) while going so fast that he would sometimes lose control of the ball. The idea was to practice dribbling moves at high speeds to develop gamelike skills. If he was not losing the ball occasionally, it meant he was practicing at a speed he had already mastered. To gain more skill, he needed to push himself to go faster and occasionally fail.

Lastly, Matt was never a "hot dog" in games, and he was very efficient. But, to develop skill, he would practice the toughest combinations of spins, behind-the-back dribbles, between-the-legs dribbles, and crossover moves that he could possibly imagine. He was forcing himself to dribble with a higher level of skill and complexity than he would need in a game. He was making practice more difficult than a game. This time spent between a player and his basketball—with no one else necessary—resulted in the highest level of ballhandling skill.

Maximized Repetitions

Occasionally, a young superstar can lead a team to success; examples are Carmelo Anthony, Kevin Durant, Greg Oden, Mike Beasley, Kevin Love, and Derrick Rose. However, these young, NBA-ready phenoms are the exception. Most often, more experienced teams are more successful. In high school, senior-dominated teams typically achieve the greatest success. In college, having most of your team returning with few senior losses is usually the key to success. At the professional level, older teams tend to win even against younger teams that are quicker and more athletic. The reason for this is that greater knowledge and skill are gained through experience. This all comes from repetition, having done things over and over again.

A player can speed up the learning process and skill development by getting in as many repetitions as possible. Once again, a player must like to work at skills over and over again as opposed to just playing the game. For example, in one pickup game, a player may take 15 shots. That is not enough to create improvement. It would be better to shoot hundreds of shots individually that day in order to create true shooting improvement.

Many players who love to play may take part in hundreds of AAU and pickup games during the off-season but never improve their skills. They may improve their instincts, decisions, defense, rebounding, and competitiveness, but they do not get enough shooting instruction, correction, or repetition to make shots more consistently. To improve shooting consistency, a player needs to seek out tough, competitive game experience as well as daily individual workouts to get the repetition necessary to build skill.

A coach who develops daily practice plans would be wise to maximize practice repetition for his players. Teams often waste practice time with players waiting in long lines for their turn to do a drill. To avoid this, a coach should use all available baskets to keep players active instead of waiting for turns. For example, players can get more shots up in smaller groups at more baskets than with large groups at one or two baskets. If only one or two baskets are available, players should practice ballhandling, passing, or defensive footwork without a basket until their turn comes to work on shooting. In this situation, most coaches develop stations that their players rotate through. This maximizes activity and repetition for the players. Coaches must remember the following: "Repetition is the mother of all learning."

Practice That Is More Difficult Than Games

One way to make practice conditions more challenging is to minimize breaks between drills and between repetitions within drills. This will create a more gamelike fatigue that requires a player to perform at a high level while tired. Physically demanding workouts are also an opportunity to build conditioning. Short breaks can be taken for water and to make free throws under gamelike physical conditions. For example, players could be required to make two consecutive free throws between each drill to simulate game conditions, with a quick sprint up and down the court if a free throw is missed.

The debate continues concerning the effectiveness or appropriateness of self- or coach-imposed penalties requiring players to run (or perform some kind of conditioning drill or exercise) for poor execution or effort. The merits of using such penalties hinge on how and to what extent they are applied. If the penalties are so severe that they become the focus of the players' attention—rather than the performance—then something is wrong. Certainly, at the youth and high school levels, the first priorities are the athletes' skill and physical development, as well as their enjoyment of the game through participation. And athletes who are trying to acquire new skills can be distracted and discouraged when penalties interfere with the learning process.

When a player has gained the skills and maturity to compete at a high level, a different mentality takes over. Maximum enjoyment is no longer gained from merely participating. Instead, enjoyment comes from testing one's abilities against another, as well as against a player's own performance standards. At this point, the positive and negative consequences of performance goals can be beneficial. The mature and highly motivated athlete accepts self-imposed penalties for not reaching standards of excellence. However, the penalty should have a purpose—making the athlete better. For this reason, physically demanding penalties produce more well-conditioned and mentally tough athletes. And, because elite athletes already value conditioning, they know such penalties are purposeful.

Role-Related Work

Every player wants to expand his skills, and this is generally a positive thing to do. However, trying to expand on a role can sometimes be counterproductive for an older player. For example, Malik Rose has enjoyed great success in the NBA, and he was a dominant rebounder and post player at Drexel University. Malik thought he might need to become more of a wing player because he could be too short (six-foot-seven) to be a power forward at the pro level.

His coach, Bill Herrion (now head coach at the University of New Hampshire), was concerned that if Malik focused too much on his weaknesses and stopped focusing on his strengths, he might hurt his chances at the professional level. The two of them decided that going into Malik's senior year, he should work on his shooting and ballhandling to prepare to expand his skills.

However, they also decided that what made him a great player was his rebounding and post play. He kept lifting weights to get even stronger.

He ended up proving that he could be one of the best rebounders in the country and that he was a better power forward than many taller players. Malik also became a solid ball handler and mid-range shooter in the NBA, but he never would have been so successful without his inside strength, which remained his primary role. In fact, when with the San Antonio Spurs, he was called on to use his strength to defend Shaquille O'Neal despite giving up six inches in height and was key in helping the Spurs beat the Lakers en route to the NBA championship.

As in Malik's case, players are sometimes better off focusing primarily on what they can already do well—as opposed to what, in an ideal world, they *might* be able to do well. Perhaps the role for a smaller player is to be a point guard who is a flawless ball handler. Or, a particular offensive system may require a power forward to be able to consistently hit three-point shots from the top of the key. Those are defined roles and skills that are essential for those players to contribute to their respective teams. In other words, players can focus on becoming outstanding at very specific skills. At the NBA level, some players are clearly superstars. However, most of the players in the league are not superstars but rather special-ists who can do something at an outstanding level. Examples of the roles

During off-seasons in college, Malik Rose spent time improving his weaknesses while maintaining his strengths—post play and rebounding.

Ron Turenne/NBAE/Getty Images

that many successful players have include being an outstanding post defender, perimeter defender, three-point shooter, low-post scorer, or point guard. Thus, understanding one's strengths and focusing on those skills to become a specialist—while also working to improve and minimize weaknesses—is the true path to growing as a player.

Goal-Directed Practice

Some players may work on everything in an effort to become a complete player (this is recommended for young players unless they are unusually big or small). Others may work on very specific skills that will enable them to better help their team. To determine the proper focus for their individual practice, players should use self-evaluation and should consult with their coach. The coach and player should discuss key areas that the player needs to work on as well as specific daily goals.

For example, Steve Alford, former Indiana All-American and current University of New Mexico coach, learned very early in his career that his shooting accuracy would determine how far he progressed as a player and how much he would contribute to his team. And because he was often fouled when releasing his shots—and was often in possession of the ball late in games with his team ahead and the opponent having to foul—he devoted an extraordinary amount of time to free-throw shooting. Indeed, Steve would not consider a workout complete until he made 100 straight free throws. He would even do push-ups for every free throw he missed.

For individual workouts, the goals should be tailored to specific skills that need work or enhancement for the player and the team to be successful. A point system can be used for motivation and to measure progress.

For example, a drill could be run in which a player breaks out from under the basket to the left wing, then catches and pivots into triple-threat position. The guard then fakes a shot before exploding to the right, driving deep into the paint in one dribble, and jump stopping for a short jump shot. For scoring, start with the number 5. A made shot decreases the number to 4. A missed shot increases the number to 6. Every made shot decreases the number by one, and every missed shot increases the number by one. The goal is to get the score to 0. When the number gets to 1, the next attempt should be thought of as the game winner. This puts a bit more pressure on the player to end the drill, achieve the goal, and make a big shot. If the score ever rises to 7, the player must perform some beneficial but taxing conditioning drill and then start the drill over. You could use this type of point system for any shooting drill.

WORK AND PLAY

All players like to play basketball; fewer like to work at it. Why would someone like work? Because when it comes to the game of basketball, work should be fun.

Larry Bird once commented that he had an amazing job because he was paid to shoot baskets and play games. Some NBA players complain about the taxing travel, mandatory off-day practices, recurring injuries, media criticism, and fans' unrealistic expectations through an 82-game schedule (which can easily extend to more than 100 games with exhibitions and playoff games). However, Larry Bird never lost his love for competition and for playing and practicing the game.

All players start playing because they like the game. Hey, putting the ball through the hoop is fun, right? But the players who grow to love the game are the ones who will love working at it. At that point, practicing hard is fun. Seeing one's shooting, ballhandling, and strength improve only reinforces that great feeling.

Michael Jordan had a well-publicized "love of the game" clause in his contract. This allowed him to play anywhere and anytime he wanted, because he loved to play.

As the saying goes, "Everyone likes to play. Champions like to work." The best players in the sport enjoy the practice, the training, and the games. They love improving and winning. They don't just like to play; they also like to work. They find the work intrinsically rewarding, knowing that they have invested themselves fully into something and have achieved results that are satisfying to them.

OFF-SEASON EFFORT

Putting the proper effort into off-season work really comes down to whether you accept this simple fact: The only way to have a successful career in this game is to continue to elevate your level of play, or, as a coach, your players' level of play. No one excels to his potential on talent alone or by being satisfied with the status quo. In fact, many coaches believe that players never stay the same. They either get better or get worse. If they work properly, they get better. Of course, doing nothing and maintaining bad habits lead to getting worse.

The one piece of information about an athlete that a potential employer would find most valuable before offering a job would be how hard and how smart that player worked in the off-season. This is a very good predictor of what type of work ethic and how much potential to improve that prospective employee brings to the workplace.

Even the cream of the crop—LeBron James, Kevin Garnett, Dwight Howard (kids who as seniors in high school seemed destined for the Hall of Fame)—have excelled as pros not because of their enormous physical talent alone, but because they have always been among the hardest workers in the off-season. Great basketball programs do not win each season simply by hoarding the most talent; rather, they recruit athletes who will push themselves to improve each year during the time between the final buzzer of the past season and the start of organized practices the next.

_____ CHAPTER _____

5

In-Season Accountability

Off-season work is primarily an individually driven pursuit, but once the season begins, the *team* must become players' first priority. This shift in focus from personal interests to group achievements is essential for a successful season in any basketball program. Conversely, any squad with players who fail to buy into the team-first approach is destined to have difficulties.

Think that's too simplistic? Consider this stark contrast between two teams during the 2005 to 2006 NBA season. The Detroit Pistons set a record with 73 consecutive games in which the same five starters were on the floor, ready for action, at the opening tip. Conversely, the New York Knicks' starting lineup was a revolving door, constantly changing from one game to the next. The Pistons' starters fought through illness, injuries, and a host of other obstacles throughout the grueling season; each player fulfilled his respective role and stepped up to support his teammates when needed. The Knicks' starters seemed to invent ways to miss games or otherwise be consigned to the bench. The club's more talented players resisted the roles that Coach Larry Brown assigned them. The Pistons compiled the league's best record (64-18); the Knicks—despite having the league's highest paid roster—lost 59 of 82 games, second worst in the NBA.

The 2008 Xavier team that won the Atlantic 10 championship had their three most talented players accept completely unselfish roles to help their team achieve great success. Perhaps their best overall player, Josh Duncan, a senior, accepted a role coming off the bench as the sixth man. He was still an all-conference player and provided his team with incredible talent. Previous leading scorer Stan Burrell became the best defender in the conference and took fewer shots. Drew Lavander, a high school All-American capable of scoring a lot, became a high-assist floor leader. All three were willing to sacrifice individual stats and emphasize what the team needed them to do for Xavier to maximize its potential as a national power.

Sculptors, solo musicians, computer software programmers, golfers, master chefs, and many more skilled individuals can operate fairly autonomously and achieve great personal and professional success. Having gained the necessary knowledge, these people perform a unique skill that allows them to create the desired results independently, or with minor assistance from others. In other words, they can do their own thing. In contrast, the desired outcome in basketball—winning—requires a collective effort in which all members share a sense of obligation toward the team.

This accountability to a group and to its mission—to something larger than oneself—is one of the key life lessons that can be gained through participation in team sports. Yet learning and embracing this approach is difficult for some players. Perhaps they were the only child in their family and had never really been required to share; maybe they matured early and received a tremendous amount of praise for superior individual

AP Photo/Ed Reinke

Motivation is demonstrated by players' efforts in all facets of the game, as here, where North Carolina's Tyler Hansbrough shows great determination to gain and keep possession of the ball.

performances earlier in their career; or they might simply come from a lax or dysfunctional home situation in which they fended for themselves and rarely engaged in activities with others. Such backgrounds don't prevent players from being dependable, contributing team members. And later in this chapter, you'll find ideas on how to nurture and develop such accountability. But be prepared for challenges along the way.

As noted by Roonie Scovel, women's basketball coach at Gulf Coast Community College, today's athletes have grown up in an "I" generation in which not much is demanded of youngsters individually, and they are rarely required to function as contributing members of a group. Thus, they find it difficult in a team situation to sacrifice their own interests for the sake of a collective effort. But as Scovel says, "You gotta decide as a team to work on things, practice with a great attitude, run faster, work harder. When I don't see that happening, it needs to be changed." Obviously, she's been successful doing so, as her teams have won 90 percent of their games and a national title since she took over the program in 1996.

RESPONSIBILITY AND DUTY

Being part of a team carries with it a great responsibility. Everything one does affects everyone else. Every shot, defensive slide, pass, rebound, screen, and loose ball will help or hurt everyone's chance to be victorious. How well a player plays in practice every day determines how prepared the player and his teammates are to win. Everyone counts on each other. Everyone either contributes or detracts—no one has a neutral effect.

The graduation of each class is a time for coaches and players to reflect on the important years of life shared together. Through the course of a season and a career, the athletes and staff have worked together, struggled together, fought together, and celebrated together. They have at times consoled each other—and at all times tried to help each other. These are the responsibilities that team members have to each other.

Each new player joins the team pledging that he will be a serious student, committed basketball player, unselfish team member, and the best person possible. Everyone agrees to these responsibilities when they join a team. Unfortunately, not everyone fulfills them. But when they do, wonderful relationships and teams can rise above whatever obstacles might block success when going it alone.

Fulfilling team responsibilities is as simple as doing what you say you are going to do. Each year we have a special dinner during graduation week with the seniors only. As a coach, my hope is to be able to tell those players, "You did what you said you were going to do when we recruited you. You worked. You were a good player on good teams. You earned your degree. You conducted yourself well. We are proud of you and know you will succeed in life."

Desire and Unselfishness

A useful saying to learn is, "Work as if everything depends on you. Act as if nothing does." First, consider the enormous responsibility if everything depended on one person. Imagine if someone thought he had to get every rebound, make every defensive stop, make every correct offensive decision, and get every loose ball. This individual would be incredibly forceful with his will and desire, always playing at maximum intensity and inspiring others to do the same.

Great players do not wait for others to do the right thing; they take the responsibility on themselves. This often does not mean scoring points or accumulating impressive statistics. It does mean taking responsibility to do everything possible to help a team win. This includes working to be the player who can and will deliver what is needed when it is needed.

This responsibility involves being aware that personal play affects the whole team and working as if the game depends on one's own effort. In fact, the outcome rests on everyone's effort, because a single weakness that breaks one link in a chain breaks the whole chain. Everything depends on each player being a strong link in the chain. As the saying goes, "Every chain is only as strong as its weakest link." A responsible player gives every effort not to be that weak link.

The second part of the quote mentioned earlier is, "Act as if nothing depends on you." This comes from the realization that all the other parts of the chain are also doing their part. In fact, without the other links in the chain, a single link would have nothing to be a part of! Consider the humility of the teammate who thanks teammates for assists, who congratulates teammates on big defensive plays and rebounds, and who encourages the player whose critical contributions are not seen by the fans and media. Having a caring and unselfish attitude toward teammates is a very important responsibility.

One of the most impressive performances I have seen came in a single play that exemplified a combination of intense effort and extreme unselfishness. Sherman Diaz, a player at La Salle, did not play in the first 59 minutes of a four-overtime game. Sherman was a good wing player, but our best lineup at the time had three guards and two big guys. Instead of feeling sorry for himself, Sherman encouraged his teammates and was into the game ("act as if nothing depends on you"). As players fouled out, we needed Sherman in the last minute of the fourth overtime. In his first play, Sherman out-hustled every player on the court for a long offensive rebound ("work as if everything depends on you") and kicked it to an open teammate who made a three-point shot that propelled us to a dramatic win. His attitude reflected unselfishness by supporting others even though he surely wanted to play more in that game. When his time came, he was ready and responded with a desire to win that made the difference in the game. He demonstrated great character and played a larger role in future wins.

LOYALTY

When players and coaches express their support of others who count on them, they show loyalty. Players and coaches who are loyal to each other are a true team or, more accurately, a basketball family. They care for each other and show it in their words and actions. They will fight for each other.

The 2003 University of Kansas team epitomized this responsibility to the team concept. After a 3-3 start, they were widely criticized and questioned by local fans and media. Whose fault was it? What was wrong? After making it to another Final Four and the national championship game at the end of the season, players reflected on the early-season struggles, describing them as a positive turning point because players did not blame coaches or teammates. They stuck together and believed they would work out their problems, which is exactly what they did. They had to ignore negativity from many sources in order to be positive about each other and keep working hard. This is exactly what made the 2003 Kansas Jayhawks a major success story.

The opposite occurs when disloyalty affects a team. Players can neglect their own shortcomings and blame others while talking poorly of teammates and coaches. Worse yet, they can act supportive of each other when they are actually not. This disloyalty ultimately creates dissension that further harms a struggling team and diminishes the character of those involved.

This does not mean that everyone on a team is required to like everyone else the same way. However, players must always play hard and together, and they must honestly communicate differences when necessary. Loyal teammates do not turn against each other.

In his book *Showtime,* Pat Riley, then coach of the Los Angeles Lakers, described a humiliating 148-114 loss to the Boston Celtics in game 1 of the 1985 NBA finals, which some referred to as the "Memorial Day Massacre." The day after, the Lakers gathered for a video session.

Kareem Abdul-Jabbar—the captain of the team and one of the best to ever play the game—arrived early and sat directly in front of the video monitor. Kareem knew he had performed just as poorly as everyone else on the club. His expression and demeanor were intense. He was eager to accept responsibility for his poor play and to lead the team the rest of the way.

Coach Riley picked up on Kareem's leadership and intensity. So, the coach decided to make Kareem a focal point of his criticism, seeing that Kareem wanted to set an example and sensing the impact it would have on his teammates. Certainly, the previous day's loss was not all Kareem's fault. However, the coach and captain alike knew that total responsibility and commitment were needed or the Lakers would be beaten in the series.

Coach Riley made a point of how Kareem was repeatedly being beaten down the court by Celtics players. The captain listened and took the criticism with great maturity, resolving to perform at a higher level in game 2.

The rest of the Lakers fed off Kareem's example. They did not finger-point. They looked within themselves, as Kareem did, and were committed to turning the series around. They went on to win the NBA championship that season, in no small measure because of the accountability and leadership of their captain.

More recently, a similar incident involving a star player's accountability for a loss occurred with the Orlando Magic. Dwight Howard, who seems destined to become one of modern basketball's superstars, was removed from a game by Coach Stan Van Gundy for not applying himself fully on the defensive end. On defense, the Magic rely on Howard's rebounding, shot blocking, and general domination in the lane area. Howard and Van Gundy had a heated exchange on the bench, and afterward the coach called out his player: "His [Howard's] focus is on the offensive end. He gets discouraged when he doesn't get the ball. I think the numbers prove that what we need him to focus on to win is defensive rebounding, but that's not what he wants to do right now, and we've got a bit of a conflict." Howard, to his credit, has been nothing but a class act since entering the NBA at the age of 18; he reflected on the matter and accepted his role and responsibilities to the team. "I got to do what's right for my team," he said. "They need me to be focused on what I can do. . . . If I don't do those things, we're going to be a mediocre team."

Now that doesn't mean that the solution to all teams' problems is simply to blame the best player—or any players for that matter—and the club will start playing better. Indeed, teams that make a habit of finger-pointing when they lose will become perpetual losers.

A wise coach once said that whenever one points a finger at someone else to place blame, there are more fingers on his hand pointed back at him. The "winner" always looks in the mirror first when analyzing faults.

A player must be mature enough to acknowledge what he could have done better after any performance. But this is especially the case after close losses. When a game comes down to the last possession, as normally happens several times during the season, any single play during the whole game could have provided the extra point or two to change the outcome. One player getting one more rebound, one more defensive stop, or one less turnover at any point in the game could have turned a team's loss into a win. Every player should reflect on what extra play he could have made that would have made the difference for the team. This helps create learning and improvement, and it also shows loyalty to teammates. In fact, a whole season can come down to a single possession. The intense coach or player constantly pays attention to execution and effort because any possession can ultimately be the difference maker. The only way to be prepared for that critical moment is to make every moment critical. This is the mind frame of winners who never take a play off.

PRIDE AND OWNERSHIP

Sometimes the tradition of a program is such that every player entering it feels a sense of pride, and every player accepts the responsibility of upholding those characteristics that have made the program so successful. Through the years, coaches have tried a variety of ways to cultivate such an aura around their team, but the only ones who pull it off are those who genuinely feel that same obligation themselves.

Michigan State University has been one of the nation's elite college basketball programs for many years. Within the Spartans' basketball facilities, the sense of tradition they have established with their players and teams is very clear. One wall is filled with framed *Sports Illustrated* covers of Magic Johnson. Another wall features the names of former all-conference players. The college jerseys of former and current NBA players are framed and displayed to highlight those alums who have excelled at the next level. In addition, national championship, Big Ten championship, Final Four, and NCAA tournament teams are honored as representing the best squads ever to represent the school.

Developing pride in a program is certainly one purpose of such displays. However, another purpose is to convey to current players that *they* are now responsible for the continued success of the program. Through the environment created in East Lansing, Coach Tom Izzo sends a clear message to his players: You are responsible to play like champions. And, by their performance, it is clear that his athletes have embraced that message—and that they hold themselves accountable for sustaining the same high level of play exhibited by previous MSU players and teams.

To reinforce that point, the initials PP and TPW appear on each Michigan State player's locker. TPW means "tough players win," and PP means "players play." In other words, players don't complain, make excuses, or try to coach or officiate. Players play!

One of life's most important lessons is that we control our own destiny more than anyone else controls it. Less successful individuals blame shortcomings in life on bad luck or others, and they do little to better themselves. As football coach Lou Holtz says, "Life is 10 percent what happens to us and 90 percent how we respond." The reality is that the attainment of our goals is up to the person we see when we look in the mirror, especially when we face adversity. Success is a personal responsibility. That's true for the player and also for the coach.

PLAYING TIME

Some players think they cannot succeed because they do not get a chance to play enough. When players of the same ability compete for playing time, a coach must make a difficult choice if neither player has performed significantly better than the other. To ensure playing opportunities, a player must clearly demonstrate that she is best for the job.

Pat Riley says, "Hard work guarantees nothing, but without it you don't have a chance." Success must be earned on the court by doing "winning" things. These winning things include helping one's team and outcompeting others. When a player is more of a winner and consistently shows more ability, he will be given more playing opportunities. It is under the player's control.

A player has control over how he plays and how he works to develop. The only thing he cannot totally control is the competition. In many cases, fine players simply have an even better player in front of them, and as a result, they do not get to play much. The best example of this was Swen Nater, who in 1973 was the 16th player taken in the NBA draft, the only NBA first-round draft choice to *never* start a college game. He had a successful 11-year career in the ABA and NBA, but in college he backed up Bill Walton, who was one of the best centers to ever play. Sometimes a good player must simply respect the teammate who is ahead of him in the lineup.

At the same time, a player should absolutely believe he can beat anyone and should work to do so. This is the best part of mature confidence—the constant belief in oneself. In a situation like Swen Nater's, the player must respect not only the abilities of teammates, but also the sanctity of the team, not begrudging teammates' success or having a negative influence on the group. Every player is expected to support teammates and to work to improve. The player who maintains a positive attitude in a tough situation like this is a winner for his team and is preparing to become a winner in life.

While a good player may face the challenge of having a very talented player in front of him, the very talented player also faces challenges that can limit success. Very talented players can be thrown off course by complacency when competing against less gifted players. Too often, the more talented player coasts in practice, because even with a lesser effort he can still be the most productive player on the court. Such a player will never reach his potential. Nor will he help raise the level of play of his team.

Conversely, a winner is never satisfied with less than maximum effort—both from himself and his teammates. This player's aim each time on the court is complete excellence in all areas of basketball. And the motive behind this expectation is not personal accolades but rather to make his team the best it can be. Whether this means helping teammates more on defense or looking for open teammates when attracting defensive help, the player will modify his game to make the team better as a whole.

Michael Jordan is the prototype of a very gifted player who is also a winner. Michael was never satisfied with his game, and he continually sought ways to better himself. He also desperately wanted to win. This was evident in his defensive pride as a regular on the NBA All-Defensive team and his desire to have the ball with the game on the line. The turning point in his career came when Coach Phil Jackson convinced him that he could not win championships unless his teammates could do more. Because of his leadership and extraordinary physical gifts, Michael was able to unselfishly create more scoring opportunities for his teammates, thereby building their skills and confidence. This was a key part of the process in making the Chicago Bulls six-time NBA champions.

MAKING OTHERS BETTER

Interestingly, Chicago Bulls teammates John Paxson and Steve Kerr both hit game-winning shots off Michael Jordan assists in games that decided championships. Jordan's personal standards were high, he made others better, and he won big—the consummate gifted winner. Consistency, making others better, and winning define the great player.

The early San Antonio Spurs championship teams resulted from an established all-star welcoming and deferring to a rising star. David Robinson—"The Admiral"—demonstrated the utmost in team accountability and loyalty in how he tutored, praised, and conceded playing time to a young Tim Duncan. Had Robinson instead been more worried about his point totals and personal fame, the Spurs would never have accomplished so much. And that same selflessness has permeated that ball club ever since, so not only did Robinson help the team win during his final seasons in the league, he also left a legacy that has been a driving force in the club's more recent title-winning seasons.

When a player is said to "make others better," he is receiving a very special compliment and the highest level of respect. Making others better on the basketball court can be done in many ways, just as there are many ways to help others off the court. This section covers the two most common ways to make others better on the court. The first way is to compete all out against teammates in every second of practice, trying to beat them in every way. One of the reasons very young teams or immature teams do not succeed is that they do not practice against each other with 100 percent intensity. The players get used to getting open easily or handling the ball without facing intense pressure. They get used to not having to box out because teammates do not crash the boards hard. And they get used to jogging back on defense because the offense does not sprint. When this team plays a game against a team that practices harder, they

© Greg Carroccio/Sideline Photos

Making decisions that are best for the team, not for personal glory, is what teamwork is all about. Often this is reflected by how unselfishly and effectively a team passes the basketball.

find themselves unprepared. Teammates who do not push each other actually make each other worse. Conversely, teammates who get after each other and push each other make others better.

The immature attitude is that it's not cool to make your teammate—who is often a friend—look bad. Outhustling your friend means you're making things hard for him, trying to show him up, or trying to embarrass him. "Losing" teams have players who think it's admirable to take it easy on each other. The mature outlook is to push your teammate and try to beat him in order to maximize your potential and to make him better. Great teams and great players always compete with fierce intensity and personal pride. They are not only trying to beat their teammates every day, they are also trying to make those teammates better.

The other common way that teammates make each other better is by passing. Many coaches like the saying, "Good passers make good shooters." The teammate who can beat his defender off dribble penetration, draw help, and get his teammates open shots is making those teammates better. The post player who draws double teams and passes the ball to open cutters for layups or to weak-side shooters is making his teammates better. Many talented scorers put up impressive statistics but do not use their talents to draw extra attention and make scoring easier for others. Great offensive players make their whole team better by passing and scoring.

ROLE PLAYING

Each player has a different role on a team. Each shares the common responsibility to show up every day, to put forth great effort, to play one's best, to accept both criticism and praise, and to be unselfish and loyal. However, each player is also expected to fulfill different team needs. The importance of each role is explained in the following sections.

Exceptional Players

Great teams usually have great players. When the most talented players on a team are true winners and positive leaders, they become great players. More specifically, whenever the best player accepts the responsibility to be on time, take criticism, and work hard, other players think they should do it too. Thus, the best players become effective leaders. A very talented player needs to lead by example, showing teammates that everyone is responsible to each other. The player must make others live up to high standards. This is why many coaches are toughest on the players with the most ability. Coaches see the potential for a talented player to become great, but they also know that if this player accepts the coach's challenges, it will set a great example and will help the whole team be more responsible. Visible, responsible leadership by outstanding players is foremost to having a great team.

On the other hand, consider what happens when the most talented player does not practice hard or at all. Immature teammates will conclude that they do not have to work either. The mature, winning players on the team will be discouraged that their talented teammate does not care enough to make others better or to help in critical game preparation. The lack of commitment by the talented player divides the team. A talented individual—based on the example he sets—will have a tremendous effect on the team.

Special Role Players

Great teams have great players *and* great role players. Great role players provide intelligence, strong skills (other than scoring), and a high level of unselfishness to complement outstanding offensive players. They usually provide an extremely high level of skill or toughness in special areas. As the best defender and rebounder in the NBA, Ben Wallace is a perfect example of how a great role player can be the most valuable player in winning a championship.

Team-First Mentality

Joanne P. McCallie–Duke University

As a college coach, I search for student-athletes who have a sense of confidence and self-worth. Players must value themselves first; then they can value the team and make decisions that serve the best interests of both.

Though it might be counterintuitive, I believe there is virtue in selfishness. By that I mean we seek student-athletes who value themselves to such a high degree that they are willing to maximize everything possible to be the very best they can and at the same time be driven to be better. From there I can work with those slightly more confident individuals to help them see the broader picture, realize the importance of the team, and help fulfill its needs. We work hard with our young players so that by the time they reach their junior year, they have fully embraced the priority of the team and accept that they have an accountability that is beyond them.

Freshmen are really only capable of being accountable to themselves because of all the challenges in transitioning from high school to college. Only exceptional sophomores really get it by their second year in school to the point that they can take on any kind of leadership role. We facilitate and monitor underclassmen's maturation process through individual meetings and through shared experiences during the season and off-season. But growth doesn't happen just by talking about it; players must evolve through situations and challenges that broaden and shape their perspectives. By junior year, players grasp their accountability to the program and truly appreciate that we are building something bigger than them. We expect juniors and seniors to demonstrate on a daily basis the motto, "Get out of yourself and into the team."

It's rewarding to see it happen every year as another group of players develops that level of maturity. Just recently I was meeting informally with four veteran players and talking about the incoming freshmen and how we were going to welcome them into the program. Somehow our conversation shifted to the 1.5-mile run, which is one of our mental and physical tests of fall training. At that point, one of the players, Keturah Jackson, who would be entering her junior year, spoke up and admitted that she was thinking only about herself right then and how she would do in the 1.5-mile run that October. My response was that such thinking would have been understandable when she was a sophomore, but as a junior she not only had to take care of her own business, but she needed to look out for other people as well. Even in that very relaxed meeting, the focus was on getting out of ourselves and into the team.

We have kids who are in that transition now figuring it all out. They aren't captains yet, but they will be captains after they show they can take responsibility for empowering the team while taking care of themselves. That is what an All-American is. It's a process, and it's not easy. And sometimes there is a selfish player who doesn't get it. Her own personal concerns take priority over the team's needs. At some point we realize that the person just doesn't have the make-up to get beyond herself, and we try to give her a role that can benefit the team, but it's not a position of leadership. Not every player will be a leader; a coach can't dictate that.

On the court, players in our program understand that they are expected to defend and rebound like crazy. That is what champions do. Their offensive game will be more of a product of their personality and their talent. As coach I need to determine the complementary pieces among the various styles and skills, then fit them together into a smooth-functioning unit.

We believe in the concept of a competitive caldron. Players earn playing time in the preseason, and their performances on various physical conditioning tests are a factor. We also consider grades. If two players are equal in ability and work ethic, we'll play the one with higher grades. Players know that if they skip class or fail to keep up with their academic work, they're essentially disqualifying themselves from the team.

Each team member's awareness of continual accountability is important. Players should never feel that they have it made and can slack off or bend a few rules here and there. How they behave, how they interact and treat people inside and outside the program, how productive they are in the classroom and on the court—all of these things are under constant evaluation.

Playing time is earned. Players can earn it and they can lose it. The head coach decides who plays and when, but in my way of thinking, players themselves really determine who merits time on the court. It's almost always apparent in practice who deserves to be playing. If those players are equally productive and responsible off the court, they will get the most minutes.

There is a point in the season, say November when the games start, when playing time has been determined and the focus shifts to fulfilling roles on the team. If a player's role is that of 12th person on a 12-member team, then she needs to accept that role and make the most of it. Young people today often struggle with accepting such role assignments. That's a major reason that so many athletes transfer from one school to another. The fact is that learning one's limits and role in various walks of life is a good thing. And many of the kids who transfer in hopes of finding greener pastures elsewhere usually encounter the same challenges at their new schools. They transfer and you never hear from them again because they can never function effectively within the constraints of a team. And basketball is a team sport. It takes a team to get it done.

The great role player plays according to his strengths and does not attempt things that other teammates can do better. For example, the big man may let the more skilled guard push the ball up the court instead of doing it himself. The average shooter makes the extra pass or is happy to set screens to get the best shooter an open shot. The responsibility of the role players is to bring their particular strengths to the court. They must be willing to sacrifice certain things for the team so that individuals with strengths in those areas can better use those strengths. There has never been a great team without great role players. This is a critical role.

Key Substitutes

Key substitutes have the responsibility of improving or maintaining the score for their team when entering the game. They must also accept their role as a nonstarter and must recognize the importance of all playing time, not just starting the game. This takes a mature player. Players who embrace this role have a profound impact not only on certain games, but also on the success of the team over the course of a season. For example, Boston's Kevin McHale had all the credentials and capabilities of a starter, but instead he agreed to come off the bench. In this role, McHale was a key factor in the Celtics winning the 1984 and 1985 NBA titles (he also won two NBA Sixth Man Awards). A sixth man can provide a much-needed injection of instant offense when the starters have been stymied on the offensive end. Substitutes who are good shooters can be zone busters and open up more opportunities for other offensive players in the attack. Another important role is a backup point guard who can bring extra quickness to speed up the game or to create defensive pressure. Hardworking, shut-down defenders and scrappy rebounders also provide key services off the bench. Great teams rely on substitutes who will maintain or increase a lead—and when needed, provide a spark that helps close a scoring deficit. These players are critical and just as valuable as any starter.

Coach Fran Dunphy of Temple University shared a wonderful story regarding his 2008 NCAA tournament team and senior guard Chris Clark. Chris was exactly the type of consistently improving, unselfish, winning teammate this book encourages players to become. All during his senior season, he provided great game-changing performances while coming off the bench. At Temple—and many other colleges—they have a custom of starting all their seniors for their last home game so that those seniors can receive special recognition. Before his last senior home game, Chris approached Coach Dunphy and said, "Forget starting me on Senior Day. We have been winning with me coming off the bench, and we shouldn't change anything. I just want to win." This positive attitude contributed to his team's success and to his great individual performances off the bench.

Playing well off the bench has other requirements in addition to accepting this important role. First, players need to be vocal on the bench. To improve coach–player communication, the players on the bench can help the coach call out plays and defenses. At La Salle, if I call out a play or defense, I want the whole bench to call it out as soon as they hear me call it. In this way, the bench stays mentally involved in strategic adjustments and in communicating with teammates, which they will need to continue doing when they get in the game. We also tell individuals to either watch the teammate they are likely to sub in for (e.g., "Watch Darnell because you will guard that guy") or watch for a key execution point (e.g., "Watch the open high post against the zone"). Focus, communication, and emotional energy (i.e., cheering, encouraging) start on the bench. If a player waits until he is on the court to start getting focused or intense, this will be too little too late.

Great Practice Players

Great practice players are the true unsung heroes. People outside the team do not see the skills of these players—or even hear about them—because these players do not play in games consistently. But without these players, intense and competitive practice is impossible. Without them, scouting reports become useless because no one can simulate the competition in practice and get the team fully prepared to win.

The team knows the talent and dedication of these players and appreciates them greatly. Although this role carries less recognition, it still includes the chance to make important contributions, the opportunity to improve as a player, the challenge of competing every day in practice, the chance to be a key part of something special, and the respect of people who care for you. No team can be successful without dedicated, competitive players in practice.

Every player has a needed and critical role for team success. It is a player's responsibility to accept and flourish in that role. Different roles may be more or less glamorous or more or less difficult, but they are all necessary. Players must also keep in mind that roles are seldom permanent. As a player's abilities improve and opportunities become available, roles often change. For example, Chris Clark at Temple began as a practice player, receiving little playing time as a freshman and sophomore. Chris later became one of the best players off the bench in the Atlantic 10 and a consistent double-figure scorer.

The key to success is to unselfishly accept a role while confidently working hard to earn a greater role and to push teammates to improve. In the 2008 NCAA tournament, for example, former walk-ons who were expected to be practice players (and did not receive scholarships) when they arrived on campus as freshmen ended up playing critical roles as upperclassmen starters for very good teams. Among these players were Adam Emmenecker of Drake (2008 Missouri Valley Conference Player of the Year), Drew Streicher of Butler (2008 Horizon League All-Defensive Team), and Curtis Terry of UNLV (Mountain West Conference All-Tournament Team).

DEVELOPING RESPONSIBILITY

Accepting a role and being more committed to team success than individual success are challenges every team-sport athlete must face. It is natural for players to want individual success. And our culture certainly emphasizes individuality. The NBA, which is the ultimate dream for most young players, markets itself by promoting its superstars more than teams. Every impressionable young player would love to be one of those superstars in those ads.

To overcome the powerful influence of self-interest and maximize team contributions, the coach can consider the following suggestions. These suggestions summarize major points in this chapter and preceding ones that will hopefully culminate in responsible, unselfish, highly-motivated players.

- Show how increased team success leads to greater individual recognition.
- Increase loyalty. Chapter 9 critically discusses how to build team cohesion, which makes loyalty and sacrifice between teammates possible.
- Develop pride and ownership in the program.
- Create an inspiring team mission.
- Emphasize responsibility by eliminating excuses.
- Challenge players to perform at higher levels by setting goals for them and focusing on what they can control (i.e., their performance).
- Develop "commandments" or standards of how to play the game that demand unselfishness on the court (passing to open people, not criticizing others, recognizing assists) and have consequences (e.g., reduced playing time for not following them).
- Communicate that each player is important and valued in their role. Chapter 8 talks at length about effective communication.

The coach can use educational team meetings and team retreats to further help foster an overall sense of shared values and purpose. Following are guest speakers who have presented at our team meetings along with some of the topics we've covered: marines talking about teamwork, responsibility, and toughness; world-class athletes from other sports and great basketball players talking about commitment, sacrifice, and unselfishness; successful alumni talking about academic and life responsibilities; and players reading excerpts from biographies of great athletes, stories of successful teams, and current newspaper articles on who is winning and why. These topics allow for discussion of common problems long before they arise, which can prevent a lot of those problems.

A coach should schedule a series of such team meetings to cover a variety of important topics in a thorough manner. These meetings should also be interesting and enjoyable. Having good guest speakers and involving players in the discussions can help prevent boredom. Some programs have these meetings at regularly scheduled times (e.g., Thursday nights) to stress their importance. They can be particularly useful in the preseason when laying a foundation of core values for the upcoming season. Former players who have taken part in such a program insist these meetings were key for personal and team development.

In chapter 9, we'll discuss team retreats as a way to build team cohesion. However, a simple discussion question used in these retreats heightens awareness of team responsibility and deserves mention here. Players simply discuss when they are most proud of the team and when they are most disappointed in the team. The contrast of these answers often makes team responsibilities very clear. The coach can moderate and guide this discussion to ensure that valuable points and lessons of responsibility are covered.

6

Off-Court Conduct

Make no mistake about it, there is a definite relationship between accountability on the court and off the court. By stressing accountability, a coach is building character. Players should know that the coach values character above all. That is why many coaches don't like giving MVP awards and emphasize effort-based awards instead.

A coach can send a clear message about what he values in a person. For example, a coach could say, "I will not admire you because you are a good basketball player. Being big, strong, fast, or skilled does not mean you are a good person. I want to admire you for your work ethic and character, not your talent or skills." Thus, a coach can challenge players to be good people first and foremost. A coach can teach players to be good people by paying attention to personal habits (manners, language, showing respect and consideration) and life's larger issues (honesty, alcohol and drug use, dating behavior, conflict resolution, academic motivation).

Just as coaches need to teach players why basketball fundamentals are important, they also must teach why character is important. Actions affect the doer's own future and many others (family, friends, teammates, coaches). Being aware that we affect others and are accountable to them decreases selfishness.

Most negative behaviors are selfish in nature and are based on emotion. People who engage in substance abuse, violence, or dishonesty do so knowing others who care about them would disapprove. They feel like doing these things even though they know they are wrong. Conversely, positive behavior is usually based on values. Thus, teaching character requires teaching values. From there a coach can promote positive behaviors, such as being honest, demonstrating good manners, using proper language, and showing respect and consideration for others, as well as taking responsibility with regard to life issues like alcohol and drug use, dating, academics, and social conflicts.

Legendary UCLA coach John Wooden's Pyramid of Success specifies the character-based behaviors that are the building blocks for individual and group achievement. The blocks are industriousness, friendship, loyalty, cooperation, enthusiasm, condition, self-control, alertness, initiative, intentness, skill, team spirit, poise, confidence, and competitive greatness. By educating his players on these characteristics, he made sure his superbly talented teams reached their potential. His 11 NCAA championships are a testament to his team's talent, but this incredible level of consistent excellence cannot be attained without unwavering commitment to successful habits on and off the court.

The concept of the pyramid is a wonderful teaching tool. In fact, a coach can construct his own pyramid to highlight principles he believes ultimately result in success. The coach can define and explain the importance of each block during team meetings. This format can become a course in character education and development. It provides a plan to teach the lessons a coach feels are important. The pyramid can be a constant visual reminder of values posted in the locker room and copied for players to take home as well. All-time greats Bill Walton and Kareem Abdul-Jabbar credit Coach Wooden and cite the lessons from the pyramid as the greatest reasons for their success. In fact, Luke Walton of the Los

Harry How/Getty Images Sport

Former UCLA coach John Wooden's positive influence, on both the players he coached and subsequent generations of coaches and players who've learned from him, continues long after his retirement from coaching.

Angeles Lakers says his father used the pyramid to teach him the keys to success as he was growing up.

Before a player can be successful, he must be successful as a person. The most common way that talented young players fail to succeed is by making mistakes off the court. People of all ages vary in their ability to make wise life choices. Off-the-court behavior can frequently be traced back to the quality of adult guidance the player has received. Many young people are now raised by single mothers. Of course, many single mothers are loving, strong-willed parents who provide for, care for, and discipline their children to overcome all obstacles on their way to success. However, some young people have undeniably poor adult guidance and have never been taught the keys to success off the court. Unfortunately, this lack of guidance is never the choice of the young person, and the young person does not usually realize he has been deprived. This chapter provides ideas to help reinforce the positive behaviors of players, as well as ways to begin the often difficult process of changing negative, self-defeating behaviors.

MODELING PROPER BEHAVIOR

First and foremost, the coaching staff should set the example for players' behavior by conducting themselves properly. Expecting athletes to do as you say, not as you do, is naive. Coaches should show respect to others, be punctual, work hard, obey the rules, be enthusiastic, and represent themselves and the school positively. The coach must accept responsibility not only to teach positive behaviors but, in some situations, to adopt a type of parental relationship with players. One-on-one communication explaining why certain behaviors are important is just as necessary as modeling the behavior. Second, whatever the behavioral expectations are within a program, they need to be communicated clearly and forcefully— and then enforced fairly and equitably. Allowing a star player to stray from standards while penalizing a reserve for the same transgressions will undermine the trust and commitment that are essential to a healthy team core. A team code of conduct can establish these expectations.

Codes of Conduct

A code of conduct for off-the-court behavior is critical for educating players about proper behavior and determining consequences for problem behavior that will maintain discipline and accountability. The code of conduct can be put in writing and agreed to by the player with a signature, like a contract. Laminating the contract and placing it in the player's locker serves as a continual reminder of the commitment to the code of conduct.

The type of code of conduct a coach uses will be determined by his philosophy and the school's philosophy and will also be influenced by the state of the basketball program. Some coaches, usually those in very solid programs without a history of off-court problems, have very simple codes of conduct. The most simple code is, "Don't do anything to embarrass the program." The generality of this statement requires explanation for players to apply it to their conduct, but it is a good concept. Another common simple code used in colleges is, "Attend class and be a good citizen." Again, this requires explanation about following rules and the law. These types of general codes allow a coach great flexibility to handle issues on a case-by-case basis and to use his own discretion in administering discipline.

In situations where philosophy or negative conditions warrant a more stringent code, rules can directly address issues such as alcohol, drugs, violence, dishonesty, and academic integrity. A comprehensive code of conduct with specific penalties for violations ensures all student-athletes will be treated equally. The penalties are clear and definite.

There are two schools of thought among coaches about penalties for misbehavior. The first is that any violation of the code results in missed playing time. The belief here is that this is the greatest deterrent and keeps the highest standards. Jerry Wainwright, the coach at DePaul University, believes young people will only do what they can "get away with" and that they will meet the standards set if the consequences for not doing so are serious. This approach produces two outcomes. First, there will be initial violations. With strict standards, one must expect some problems, and suspensions will potentially create short-term disadvantages for teams. It is useless to have high standards unless they are held up and enforced by consequences for offenses. Second, irresponsible behavior soon decreases once the code and its consequences are understood as being serious. Thus, there are definite long-term benefits to a well-conceived and executed code of conduct.

The other philosophy for penalties in a comprehensive code of conduct is that penalties should fit the crime. Progressive discipline is often used—first offenses are treated differently from second or third offenses. There are also varying levels of penalties based on the seriousness of the misconduct. For example, a felony and an unexcused absence from a class may be treated quite differently. Some coaches also feel that the harshest penalties—game suspensions and team dismissals—should be reserved for the most serious misbehaviors, because these penalties affect others (i.e., teammates, coaches, fans) besides the one who committed the violation. Examples of alternative corrective measures could include extra required study hours for academic irresponsibility and community or school service for poor social judgment.

The intent here is not to say that one code of conduct fits all coaches, teams, and schools. The intent is to emphasize the need to educate young people about proper behavior, set standards, try to prevent problems before they occur, and provide consequences at teachable moments in life that lead to personal growth when mistakes are made. Coaches should consider their beliefs and how they can be expressed in a beneficial code of conduct that truly affects behavior in a positive way. Strategies to motivate players to be responsible off the court and abide by a code of conduct follow.

Breaking Stereotypes

A coach can challenge players to break stereotypes. Simply ask players to describe the stereotypes people have for college students, college athletes, males, African Americans, and Caucasians. Negative descriptions such as spoiled, arrogant, partyers, violent, and stupid are among the terms that could come out. After discussing these stereotypes, the next step is to challenge the student-athletes to prove the stereotypes wrong. The keys to proving stereotypes wrong are to display positive behaviors and to let others get to know you. The coach can then lead a discussion regarding how team members can build positive images of themselves.

BUILDING A POSITIVE IMAGE

From listening to sports talk shows, reading the sports page, or watching the day's sports news, it would be easy to draw the conclusion that athletes are delinquents and criminals in far disproportionate numbers to others their age. But, for the most part, players are simply kids and young adults who are very much like their peers.

The big difference is that basketball players' off-court actions are subject to public scrutiny and are closely monitored by outsiders. Unfortunately, it's usually the case that those making the observations catch only glimpses—a partial picture—of what the coaches and athletes in a program are really like. And when that limited amount of empirical data is combined with an existing bias, any number of misconceptions about an athlete's character can surface.

Abraham Lincoln once said, "Character is like a tree, and reputation like its shadow. The shadow is what we think of it; the tree is the real thing." Like it or not, that shadow is often what defines individuals, teams, and programs. Once a reputation is formed and widely disseminated, it's likely to stick. That's OK if it's a positive impression, but it can be devastating if the reputation is negative. If Honest Abe were alive today, he would certainly concede that image *does* matter.

And, not in Lincoln's day or until the last decade did technology and the means of communicating put players and coaches on public display nearly 24 hours a day, 7 days a week. Camera-equipped cell phones, YouTube, blogs of all sorts, e-mail, and so on have made privacy nearly impossible. Any number of these means of recording and spreading images can serve to expose athletes and coaches to more public presentation and ridicule than ever before.

Without question, the media focuses more on negative behaviors. Give them a story such as that of Shawn Kemp or Jayson Williams, and a feeding frenzy ensues. As singer Don Henley lamented in his once popular song, "they love dirty laundry."

Less compelling to the media are the many examples of dedication, generosity, and compassion exhibited by sports figures. Although most players and coaches would rather perform these acts outside of the media's view, such behaviors need to be noted publicly in an effort to offset the preponderance of negative portrayals with positive ones.

In chapter 5, I mentioned how David Robinson tutored and then turned over his central role on the Spurs to Tim Duncan. That smooth succession process was probably made possible not only by the great effort, leadership, self-control, and respect both players exhibited on the court, but also by the way they conducted themselves off the court. Both are solid family men who give to their communities and treat others as they would wish to be treated. For all these reasons, they were named *Sports Illustrated* 2003 co-Sportsmen of the Year.

Because of their great visibility, Robinson and Duncan were able to carve out their reputations for all to see. Their success on the court increased the amount of attention and media coverage they received, so their charitable, humble, and respectful behaviors were irrefutable, even to the cynical segments of the press and public. Such exposure is rare, however, so someone within a basketball program needs to cast light

AP Photo/Eric Gay

Not only were Tim Duncan and David Robinson a championship-winning combination on the court, they also represented their team and presented themselves in a very positive manner off the court.

on the positive acts of players and coaches in order to reveal their true character. This will help eliminate the misperceptions formed by the "shadows."

To portray a more positive image, NBA commissioner David Stern established standards of dress for players' off-court apparel on game day. The standard of dress called business casual was instituted in recent years to emphasize a more mature, conservative, corporate culture compared to the popular, younger, hip-hop image. The NBA's off-the-court dress code bans sleeveless shirts, jerseys, T-shirts, sneakers, shorts, headgear, sunglasses indoors, and bling (including chains, pendants, or medallions). Players are required to wear dress shirts (either collared or turtleneck), shoes, slacks, or jeans. Players out of uniform on the bench must add a sport coat as well.

Obviously, with the average NBA player making over $5 million and the minimum annual contract being more than $420,000, purchasing the new clothes posed no problem. Still, several star players voiced concern that the new wardrobe rules stepped over the line concerning freedom and individual choice. Others argued that the rules prevented them from wearing the latest fashions and clothes that were most comfortable for them. But the commissioner, like any employer with a good rationale for a dress code and the ability to enforce it, simply said this about the disgruntled players: "If they are really going to have a problem, they will have to make a decision about how they want to spend their adult life in terms of playing in the NBA or not."

The most interesting words in Stern's quote are *adult life*. Those words are critical because basketball players tend to be young; most are in their teens or their 20s. But because they are in the public eye, they are forced to appear more adult than their peers who are not observed by big crowds or covered by the media—and who do not carry school and community names on the chest of their jersey. Coaches should point out that the privileges of being a student-athlete (i.e., attention, scholarships, travel, gear) come with adultlike responsibilities. Players must realize that they are in the process of becoming adults. At La Salle, we frequently use the biblical quote, "When I was a child, I did childish things. When I became a man, I put childish things away." Having a positive image is more easily accomplished when players accept the need to become more adultlike. Invoking the process of becoming a man strikes an emotional chord with most male players who want to see themselves as men as opposed to children.

Coaches need to realize that basketball culture is just a part of the larger culture that shapes the thoughts of players. Much of this larger culture has always been and still is dictated by entertainers. The tremendous impact of hip-hop culture is undeniable but carries with it a negative stereotype. The reality is that some hip-hop stars break that stereotype. Performers such as Jay-Z and Will Smith lead highly disciplined lives of early-morning meetings and workouts, business travel, media and promotional functions, and constant work on creating and performing music. In many cases, hip-hop performers have overcome poverty to achieve great success. They also often dress in business fashion when in the public eye, just as David Stern has required NBA players to do. Most likely, players are going to look up to entertainers, so the entertainers who don't fit the negative stereotypes are the ones players should be encouraged to look up to.

In summary, the coach must lead young players to see connections between their visibility as basketball players, positive role models in their culture outside of basketball, and the realities of the adult life they are entering.

PROMOTING EDUCATIONAL SUCCESS

Athletes' attitudes and actions away from the gym have far greater implications for their future than what they do on the court. Except for the very small percentage of athletes who become pros, players' career options, personal income, and leadership opportunities will be based largely on their level of education. Education lasts an entire lifetime, whereas athleticism fades with age.

Pete Carril, legendary former coach at Princeton University and Sacramento Kings assistant, was once honored as Coach of the Year for another outstanding season at Princeton. At the banquet, awards were also given to many players for being named to various all-star teams. Instead of simply thanking people for his award, Coach Carril gave the players an important message about life. He told them, "If I try to take the bus home tonight, I better have 75 cents, because the bus driver will not care about this trophy." The point is clear: Basketball success does not usually matter in school, business, or life outside sports.

Just as everything must be earned on the basketball court, everything must be earned off the court. Off the court, personal respect and job opportunities are only earned in two ways.

First, people tend to listen to and respect others with knowledge. The more knowledge a person has, the more helpful he can be to himself and others. Thus, the pursuit of knowledge in school and life is a truly wise undertaking. A more knowledgeable person has a distinct advantage.

Second, others trust people with high character. Having high character means the person possesses honesty, dedication, integrity, and dependability. Great responsibility is only given to those who have proven themselves trustworthy. Thus, a young person's decisions and actions will be strongly considered by those who can help him in life.

Education and personal character are keys to success in life, but there are still numerous reasons to pursue basketball goals. Basketball can build character; provide enjoyment, great memories, excitement, and friendship; and provide a journey that can take a young person far, including college and professional careers for a select few.

Basketball is also a means by which a young adult can get into the best schools possible, travel, meet people, and, for the truly exceptional, earn a scholarship. However, although the sport has opened up many doors for extremely successful people, it has also been a dead end for other players. Many very talented basketball players have struggled in life after basketball. These players did not see the doors available to them. Opportunities to learn, build a strong future, and become a better person are available every day. Players will either walk through those doors to a great life, or they will hit a dead end.

To be successful as a student, one must spend a lot of time studying, reading, and writing. To be successful as a basketball player, one must spend a lot of time playing, drilling, and training. Many young people spend the majority of their time relaxing or having fun. Music, movies, computer games, and socializing consume most of their time. Those things are enjoyable, but they don't make a player any more successful in the classroom or on the court. A coach should teach players that the truest measure of commitment is how a person spends his time. A person is truly committed to those activities that he devotes the most time to. For this reason, setting daily schedules for players with class times, study times, basketball commitments, and rest time provides the planning and structure that many young people need. Having the daily schedules in writing prevents confusion about where players are supposed to be. The whole organization of a program is enhanced with daily planning.

The Ivy League boasts very good basketball and equally good students who typically go on to be extremely successful alumni. The challenge of applying oneself fully to both basketball and books can only be met by eliminating nonproductive time on things such as watching television and playing computer games. Ivy League athletes who meet the on- and off-court demands in their lives gain a leg up on most of their peers.

Those athletes who face less rigorous academic demands can still learn valuable lessons in discipline and time management by applying themselves in their schoolwork. An applicable saying in that regard is, "After the work, the rest is easy." In other words, athletes who work hard training, practicing, playing, studying, and participating in classes will appreciate the physical and mental break that comes when they're through. They will also take pride in what they have done. Procrastinating or loafing reduces the amount of work accomplished, and it also increases stress, because the anxiety over the work waiting to be done will only continue to grow. The habit of getting one's work done first—then relaxing and recreating afterward—will serve athletes well both in school and in subsequent years of employment.

Graduation rates are highly publicized because the government requires each college to publish these rates. This allows high school students to see how well a school retains and graduates its students. The national graduation rate for all students, not just student-athletes, is about 62 percent. This shows that not all students succeed. To succeed, a student must know when to work and when to have fun. Good students regularly spend significant amounts of time on their academic work. They give priority to academic time over leisure time. This takes the maturity to know when to work and when to have fun. Remember, after the work, the rest is easy.

Here's another useful quote: "If you value life, you must value time because life is made up of time." In other words, wasting a lot of time is the same as gradually wasting life. Researchers have asked students why they did not study more or receive better grades. Many students thought that studying and trying hard to be a great student was not cool. Socially, other things were much more important to them. Many peer groups base their acceptance more on appearance and popularity. But in a few short years, those same students will be judged in universities and workplaces on their knowledge and personal character, not on looks or popularity. The mature student understands this and separates himself from academic underachievers.

The University of North Carolina has produced some of the world's best basketball players. Michael Jordan, Vince Carter, Jerry Stackhouse, and Antawn Jamison have all been great NBA players. They all were so highly valued by the NBA that they were able to leave school before their senior year to be picked high in the draft and be guaranteed millions of dollars. All of these players also continued to study, take tests, and do papers to finish their degrees. They are all UNC alumni.

These millionaire Tar Heels continued their education when they already had money and fame. The same stories of success can be found at rival Duke University. Players such as Shane Battier and Jay Williams, who took extra coursework to graduate in three years, exemplify what it means to be a student-athlete. These NBA players and many others cite numerous reasons for finishing their college education: family values on education, personal pride, preparation for life after basketball (or in case of injury), and the value of knowledge—no one can take it away. Many also speak of keeping promises to their parents to finish school because of the encouragement and sacrifices their parents made.

The sense of accomplishment that one can get from education is enormous. Nothing worth achieving is ever easy. Rigorous academic work strengthens the mind and character. Graduation is something important that will be respected by all and will last forever. Players should understand that not everyone can play in the NBA, but everyone can learn.

Many more success stories can be told of basketball players at major colleges and small colleges in addition to more well-known pro players.

An excellent example of this is Tyrone McCloud, a former small-college player at Rowan University. Like most players, Tyrone did not achieve great fame, but he did achieve a highly rewarding life outside basketball. Tyrone grew up in a deprived community surrounded by violent crime and rampant drug use. His family experienced extreme difficulties. He did not know his father. He came out of a very weak school system.

However, everyone who knew Tyrone, especially his coach, Rick Barrett, knew he was special. He understood the tragedy that violence and drugs created. He stayed away from trouble. It was clear he had a good heart and wanted badly to succeed in life. He was admitted to college through an equal opportunity program. This program was designed to give disadvantaged students a chance at a college education by building up their skills and work habits through a variety of activities—extra summer school courses, required study sessions, basic skills testing, remedial classes, and constant monitoring and advising. Tyrone loved it! He loved the peace of a college campus. He loved the helpful people.

Tyrone graduated with a degree in sociology, but his favorite class was Introduction to Computers. He aced the class, worked as a computer tutor for other students, and got a computer graphics job after graduation. He used his computer skills to begin a newsletter and Web site devoted to South Jersey basketball (and he sold advertising for profit). He even taught Introduction to Computers at a local college. He then went on to direct the computer network at the Philadelphia Art Museum. He is a great family man and successful by any standard. Indeed, everyone can learn, and nothing can stop a committed person from achieving success in academics and life.

CULTIVATING SOCIAL AND INNER DISCIPLINE

An important quality in life is the ability to learn from the experiences of others in addition to our own experiences. Learning a lesson from others' mistakes is far better than having to suffer the consequences ourselves. Many coaches collect articles about athletes getting in trouble. They post these articles on a bulletin board in the locker room so that their players can read them and learn from them. Discussing such real-life situations on a regular basis is a good preventive method.

Some coaches favor early-morning workouts. Coach John Chaney at Temple University was well known for the use of morning practices. One benefit of morning practice is that after the practice ends, the players have the remainder of the day available for academics and rest. In addition, morning practices make late-night activities, such as partying, very difficult. Even if a coach does not like the idea of daily morning practice, some morning practices can be scheduled strategically. For example, practices could be scheduled for Friday or Saturday mornings, anticipating that a lot of students may want to party on Thursday and Friday nights. As Morgan

Good Habits

Oliver Purnell—Clemson University

One thing our players must understand is that we are in a highly competitive situation, vying against more than 300 other schools to win a national championship and 12 very strong programs striving to win our conference. We explain that teams that do not have off-court distractions have a huge advantage over teams with players who get into trouble. In other words, off the court just as on it, one error in judgment by one player can cost the whole team. That doesn't mean we keep a very tight leash on all our student-athletes. Instead of an elaborate set of formal rules, we simply make clear to every player that he is to follow these four guidelines:

1. No drugs.
2. No alcohol.
3. Don't do anything that would embarrass yourself, your family, or your institution.
4. Fulfill your academic obligations.

Aside from the legal issues surrounding alcohol and drugs, they have an adverse effect on athletic performance. Early each academic year we usually have speakers talk to the team about the ill effects of using and abusing those substances. The speakers share a variety of experiences that players relate to, and players can see the negative consequences of drug and alcohol use—not just during their college years but throughout the rest of their lives.

Players also need to understand that their participation in our program gives them a high profile in the community, if not the state and the nation. The high interest in athletics means coaches and players operate in a fishbowl. And, with today's technology, any indiscretion is likely to be posted on the Internet within minutes of its occurrence. So we'd all better realize that everything we do can, and often does, become public. That's why the third rule—avoiding situations that would embarrass a player, a family, or the institution—must be stressed at the outset of each year and throughout the year. This reminds players that they have more than themselves to consider, and it's crucial that they behave responsibly or others will be adversely affected in some way.

We talk with players about academics every day, not just officially in front of the team but also before practice, after practice, and in informal meetings. We constantly show interest in how they are doing academically, and we keep apprised of their course load and academic progress. This lets them know that we are aware of their classroom performance, that we believe it is important, and that we care about their education. We don't address academics just when a player is struggling; we also emphasize it when a student-athlete is performing well in the classroom. That player needs that positive reinforcement in order to motivate him even more.

Off-court conduct comes down to this: We are creatures of habit. Whenever there is an important situation, whenever there is pressure, and whenever the lights are turned up high, a player's habits, good or bad, will come to the forefront. So we tell every camper, every recruit, and every player in our program that if they want to grow on the court, in the classroom, and in social situations, they will succeed if they develop good habits.

Something as simple as saying, "Yes, sir" or "No, sir" when responding to an older man not only shows proper respect but also makes a good impression on him and everyone else in the vicinity. If this response becomes habit, it reflects well on the individual and is likely to encourage the development of other similarly respectful behaviors. Conversely, bad habits, whether on the court or off, always come back to haunt players, seemingly at the worst moment. For instance, a player makes jump passes every time he is trapped or guarded closely. Chances are that if that player is pressured hard by the defense in the closing seconds of a game, he's going to leave his feet and get called for a charge or make a turnover. In other words, a player's development of a poor habit led to a costly error for the whole team at a crucial time.

When players make decisions on and off the court, habits often take over. Whether it's declining a friend's offer to have a beer or blocking out for a key rebound, people revert to what is ingrained through experience when placed in a position to act. If you develop good habits, then those habits take over when you need them to. That's why the conversations we have every day with players are so important. We understand as a coaching staff that we are competing for the hearts and minds of these young people every day—things they are exposed to, the decisions they have to make. We have to be a major influence on them if we are to ensure their behavior reflects positively on them, their team, and their institution. They must be taught the right things, and consistently. It all comes down to building those habits.

My favorite student-athlete is Cliff Hammonds. Cliff received the Skip Prosser Award as the top student-athlete in the ACC. He had a double major in architecture and psychology and graduated with roughly a 3.8 GPA. He also was a four-year starter and senior captain on our team. When he came in, he was very quiet; as a sophomore we wanted him to start to be a leader. By the time he was a junior, we asked him to be a vocal leader. Everything that we asked him to do he did. The reason we were able to get better and better for the last four years as a team was that he was such a great role model for the rest of our guys. He was a shining light.

(continued)

Many kids don't have positive, stable, two-parent family situations at home like Cliff had. That is why teachers, coaches, Boys' and Girls' Club coordinators, Boy Scout leaders, and other adults in the community are so important. Those adults can have a tremendous effect as strong role models that the kids might not have at home.

We have a young man right now who finally appears to be grasping the positive attitude and conduct we're trying to reinforce. We hammer away at what the expectations are, show how to build constructive habits, discipline him when he gets off track, and reward him when he does things well. If kids—even those from a tough background—hear consistent and positive messages in their academic and athletic environments, those messages will rub off. When a young person hasn't had a healthy upbringing or good direction, it can take more time, patience, and caring before changes take place.

Coaches who are so caught up in winning and winning now can wash out a kid who is struggling. That is where I think compassion and caring are most important. We as coaches have to know right from wrong: If we continue to work with these types of kids, the light will come on, and those are the most gratifying situations. A player who is struggling to make the grades and doesn't want to go to class but is willing to listen and will work on academics with a little direction and prodding can get better every year in the classroom. And maybe by junior year, the light goes on, and he becomes more self-motivated to study and graduate.

One of the best rewards of coaching is having a former player return years later and say, "I'm glad you stuck with me. The same things you said to me are the same things I am saying to young people today." A young man I coached at Old Dominion, David Harvey, now a teacher and a coach in Atlanta, did that. David also works our basketball camp, and when he talks to the campers about his experience, it warms our hearts and makes us feel good that we could affect someone in that way. The consistent, disciplined, and patient manner in which he was treated in our program allowed him to blossom, and now he is affecting other young people's lives in a positive way.

Wootten, legendary coach at DeMatha High School, has said, "You cannot run with the wolves at night and fly with the eagles in the morning."

Unfortunately, too many players fail to learn from the mistakes of others and make the same poor decisions off the court. Those misguided choices and negative behaviors can seriously hurt people. From a basketball perspective, players have been dismissed from teams and from school and have lost scholarships. Their actions not only hurt themselves but also hurt others—their schools, their teams, and their families. Following are several ways that athletes—and coaches, for that matter—can avoid the common pitfalls related to conduct.

Avoidance of Alcohol and Drugs

Most teenagers in our society are exposed to illegal substances and must make their own personal choices. Too many use alcohol and drugs without being aware of the dangers. Therefore, education about the consequences is critical. The use of illegal drugs can lead to a criminal record and penalties. Driving while under the influence of alcohol and underage drinking are also against the law. Those offenses might result in stiff fines, requirements to do community service, suspension of a driver's license, higher insurance rates, and a permanent police record.

Furthermore, alcohol and drug use is habit forming. Studies show that a large percentage of individuals who use these substances tend to do so regularly. With regular use comes greater risk, harm to the body, and psychological dependency. The substances and the behavior become addictive. At this point, dependency or addiction affects one's whole life, including motivation, relationships, and lifestyle.

Al Szolack is a recovered alcoholic and drug addict who speaks to many groups about the dangers of those substances. Al points out, "Later in life no one ever wishes they used drugs or alcohol more." In fact, many people have lost their families, their careers, or even their lives because of drugs and alcohol, and every one of them would regret ever getting started. We can learn from the mistakes of others if we are wise.

A coach can talk all he wants about this topic, but the behavior of players is most influenced by peer behavior and the culture of partying or not partying found within a team and school community. Developing leaders who will encourage a more responsible team culture is very important. Another key is identifying the high-risk student-athletes. A coach should try to maximize the influence of positive leaders, minimize the influence of high-risk individuals, and make one-on-one efforts to change the behavior of individuals when necessary. A coach can informally assign team leaders to try to make sure high-risk individuals behave responsibly. This is the most important aspect of forming a positive team culture—teammates who care about each other and hold each other accountable.

Nonviolent Behavior

Confrontations occur in life, but how they are handled will determine the seriousness of the consequences. The combination of alcohol and confrontation often creates situations that can lead to violence. Players can be cautioned that fights, assaults, lawsuits, and criminal charges usually don't happen at midday with sober, rational individuals. Violence usually occurs during late-night hours when alcohol is involved. The mature individual knows how to avoid these situations.

Consider the following situation: An athlete is behaving responsibly but is then confronted, insulted, and challenged by someone. Athletes have a sense of pride and toughness that brings them to accept and win challenges. The correct decision in this case goes against the athletic instinct to never back down. The reality of the situation is this: The nonathlete involved will not be embarrassed by media coverage of the incident, and the nonathlete will not lose a scholarship or a place on a team. Quite simply, an athlete has much more to lose in this situation.

In the situation described, an athlete must make a choice between (a) losing some pride for a short period of time by walking away or (b) harming his reputation, team, and opportunities for a longer time. This is a negative situation, but the mature, wise choice is obvious. Teammates should help each other avoid and walk away from these situations. The consequences of fighting are not worth it.

Healthy Relationships

Everyone is positively or negatively influenced by those close to them. A coach should emphasize that players must choose friends and social acquaintances carefully. It only takes one slip. Even if a person is innocent, he can be considered guilty by association. For example, if illegal drugs are found in a vehicle or home, everyone present in that vehicle or home is charged. If a person drinks and drives, gets in fights, or steals, others present are automatically involved. People who skip school or do not study will try to get others to do so too.

A player should surround himself with others who have maturity and commitment to strong values and goals. This will make it much easier to avoid problems and achieve goals successfully. An insightful quote about choosing friends wisely is, "You can't lie with dogs and not get fleas."

Dating relationships are also common for student-athletes. To help ensure positive, nonviolent relationships, athletes should be encouraged to respect others and to make serious commitments only with people whom they greatly admire. Unfortunately, young people often enter emotional and physical relationships too soon—and not with the right people. This usually leads to emotional distress and conflict, which affects one's whole life. Even worse are the well-publicized cases of famous athletes being charged with sex crimes. These cases typically involve inappropriate sexual relationships with mere strangers. Patience and selectivity must be encouraged to ensure healthy relationships that are enjoyable and helpful. A healthy relationship will involve mature people who encourage each other to excel in life.

ESTABLISHING A STANDARD OF CONDUCT

The privileges enjoyed as a member of a team are earned through dedicated effort on the court every day. Off the court, everything must be earned as well. Some players who have earned success on the court have made grave errors off the court by trying to take things they have not earned. There have been highly publicized cases of athletes involved in theft, use of stolen credit cards, use of long-distance calling cards, and improper discounts. All of these acts have criminal consequences. They can also lead to NCAA ineligibility—receiving extra benefits because of athletic ability or reputation is against the rules. Remember, nothing should be offered, taken, or accepted unless it is honestly earned and paid for fully.

A person who does not speak or act truthfully does great harm to himself and others. Academic dishonesty has been another pitfall for some student-athletes. Plagiarism (using someone else's writing and claiming it as your own work) and cheating are obvious cases of dishonesty. Such behaviors are unacceptable and reflect a deficient moral compass that can also spill over into shortcutting and a lack of discipline in the athletic arena.

Long-term success follows the individual who speaks and acts honestly, earns everything he has, is surrounded with positive friends, and avoids violence, alcohol, and drugs. Such a person builds strong values, successful habits, and an admirable reputation. He is free of negative distractions and is free to fully commit himself to important goals.

Remember the wise words of the prison warden from chapter 2. He knew that one mistake could make a free man a prisoner. Make the right choices off the court, not merely to avoid trouble, but to represent yourself, your program, and the sport in a positive light.

Finally, few easy answers exist for coaches trying to prevent off-the-court problems. The intent of this chapter is to present the most common problems athletes face and encourage communication, setting standards, positively influencing behavior, and teaching life lessons.

PART II

The Six Cs of On-Court Success

Much of the first six chapters of this book dealt with the "stuff" players and coaches bring to the table in terms of their skill set, work ethic, attitude, discipline, and conduct. All of these things help lay the foundation for success, but many of them are global and off-court factors that might not seem so directly connected to performance on the court.

For those of you seeking more specific, performance-related information, fear not. The rest of the book addresses the methods, tactics, and actions that coaches and players can employ to maximize both team and individual performance, as well as to optimize the team environment. These aspects are referred to as the six Cs as a way to help you remember the half dozen topics that are critical to developing a high level of court sense.

CHAPTER

7

Coachability

Back in January of 2006, Steve Francis refused to reenter a game when directed to do so by then New York Knicks head coach Larry Brown. Francis was fined and received a one-game suspension by the club. In April of that same season, Ben Wallace declined to go back into a game when requested to do so by Detroit Pistons head coach Flip Saunders. Wallace was neither fined nor suspended.

The fallout from the two incidents couldn't have been more different. It appeared that Francis continued to be unhappy, and a poorly functioning Knicks team went through one of the worst seasons in team history.

In Detroit, on the other hand, the matter was resolved, and Wallace resumed his starting, inspirational role as a key team leader as the Pistons compiled the league's best record. Here's what Coach Saunders had to say about the incident: "I talked to Ben. Ben talked to me. Ben talked to his teammates." In other words, Wallace recognized he was wrong and apologized for his actions behind closed doors to his teammates. They accepted his apology, retained their respect for him as a leader, and resumed their effort to win another NBA championship.

Obviously, no team can function efficiently or effectively when players disregard the directives of their coaching staff. So Francis' and Wallace's refusals to reenter a game when asked to do so by their coach were clearly unacceptable. However, the manner in which the coaching staffs and organizations dealt with the two players differed significantly. Which was right and which was wrong? Or were they both right? Or both wrong? And what is the player's responsibility to conform to the coaching staff's direction, whether it pleases him or not?

The topic of coachability typically puts coaches on a soapbox and puts players on the defensive. Coaches tend to complain about what a pain so-and-so was to deal with, and how this made their job all the more difficult. Players, in turn, feel as if they're being put on the spot to behave like choir boys and jump eagerly to every single coaching demand.

The concept of coachability should be broadened to encompass both the manner in which players and coaches get along and how capably they perform their respective duties. So, any definition of coachability should take into account two factors. One is the manner in which players receive and respond to coaching; the other is the extent to which the coaching staff engages players and maximizes their opportunities to excel as a team.

The nature and success of coach–player interaction hinges on the criteria for effective communication that will be covered in the next chapter. In leading up to that topic, however, this chapter provides information on various ways to help set the stage for such effective exchanges. All these strategies tend to involve players making themselves receptive to coaching. They also involve coaches giving players the respect and opportunity they need to develop, to perform, and, yes, to have a little fun along the way.

Some people say that the coaches are the stars at the college level, and that the players are the stars at the pro level. This sentiment sums up the misguided mind-set that hinders coachability. Players and coaches shouldn't be concerned about being stars; instead, they should work together to make the team the star. The two should not be competitors or adversaries. They must be cooperative coactors applying their best efforts to achieve collective success that is bigger than any individual award.

THE COACH'S ROLE

People often think of coachability as a one-way street, referring to how readily and positively players respond to the coaching staff's directives. But that's not the whole story. How coaches set up, present, and conduct their program has much to do with how players respond.

The administration must also be supportive and allow coaches to make the final calls on matters that are important to their program. Players need to know that the buck stops with the coaching staff.

New School

The old-school "my way or the highway" philosophy can be an efficient mode of operating, but it is rarely the best approach nowadays. Yes, the coaching staff must be in charge, and that line of authority must be respected by the players. However, coaches who approach their role in a more reciprocal manner tend to get better results.

Once the clear line of authority is established, the coaching staff must then specify exactly what the expectations are for players in terms of behavior and performance—what is desired, acceptable, unsatisfactory, and forbidden. The coach's explanation of those guidelines will help players understand the rationale for the policies.

Chuck Daly, former NBA coaching great, was a very successful "player's coach" who still maintained a very tough side. He said that the key to working with players is to remember that players allow you to coach them. In other words, players must want to be coached by you. A coach must work at making players want to listen and be coached.

Keys to getting players to want to play for you include the following (these keys will be elaborated on in the remainder of this chapter and in chapter 8):

- Explain the why behind strategies and rules. Don't just tell players what to do. Sell them on why doing it will help them. This is a good principle to begin any instruction with.
- Get to know your players by talking with them and learning as much as possible about them.
- Know the limits of how much criticism each player can take. Nip problems in the bud by talking with players one on one when they become overly frustrated.
- Show honesty, loyalty, and caring toward players, especially with regard to their personal lives.
- Do not emotionally beat up the players when they are losing. If a coach is constantly blaming players during a losing streak, the coach can "lose" the team. Problem solving, increased effort, and encouragement are what is needed during a losing streak.
- Publicly praise individuals, and limit criticism to individual or team situations.
- Allow for fun and enjoyment to take place whenever possible (in ways that do not take away from focus and effort).

The Focus on Winning

The priorities and perceptions of those involved in a program can start things off on the right or wrong foot. Everyone wants to win, but if that's the sole focus, then all is lost when the inevitable loss occurs.

Sadly, the reward system for coaches is often based on the following: "Just win, baby," and you will be adulated and well compensated; lose and you will be scorned and unemployed. This system is counterproductive to the entire coachability equation. Coaches feel a tremendous amount of pressure to win. They then transfer that pressure to players, not only to perform their best and give great effort, but to make certain they total more points than their opponents. In this situation, players tend to become mere pawns that are expected to produce favorable results.

Coaches can be forgiven for falling into this trap. So much of a coach's job security, advancement opportunities, and personal reputation is tied directly to winning percentage. Add to this the continual public evaluation and media criticism, and the whole set of proper priorities that a coach may have started with can devolve into a must-win mentality. At that point, players are viewed by coaches as a means or obstacle to success, as opposed to people who depend on them and need help to grow. As a result, treatment of players can become impersonal and harsh. When this occurs, players become more defensive and less open to coaching. And then, ironically, the team has even less chance of producing the wins that the coaching staff is so desperately seeking.

So, how does the coach avoid a strictly outcome-centered approach? First, the coaching staff needs to believe that the program will enjoy more long-term success by emphasizing development, effort, teamwork, and toughness—not point totals. Administrators need to buy into this as well, because the first few seasons of implementing such a system can test one's patience and loyalty. Athletic directors and general managers face a tough decision in whether to retain and support a coaching staff that struggles out of the gate and suffers consecutive losing years. These administrators must decide whether to relent to pressure from outside the program to win immediately.

Had a certain university not believed in the philosophy and abilities of a young coach from Army in the early 1980s, the school's administration might have easily fired its unproven coach after his first three seasons. In those three seasons, the program totaled an undistinguished 38-47 record and made only one postseason (NIT) appearance. But the school and coach endured the disappointing losses and mounting criticism, and they went on to enjoy more success than any other college basketball program in the country over the next 25 years. Coach Mike Krzyzewski believed that other, more fundamental elements needed to be emphasized and established during those formative years—not the number of wins or titles—to set the stage for long-term success. The results are rather convincing, wouldn't you agree?

So the coaching staff and its approach to players will play a very significant role in either fostering or diminishing the coachability quotient on its team. Creating a more reciprocal and developmental environment will encourage players to both grow more fully and respond more favorably.

Former St. John's and New Mexico coach Fran Fraschilla once said that all coaches are positive in recruiting, but that many coaches change after the players arrive on campus. He encouraged coaches to never stop recruiting their own players. In other words, coaches should keep telling and showing players that they care. Coaches should keep reinforcing players' positives and what each player and the team can accomplish. The coaching staff should see to it that players remain positive about being members of the program. This approach should make for more coachable players.

Patience, Please

Players are more coachable when they think the coach's emphasis is on helping them, even if criticism is involved. They are also more coachable when they believe the coach can help them.

The coaching staff's use of criticism should be moderated by two factors. First, all members of the coaching staff must acknowledge that the players are people with feelings and shortcomings. This does not mean that a soft approach to coaching must be used or that coaches should withhold any criticism. However, coaches need to establish the foundation for a positive relationship before criticizing. Players may still not like receiving the negative feedback, but they will more readily accept it when they know it is being rendered in order to help them and the team improve.

Building positive, respectful, caring relationships—with the realization that this will lead to greater improvement and winning—can be described as keeping the horse ahead of the cart. Pressuring players to play harder and better without true personal consideration is placing the cart before the horse.

The second factor is that a coach must believe that his instruction with coachable players will produce success. In other words, the coach must believe in himself and his players. This results in confident teaching that puts players at ease and allows appropriate praise and criticism to be accepted.

This is easy to do with physically talented players. However, it is much more of a challenge with players of marginal or inferior talent. In such a situation, the tendency is to fear that anything less than perfect execution will lead to losing, because the margin for error is so small. Thus, every mistake seems catastrophic, and the coaching staff tends to overreact. As a result, players feel less secure and more frustrated.

At this point, the coaching staff must exercise more patience. The entire coaching staff can monitor one another to help keep themselves from being too critical and to stay under control in such situations.

Michigan State coach Tom Izzo—a very driven coach who was once known for distributing shoulder pads and football helmets for his toughness-building practice drills—has had to alter his style of coaching for certain Spartans teams. He needed to accept recent teams for what they were—what one Detroit writer characterized as having "a toughness that's gauged with an egg timer."

As Izzo put it, "Every year, the personality of your team changes, and it's up to the coach to work within that personality. People wonder why I don't yell more like I did before, but if you don't think it's going to achieve your objective, then why are you doing it? Sometimes the best course is giving a pat on the back rather than a kick in the rear."

THE PLAYER'S ROLE

Everything a player says and does could be considered as falling within a collective set of attributes defining her coachability. Only a naive and inexperienced coach expects every player to fit an ideal mold of student-citizen-athlete who is wonderfully responsive to each coaching instruction and correction.

© Aaron M. Sprecher/Icon SMI

Michigan State coach Tom Izzo understands the importance of tailoring practice sessions to the specific needs of players on each year's team.

Stanford women's coach Tara VanDerveer, a Hall of Famer with a wealth of coaching experience and expertise, knows how rare that ideal player can be. Perhaps that's why she has enjoyed coaching Candice Wiggins. Coach VanDerveer calls Candice "a dream" and openly admits what a joy it is to coach someone whom she "trusts implicitly." VanDerveer wonders why the coachability situation has to be so difficult, but she agrees that it is more common for the players and coaching staff to fail to connect on and off the court to the extent desired by both.

Rather than try to approach this topic more globally—as if trying to construct a Candice Wiggins or Tim Duncan prototype that all players should emulate—it is more realistic and useful to examine specific areas in which players and coaches often disconnect. Following are several potential points of discord, along with information on how the players and the coaching staff might conquer them.

Starter or Reserve

Which players receive the five available starting slots on a team is a much bigger deal to players than it is to coaches. Players, as well as their families and friends, perceive a starting role as being more valuable than a reserve role. They simply like the designation as a starter.

Coaches, on the other hand, think in terms of player combinations and rotations. Which groups will perform best together? Which players will give the team a boost off the bench?

Getting players who might otherwise start on a different team to accept their role as reserves is a challenge faced by every

Team leaders do more than talk; they also listen, as former Stanford star Candice Wiggins demonstrates in receiving her coach Tara VanDerveer's instruction.

coach. That's why it's helpful and refreshing to have examples of great players who have excelled in this role. A coach can refer to these examples so that disgruntled reserves may see that a starting assignment does not always mean that a player is more valuable or better than a teammate who comes off the bench.

Manu Ginobili is just one of many recent examples of a "sixth man" being just as critical to a team's success as any starter. The offensive punch and up-tempo style of play that Ginobili injects into the San Antonio Spurs when he enters the game has paid off in the form of multiple NBA titles. And to his credit, Manu recognizes that it's much better to be a reserve with three championship rings than a starter on a squad struggling to stay above .500. Once again, a coach needs to explain why a player is in a certain role for the welfare of the team in order for the player to understand and accept the decision.

Playing Time

Starter or not, every player wants to be on the court, competing as much as possible. However, the rule book limits participation to 5 players at a given time, and teams typically carry rosters of 12 to 15 players. Therefore, more players will be on the bench than in the game.

This dilemma regarding playing time has been a problem for many coaching staffs over the years, but no more so than in the past decade. The common mind-set today is one of instant gratification. In addition, a disproportionate amount of media hype surrounds young athletes with potential compared to the attention given to the proven, veteran team members who have paid their dues. As a result, many players have a "play right away" mentality, whether earned or not.

Playing time is often an important consideration when players are choosing a school to attend or a club team to join. Many recruits have declined to become a member of a program because they perceived the roster as already being full of players equally or more talented. They simply didn't want to share minutes, even for a season or two.

This kind of thinking is shortsighted and reflects misplaced priorities. A player can often benefit from entering a program without the expectation or pressure to play heavy minutes. This gives him the opportunity to learn and develop at a more realistic and beneficial pace.

Take, for example, Joakim Noah, who averaged only 9.5 minutes and 3.5 points a game his freshman season at the University of Florida. Despite the limited playing time, Noah distinguished himself by his dedicated work to improve in practice sessions and by his scrappy, hustling performance whenever he did get a chance to enter a game. Obviously, with his improvement and with veteran players leaving the program, Noah made the most of his opportunity in his sophomore season. He averaged 25 minutes and more than 14 points and 7 rebounds a contest, and he was selected the Final Four MVP in leading Florida to the 2006 NCAA championship. He helped the Gators repeat in 2007.

Athletes would do well to learn from Noah's approach to the playing time issue. He chose a program he wanted to be in, not because of guaranteed minutes from the day he stepped on campus, but because he believed it was the best place for him to develop as a player and person. Moreover, he remained highly coachable throughout a challenging freshman year in which he played less than one quarter of each game. Good things do often come to those who wait, but it's also important how a player waits—not whining and being lazy, but striving to improve and making a strong case for deserving more time on the court.

How a player handles the playing time issue also reflects on his maturity and readiness to deal with life off the court. Face it, there are very few professions or endeavors in which success is achieved individually. Great businesses and teams are so successful because their personnel function very well collaboratively, understanding and appreciating each other's role.

In short, the approach a player takes toward playing time reflects the player's level of respect for teammates and the coaching staff. It also reflects the player's level of personal selfishness and perceived worth. A player who outwardly objects to his lack of playing time is implying that his teammates do not deserve to be on the court (i.e., "I should be out there instead"), which is disrespectful. The player who insists on starting and never being rested will likely do more harm than good, simply because of immaturity and disrespect.

As a constant reminder, this definition of respect can be placed in each player's locker:

Respect: To treat considerately, courteously, and with high regard; honor, heed.

This concept is *the* key for coaches and players to work well together. To give special consideration and reverence reflects concern and liking for the other person. To heed means to listen. Understanding respect as it is defined—and understanding the importance of showing respect both in communicating and listening—will eliminate a multitude of problems.

Roster Cuts

Not all players can realistically aspire to start, much less become the most valuable player on a team. For many athletes, surviving the final cut is the goal.

For a coaching staff, decisions on which players to keep and which to cut can be among the most difficult choices made each season. Not surprisingly, coachability figures prominently into distinguishing which athletes to retain and which ones to let go.

If a player has talent but is unlikely to get a great deal of playing time, that player needs to give the coaches no reason to cut him and every reason to keep him based on factors beyond his basketball abilities. The last thing a coaching staff or team needs is problem athletes who rank from 10th to 15th on the depth chart. That's why coaches tend to choose players who will be excellent on the practice floor, in the classroom, and in the community, even if those players are a shade less skilled than peers who have not distinguished themselves in those areas.

Before any evaluation, the coaching staff must provide players with a clear explanation of what attributes are foremost in determining cuts. The coaches must then adhere to those criteria when the final selections are made. If the coaching staff is forthright and consistent, that's as much as any player can ask. Disappointment and anger are natural reactions for players who have been informed that they will not be on the roster. But a player in this situation will often know that his chances were slim based on workouts, practices, and scrimmages. And players who are cut can learn a great deal about how to bounce back from setbacks to be even stronger people in sports, their careers, and other facets of life. Many CEOs of very successful corporations—and even future sports stars—withstood being cut from teams at an earlier age and went on to do quite well.

Perhaps the most famous cut of all was when the coaching staff for varsity basketball at Laney High School in Wilmington, North Carolina, had to inform a skinny, 5-foot-11 sophomore that he just wasn't developed enough to make the roster. That high school student, like so many his

Player Responsibilities, in Writing

Tubby Smith—University of Minnesota

All of us have had coaches or mentors, be it an adult who was in charge of a sports team we played on, our parents, a big brother or big sister, or another significant figure in our lives. Someone was there telling us what the boundaries were, what we needed to do to be successful, and how to meet the inevitable challenges.

In my case, with 17 brothers and sisters, we needed the expectations and accountability to keep discipline within the household. So when my dad told me what my chores were, he didn't need to give me a deadline or tell me twice. I simply understood that the tasks were my responsibility, and I did them.

Another thing my dad taught me was the importance of finishing what I had started. And when I think about coachability in terms of my basketball program, we're looking for young people who will take on and finish the assignment, be it a practice drill or a paper for a class.

Perhaps it's old school, but I believe that the way a young man talks is a telltale sign about his character. Does he respect others and show good manners? Did he hand his teammate a cup of water? Did he respond to the team manager with a thank-you? Did he respond to an official's call in a positive way? Did he acknowledge a teammate's pass that allowed him to score? Is he a caring and giving young man, or is he a taker?

The broader breakdown in our culture—the absence of boundaries, inability to assert discipline, and lack of regard for others—makes coachability a difficult concept for some. So when I make a home visit, I watch how the young man talks to his parents. Does he respond in a positive, respectful manner when they speak? If he is defiant toward them, how can I expect him to respond positively to me? Coaches who just look at a kid's talent and not at his behavior could be compromising not only their values but the well-being of the rest of their team and program.

We ask players to think about the "man in the mirror." We constantly make them aware of how they are perceived so that it matches their own perceptions of what others think of them. And we ask them if that is how they want to be identified and received. We talk about that from day one. And then we talk about how they are going to develop—socially, academically, spiritually, and athletically—from there.

We emphasize that the steps upward in development are achieved through setting and achieving goals. But you have to be careful. If I sit down with a young man and ask him what his academic goals are for this year, he might say, "To get all A and B grades both semesters." That's all fine, and his parents are pleased to hear that, but what happens if his records show he's been a C student throughout his high school years? So it's important to talk to players and make sure they both set realistic goals and have a clear idea of what it will take to achieve them.

The next step is to have players put the goals down in writing. Copies of these goal sheets are kept by the coaching staff, each player, and their parents. That way, when I learn of a player being late for class, I can pull out his goals and ask him to explain his reasons and tell me why. Essentially, he has to verbalize and take responsibility for an action that ran contrary to achieving a goal that he had pledged in writing he was aiming to achieve. Or perhaps one of a player's goals is to average so many minutes of playing time per game. So, when we meet, I turn to his goal sheet and ask why he thinks he's not playing more. And through that discussion, he will understand where his effort and performance have been lagging and what he needs to do to make that goal possible for him to attain in the future.

So the key is to get players to commit to goals and record them on paper. At that point they are accountable and more coachable. They know that the goals are their responsibility; I didn't make them up for them. You say here you want to be a Big Ten player? Then start showing the effort and discipline in practice to get that chance. You believe you can be all-conference academically? Then attend and pay close attention in every class, and put in the required work during study sessions and at the library.

One point to keep in mind: The focus should be positive. A player shouldn't focus on the things that won't be achieved if he fails to own up to his responsibilities; he should focus on what he can do to accomplish his responsibilities and goals. What also needs to be stressed are the benefits he'll realize if he applies himself to the task. So, I might say, "If you get stronger this year, son, you can be one of the better defenders in the league and lead us in deflections and charges."

We believe in keeping accurate statistics in everything we do, including drills. When we scrimmage, we keep stats and run the clock and try to balance the minutes with various player combinations. This prevents players from saying they didn't get a fair chance or that they were stuck on a weaker team throughout the scrimmage. In the end those variables even out, and the best will rise to the top. They don't complain; they find a way to meet the challenge. In doing so, they raise the performance level of their teammates.

Tayshaun Prince, of the Detroit Pistons, was one of the most coachable players I've been fortunate to work with during my career. He is the prototype of the player who is humble and totally committed to the team. Tayshaun was on the 2008 Olympic team and has the ability to make everybody else on his team better. I get goose bumps when I recall Tayshaun blocking Reggie Miller's shot to save that tight game between the Pistons and the Pacers in the playoffs the year Detroit won the NBA championship. Most

(continued)

guys would have given up on the play. But not Tayshaun. He ran from the other side of the court to block that shot and get the win.

Another player took time to reach his potential. He was as gifted an athlete as any player I've had, but he had a lot of people in his ear. We needed him to play early on, and he had a lot of success because he was surrounded by several experienced and talented people. He was given freedom to do things defensively and went on to shatter the record in steals. But he also was very sensitive. He didn't want to be confronted in front of his peers. That's a common concern among young players today. They are often worried about how they look to others. I don't care what you look like; I just want you to be good. That is something we stress.

So, to recap, with all the subjectivity and emotions that can interfere with coachability, it's essential to have players record their goals on paper and to keep statistics on their performance in practice and games. I can show them what they aimed to achieve and where they are succeeding or falling short in their efforts. If they recommit to the goals and improve their output, that will be reflected on the statistical chart.

Every player's situation is unique. A coach might want to treat them the same, but they have varied personal backgrounds, temperaments, learning styles, and idiosyncrasies. What is soon evident through this process of goal setting and statistical analysis is whether a player is a pretender or a contender. The pretender will look for the easy way to get what he wants, blame others when he doesn't achieve it, and become a negative influence on the team. The contender doesn't need a coach to watch over him; he will perform to the best of his ability and go as hard as he can go every time.

age, grew 4 inches (10 cm) over the next several months. Not only did he make the team his junior year, he also went on to become the greatest basketball player of all time.

Yes, even Michael Jordan was cut once. So players who experience the same fate should not consider it anything more than an opportunity to work harder and find a way that they can excel in school, in basketball, or in another extracurricular activity.

Role Definition

Once a player is on the roster and receiving playing time, another issue affecting coachability is acceptance of the role designated by the coaching staff. In the past, player positions were strictly defined—point guard, two guard, small forward, power forward, and center. But today's players are given much more leeway in applying their assets on the court.

Versatility and *flexibility* are the buzzwords used to describe the ideal players of today—with players often shifting between two or three different assignments. Think in terms of LeBron James or the "Matrix" himself,

Shawn Marion. Those players can function effectively in multiple roles and positions on both ends of the court.

Yet, some structure is needed on a team. And players need to accept a specified role within that team framework to ensure that key functions are fulfilled. Essential but less glamorous duties such as playing defense, rebounding, setting screens, and so on would likely be shortchanged if team duties were left to the discretion of players. And those glaring gaps in a team's arsenal aren't likely to be filled voluntarily. (If you doubt this, just observe self-coached teams on the playground or in rec leagues.) Still, not all players will be pleased with the duties that are designated for them.

One common source of disharmony between coaching staffs and players these days concerns the role of big men and women who fashion themselves as perimeter players. They've watched the Dirk Nowitzki types excel with tremendous shooting range, ballhandling ability, and drives to the basket, and they believe that is what they should be doing too. The problem is that only a very small percentage of taller players have the quickness, coordination, and shooting skill to play that type of perimeter game. Most taller players will be more effective—and will help their team be more successful—by developing and playing a more post-oriented game.

Sometimes, the best inside players aren't even very tall. Despite standing less than six-foot-seven, Wes Unseld was one of the most impressive post players in basketball history. Unseld didn't try to be what he wasn't on the court; instead, he applied his thickly built frame, court savvy, and great determination in becoming one of the best rebounders, most feared screeners, and highly adept passers ever to play in the post. The five-time NBA all-star averaged 14 rebounds a game and totaled more than 10,000 points and nearly 4,000 assists during his pro career. But Unseld did not focus on stats; his efforts were devoted to providing his Bullets teams with the great play they needed in the post to be a winning and championship (1978) club.

Unseld, Paul Silas, Joe Dumars, Steve Nash, and many other great players have demonstrated what it takes to be a special player by fulfilling a role and not caring whether they receive credit or attention. They were willing to forgo fame in order to make their teams better, and yet they became even more appreciated and famous through their sacrifice and selflessness.

Unfortunately, too few players share this approach to the game. Most want a role that enables them to score a lot of points. Two types of players are the most difficult to coach. The first type is the poor shooter who has deceived himself into believing that he is a capable scorer (if only his teammates would get him the ball in better position to make baskets). The second type is the reluctant defender. The inaccurate but cocky shooter will kill an offense, and the matador defender will require teammates to cover for his many lapses, leaving the defense vulnerable to any competent offensive attack.

The coach must clearly show these players what deficiencies are preventing them from being successful contributors to the team. The misguided shooter can be shown objective statistics, and the weak defender can be shown videotape. The coach should also define a specific role for such players, highlighting the areas in which they can help the team. The coach must persuade them to focus on these areas in games—until they demonstrate in practice that they have shored up their weaknesses and have earned a more expanded role.

This kind of role definition is beneficial to individual players and to the team when it comes to performing. It's also helpful to athletes as they progress academically and professionally. No matter what career they move on to after basketball, players will have to learn and accept a specific job description and role outlined by their employer. Human resources staff often look to hire former athletes who have demonstrated the ability to sacrifice personal stats and be great team players during their athletic careers. Such athletes will be prepared to do the same thing in their jobs off the court.

Players should have some idea of their likely role well before the season starts—and even before they join the team. Role definition is very much tied to the system used in a program. So, a player attending the University of Tennessee to play under Bruce Pearl is going to have very different expectations than one who is playing under Tony Bennett at Washington State. The style, pace, and priorities of the two systems employed by those programs are in stark contrast. Tennessee's fast-paced, high-scoring attack is distinctively different from the half-court, controlled-tempo approach used at Washington State.

By making the style of play clear to players ahead of time—and highlighting the skills and functions that are essential to be successful within that system—coaches can avoid some of the role-definition and acceptance problems that prevail on many teams.

Substitutions

Some rosters are deeper in talent than others. Some have a handful of strong players and then a big drop-off from there. Others might have a superstar or two top players and then fairly evenly talented 3 through 10 players.

In any case, coaches and players should be clear about the pecking order and the coaching staff's philosophy concerning substitutions. And players should understand that their coaching staff, in making substitutions, is trying to develop a pattern for ensuring that the five best players are on the court for specific situations and matchups. Still, some of the substitutions made will seem arbitrary to players who don't grasp the particular player combinations, rest periods, and other factors the coaches are weighing when making replacements.

When Jay Wright took over the Villanova program, he didn't step right in and immediately achieve a nationally powerful program. He started by recruiting well and developing his first recruiting class over their freshman and sophomore seasons. By their junior year, they made it to the Sweet 16 of the 2005 tournament, barely losing to eventual NCAA champion North Carolina. The program has continued to make regular NCAA tournament appearances and has made subsequent runs to the Elite Eight and Sweet 16.

Wright recalled seeing frustration on star guard Randy Foye's face during his freshman year. Wright kept promising his players that if they worked hard and played hard, good things would come.

"I'd take Randy out of the game because he'd get two fouls, and he'd just look at me," Wright said. "I knew what he was thinking: *You tell me to play hard and now look at me, I'm sitting next to you with two fouls.* It was hard for a while."

Wright simply pushed forward. Taking the cue from him, the players did the same. They never made excuses, and they insisted that they were getting better. And they did.

In the end, when it comes to substitutions, players have to trust that the coach is exercising his best judgment in trying to give the team the best chance to be successful. No player likes to be taken out of action—even if only temporarily—but substitutions are a fact of life. No team plays all five starters every minute of the game. So the sooner players accept and grow comfortable with that fact, the better.

A coach can do a few things to help players understand substitutions and accept them emotionally. An effective tactic used by Dean Smith was to have the entire bench rise and encourage (i.e., hand slap) the player coming out of the game. This forces that player to accept encouragement from teammates and not pout. Also, a player should never be permitted to go to the end of the bench (a favorite sulking spot) after coming out of the game. Instead, the player should immediately sit next to an assistant who can explain how the player performed, describe what the situation is, and prepare the player for his next time on the court. If a player is coming out because of poor play, this practice also prevents an emotional head coach from confronting the player in a way that could be too harsh. An assistant who may be calmer under those circumstances is then able to address the situation.

Acceptance of Criticism

Players perform in a very visible, competitive classroom. And it's perfectly normal for them to want to appear competent, if not highly proficient, in front of their peers. That's why so many players resent and respond poorly to corrective feedback and criticism.

Proper communication styles as well as sending and receiving messages will be covered in the following chapter, but specific points relative to coachability and criticism must be made here.

Players must understand that even Hall of Famers were at one time critiqued and even scolded by their coaches. The key distinction between useful and harmful feedback of this type is that the useful criticism is not personally insulting. If the criticism is focused on specific behavior or performance—and if it is accompanied by a clear description of what is needed to correct the problem—then the coach is on solid ground. Any player receiving such feedback must listen and respond positively.

Bob Knight is well known for great coaching and for providing forthright criticism that was often harsh. Knight was an extremely intelligent and demanding coach, but his passion for perfection sometimes led him to deliver particularly stinging assessments to players concerning their performance.

Coach Knight once explained that he never got upset at a player who was learning something new. He only became upset if a player failed to perform something that had already been taught, drilled, and emphasized (e.g., fundamental plays, commandments, well-prepared scouting reports). He simply expected players to listen and execute what they had been taught. His excellence was found in never accepting less than this. Players who found those demands unrealistic and found the coach's critiques demeaning didn't fare well in Knight's system. Players who went into Knight's program aware and accepting of the feedback they would receive usually excelled.

Generally, players should expect a coach to treat them with respect, but they should also expect criticism when not performing critical tasks. They should also not expect infinite patience. Indeed, one of the biggest problems that coaches have in practice results from players repeatedly making the same type of mistake. After positively encouraging a player to do better when the mistake is made a first and then a second time, a coach may run out of patience. The coach might perceive further failures to execute as resulting from a failure to listen and a lack of respect for the coaching staff and the rest of the team.

The coach is right to convey concerns directly and strongly to players; however, a coach must also be mindful of not embarrassing players needlessly. Coaches should also avoid sticking a player with a nickname or label that the player finds offensive. A coach might consider a player to be soft physically because of poor defense, rebounding, and interior play. Or the coach might think the player is soft mentally because of poor reactions to criticism (e.g., pouting, depression). But this assessment, as well as any concerns about the implications for the player's chances for success, should be expressed in a private session with the player. No athlete should be subjected to a coach's public labeling of him as soft. And most players will do everything within their power to avoid such a stigma, despite their deficiencies. In fact, privately telling a player the harsh truth—that he is viewed as soft—can be very helpful. This should be done in a caring and positive way that challenges the player to reverse that perception.

COMMON GROUND

To enhance coachability, sometimes all that is needed is a direct meeting between player and coach early in the season, before signs of trouble surface. Rarely are a player and coaching staff 100 percent in sync, but an initial meeting can help them understand each other better.

In this meeting, the coach should be clear that players can expect to be uncomfortable at times during the season. The coach needs to explain that this discomfort should not be resisted by players but should be perceived as an opportunity to grow and develop. In fact, comfort means a player is only doing things he is already capable of and not being pushed to do more. These types of growing pains are healthy, and they sometimes need to be instigated by a coach to ensure that players develop to their potential. The players who accept the temporary discomfort and conquer the challenge are the ones who are most coachable *and* successful. Athletes will feel either the pain of disciplined effort (i.e., being pushed to new, uncomfortable limits) or the pain of regret.

Some players entering a program may have had great individual success playing a certain way with a previous team or at a lower level of competition. These players often have the most trouble adjusting to a different role that requires them to sacrifice some of their scoring stats for the benefit

© Greg Carroccio/Sideline Photos

The coach–player relationship is complex and can be difficult, but when it is founded on mutual trust and respect, both individuals should find the experience rewarding.

of their present team. That's why stories such as that of Mario Chalmers are so useful—they show players that they can make the transition and will be better off if they do so.

Mario was coached by his father, Ronnie, at Bartlett High School in Anchorage, Alaska. It could be said that Mario not only led the team on offense, he *was* the team's offense, averaging more than 25 points his senior season. When Mario made his way to Lawrence, Kansas, he maturely accepted the role that Coach Bill Self envisioned for him. By the end of his sophomore season, Mario was selected as the Big 12 Conference's co-Defensive Player of the Year, and he broke KU's single-season record for steals. Though his scoring average was a fairly modest 12.2 points a game, his contribution to the team effort was a big reason why the Jayhawks won 25 games, won the league title, and made it to the Elite Eight in the NCAA tournament. Of course, his coachability over the years paid off in a big way when he became "Super Mario," making the game-winning shot in the 2008 national championship game.

And yet, some players are reluctant to alter their role. They might listen to the coach, but they do not change the way they play. They resist the short-term discomfort that would be experienced by trying to learn and master a new skill or by increasing their effort level. At that point, the coach needs to explain that although it might be more comfortable to do things the same way as always, that will only produce the same—not better—results. In this way, the coach is making it clear that the player's development and enjoyment—and the team's success—are the motivating factors behind whatever criticism and discomfort-inducing methods are employed.

Sure, anyone can have a bad day and get into a mood that briefly disrupts them. Neither players nor coaches should overreact to these infrequent emotional disruptions. Over a five-month season (roughly 150 days), it's inevitable that these instances will arise. But even in the midst of such emotions, both players and coaches must maintain respect for one another and not say or do something that will result in long-term damage. This requires a certain level of maturity and restraint, which should be expected of all those who participate in the program.

In the end, however, coachability comes down to the player wanting to be coached and the coach encouraging that desire. Does the player cooperate voluntarily? Does he ask questions to understand as much as possible? Does he seek extra workout and shooting time? Does he request feedback for improvement? Does he look for ways to be an even better contributor to the team? If so, that player is highly coachable, and it is up to the coaching staff to help that athlete excel to the extent of his abilities. A key part of job or professional growth is keeping your boss happy. This sounds like a message that encourages insincerity. It is not. But the importance of keeping a boss happy is a reality. If pleasing a coach means giving great effort, being unselfish, and listening closely in order to learn as much as possible, that is ultimately a good thing for everyone involved. The coach needs to clearly communicate that following his expectations serves the interests of individuals and the team.

8

Communication

A player stalks off the court with shoulders slumped, head down, and a look of disgust when approaching the bench after being replaced by a teammate.

A coach provides a series of positive, eloquent, and respectful responses in a press conference after losing a hard-fought contest in which a late controversial call tipped the scale in favor of the opposition.

Several members of a squad continually snipe at one another on the court as they play selfishly throughout the course of a humiliating loss to their school's arch rival.

Each of the preceding scenarios conjures up all kinds of thoughts and feelings. Communication does that; it jars the memory and stirs the emotions. And that's especially true when we have a history or some stake involved with the event or individuals involved in the situation.

Communicating positively is much easier when things are going smoothly, the team is playing well, and the win column is growing. Adversity, however, tends to expose deficiencies in communication that result in dysfunctional interaction within a club. Witness, for example, the inappropriate outbursts that often happen when players become frustrated during a tight, pressure-filled game or in a losing locker room afterward.

Recall instances in which teammates and coaches were at odds, either in your program or on other teams. The frustration—even hostility—that develops is all too apparent and disruptive. And consequences can range from damaging a single player's performance in a particular game to leaving wide, seemingly intractable divisions within the team and between players and the staff.

Even winning teams sometimes succumb to the deadly fate of dysfunctional dialogue. The three-time (2000, 2001, and 2002) NBA champion Los Angeles Lakers were one of the most prolific examples of self-destruction resulting from communication breakdowns. The club's three central figures—Kobe Bryant, Shaquille O'Neal, and Phil Jackson—apparently couldn't "get on the same page" at the time, so O'Neal departed for Miami and Jackson took a year's hiatus at his ranch in Montana. Who knows how many titles that team might have totaled had that trio been able to bridge their communication gaps.

This chapter provides many useful ideas and proven methods to help avoid such troubled interactions. These techniques will produce more positive and effective communication between players and the coaching staff, between team members, and among the coaching staff. And, don't be surprised if performance on the court improves as well.

COACH-TO-PLAYER COMMUNICATION

The factors involved in the coaching staff's communication with individual players and the team are so numerous and complex that they alone could fill an entire (and lengthy) book. Just look at the long list (see table 8.1) of reactive and proactive or spontaneous communications two sport psychologists came up with when they attempted to assess coaches' behavior. Throw in all of these factors, including the often emotionally charged environment of the competitive arena, and it's no wonder that so many players and coaches encounter lapses in their communication.

Yet, how well players listen to and understand their coaches has a significant impact on how a team will play. And how well coaches listen to and attempt to understand the players' perspective largely determines the quality of athlete–coach relations.

Credibility, Immediate Belief, and Knowledge

Effective communication involves a sender (i.e., a source), a message, and a receiver who accurately interprets the desired message. The credibility of the source is critical for a message to be taken seriously by the receiver. In other words, some coaches and players communicate better than others based on who they are as opposed to what they say. The more credible the source of the communication, the more the receiver tries to receive the information and interpret it accurately. That's why communication from a coach with a winning track record or from a top veteran player tends to garner more attention—and therefore better responses—than that of an unproven coach or a rookie bench player.

Table 8.1 Response Categories
of the Coaching Behavior Assessment System

Response category	Behavioral description
CLASS I: REACTIVE BEHAVIORS	
Responses to desirable performance	
Reinforcement	A positive, rewarding reaction (verbal or nonverbal) to a good play or good effort
Nonreinforcement	Failure to respond to a good performance
Responses to mistakes	
Mistake-contingent encouragement	Encouragement given to a player following a mistake
Mistake-contingent technical instruction	Instruction on how to correct a mistake
Punishment	Negative reaction, verbal or nonverbal, following a mistake
Punitive technical instruction	Technical instruction given in a punitive or hostile manner following a mistake
Ignoring mistakes	Failure to respond to a player mistake
Response to misbehavior	
Keeping control	Reactions intended to restore or maintain order among team members
CLASS II: SPONTANEOUS BEHAVIORS	
Game-related	
General technical instruction	Spontaneous instruction in the techniques and strategies of the sport (not following a mistake)
General encouragement	Spontaneous encouragement (not following a mistake)
Organization	Administrative behavior that sets the stage for play by assigning duties, responsibilities, positions, and so on
Game-irrelevant	
General communication	Interactions with players unrelated to the game

Adapted, by permission, from F.L. Smoll and R.E. Smith, 1984, Leadership research in youth sports. In *Psychological foundations of sport,* edited by J.M. Silva and R.S. Weinberg (Champaign, IL: Human Kinetics), 375.

From a player's standpoint, the amount of attention and significance attached to the message by the rest of the team and coaching staff correlates directly to his previous experiences with and regard for the sender. Wise, all-conference veteran players are given full attention, while freshmen striving to make the team typically receive nothing more than courtesy nods. Players need to understand and accept that their stature as a communicator and leader will grow as they, through their words and deeds, increase others' appreciation and respect for what they have to contribute to the team.

For a coach, a critical goal is to maximize his credibility with players. A small number, including Hall of Fame coach Mike Krzyzewski at Duke University, command "immediate belief." Players focus on his every instruction, and they put those instructions into action. The result is great team unity with all players following the same plan for a shared purpose.

But most coaches do not have the status and automatic credibility of Coach Krzyzewski. Credibility comes from having knowledge, and any coach can have great credibility by demonstrating high knowledge of the game and how to win. Even Coach K would lose credibility with players if he could not teach offense or defense, if his practices did not produce learning or improvement, or if he appeared unprepared or confused, especially during stressful times of the game.

The coach must appear knowledgeable at all times to inspire "immediate belief." This knowledge is developed in many ways besides the normal trial-and-error process that all coaches go through. Coaches can also gain knowledge through discussing the game with other coaches, scouting opponents, and taking advantage of formal learning opportunities (e.g., books, videos, clinics).

To help a team win and to develop credibility, a coach must first have knowledge in two critical areas. First, the coach must know and use the basketball strategies and philosophies that best suit the team's personnel. For example, Pete Carril was notorious for emphasizing his team's lack of speed and jumping ability; he would often rhetorically ask, "Why should we try to run fast breaks if we are slower than the other team?" Thus, he used a style of play that suited the passing, shooting, and decision-making skills that his teams excelled with. Nolan Richardson's great Arkansas teams (1994 national champion and 1995 national runner-up) featured constant running and pressing that was referred to as "40 minutes of hell" for opponents. These Arkansas teams also took advantage of their great team depth and quickness. Many other examples could be used, but the point is that a coach must know his players and must know the systems of basketball that can benefit those players. A coach should teach what he knows and know what he's teaching. In other words, the coach should have complete knowledge of a system of basketball before determining whether to apply it to his team. He should only apply that system if it maximizes the team's assets and minimizes its liabilities. Once a coach knows a system of play that suits his team, he will be able to teach effectively, demonstrate useful knowledge, and have credibility.

Second, the coach must have the knowledge to plan for special situations. For example, a team must be prepared defensively when they are up by three points and the other team has the last shot. A team should also be prepared offensively in that situation. Other special situations include attacking different zones, presses, and matchup defenses.

A coach and the team must be knowledgeable and prepared regarding all of these situations. In fact, preparing for late-game situations may be the most important factor in determining success in close games and therefore the overall success of a season. Being knowledgeable about the game and all its situations is key to being a credible source of information to players. A coach who players trust as knowledgeable gains immediate belief. The coach must display that knowledge by confidently teaching in practice.

Wise Use of Influence

Influence is like a bank account: The more you use it, the less you have. Every parent, teacher, and coach knows that the attention span of listeners is limited. After a certain point, people lose concentration, and communication is less effective because messages are not received. This can happen during a long speech or practice. Even worse, it can happen in long-term situations when players are constantly returning to the coaches' offices with gripes and complaints, or coaches become repetitive or too negative and the team tunes them out. In either case, changes need to be made to restore and improve effective communication.

Players need to understand that their role is to contribute to, not detract from, the program. Whiners and troublemakers, no matter how skilled as players, have a negative impact on a team. So the best way for a player who's being tuned out to regain others' attention is to communicate positively and apply great effort in his or her assigned role.

Similarly, a coach must try to keep messages fresh and relevant over a long season and over the lengthy playing careers of individual players. Since players like to play much more than they like to listen to coaches talk, a coach should keep daily communications brief and to the point. The coach should then give players the opportunity to demonstrate that they understand those messages by practicing in the desired way. This makes practice more enjoyable and productive because the desired playing results are obtained quickly. This approach also increases players' level of listening and comprehension because they are expected to "get it" the first time the coach gives a message.

Unnecessary and excessive use of influence will have the same impact as excessive use of one's bank account. Resources or, in this case, influence quickly dwindle.

Helpful, Honest Interactions

The father of humanistic psychology, Carl Rogers, believed that effective helping relationships are based on unconditional acceptance and genuineness. He believed that a therapist who demonstrated these qualities to clients would be effective in helping the clients grow toward their personal potential. Consider people who have always accepted you in spite of your faults, people who have always been honest with you and have said what they truly mean instead of hiding feelings. These people win complete trust and lead others to have "immediate belief" in what they say.

Unconditional acceptance does not mean accepting negative behavior. It means being committed to helping a person no matter what that person does. For example, some coaches have dismissed players from their team, but they keep in touch with those players and continue to encourage them in life.

Criticism and discipline are absolutely necessary in coaching in order to help players identify problem behaviors and make positive changes. However, for critical messages to be well received, the player must know that the coach's criticism is intended to benefit the player and the team. The player must believe that the coach is working to help him and will never stop trying to help him. This is the nature of unconditional acceptance.

Problem behaviors are on- or off-court actions that hurt the team and the individual. A coach should avoid labeling the player as the problem. Criticism shouldn't be personal (i.e., a criticism of the person); it should

© Human Kinetics

One of the challenges of good coach–player communication is determining each player's individual needs and styles of interaction.

be professional (i.e., a criticism of actions that are harmful). Personal criticism can create personal animosity and distrust. Criticism that is professional can help create the special trust that occurs when a player knows that a coach will always work to teach the right and wrong ways to be successful.

Genuineness and honesty are necessary for any healthy relationship. Most coaches are very honest. However, circumstances can and do change. For example, in recruiting, most coaches tell recruits that the team really needs them. The message is that they are important and that they will be successful. Later, some of those players may not get to play and may not succeed. Although the coaches were not necessarily dishonest with these players, the players usually think they were. Therefore, distrust creeps in, and the coach's effectiveness as a communicator is reduced.

In this situation, the coach probably did recruit that player with the belief that the individual would be successful; however, circumstances changed. Perhaps the player did not work as hard as expected or had a difficult time adjusting to a new level or system. Or perhaps other team-mates just excelled more. These experiences happen all the time, and no coach wants to be perceived as dishonest. The key is to keep communication current and let players know where they stand and why, while also showing commitment to helping players improve (i.e., unconditional acceptance). Later in this chapter, ideas on how to keep personal communication open are discussed.

Honesty means communicating both positive and negative information. For example, consider two freshmen who did not play in their first two games. Both players were told they were recruited to provide the team with immediate help. So, while sitting idly on the sidelines, they wondered if the coach's word could be trusted.

One of the players, however, acknowledged that he was not practicing well and that the adjustment to college ball had been more difficult than expected. He also admitted that he hadn't come to school in great shape, and as a result, he had a difficult time defending quicker players. And he knew that his shot wasn't consistent, probably because he failed to do the drills the coach had recommended during the summer. So when he met with the coach to discuss his status, the coach explained that the player's opportunities would increase only if he worked harder on his game and got in better shape. The coach emphasized that he had been honest with the player in recruiting. He told the player that his playing time would have come had he demonstrated the expected work ethic and improved his readiness.

The other newcomer was doing better, but he had two juniors ahead of him playing just as well. The coach explained that these juniors had earned the first chance to play in this equal situation because of their seniority. He explained to the freshman that he would be playing if he was superior (he knew he wasn't), and that he would receive the same consideration in equal situations as an upperclassman. A coach may assume that players understand the situation, but communicating to make sure players understand is important in building trust.

Genuineness is largely a product of honesty. It is a form of emotional honesty. A genuine person truly means what he says, and others can see how the person truly feels. Genuineness includes a transparency whereby others know what the person is thinking and feeling. The person's commitment to the well-being of others and his positive or negative feelings will be clear.

Rogers believed that the key for therapists to become more accepting, genuine, and effective is their ability to be empathetic. Empathy is knowing how another person feels, or putting yourself in his shoes. By remembering how hard it was to be a player and trying to understand players' frustrations, a coach becomes a better communicator.

"Keeping it real" is important in the culture of many young players today. Putting up a false front in an attempt to win approval or manipulate others results in immediate distrust. Keeping it real means sharing the bad and the good. It also means being consistent and not changing personality based on the situation. Of course, coaches must sometimes behave differently in different situations. However, the core values of the coach and loyalty to players must be constants. "Keeping it real" may be another fleeting pop phrase, but it does reflect the values of many young people who may have previously been manipulated and disappointed by other adults. Keys to keeping it real are to follow through with promises and to say what is felt.

In summary, unconditional acceptance, honesty, genuineness, and empathy remove any doubt about the motives of the source of information. In other words, they allow a coach to have "immediate belief."

Caring is the demonstration of unconditional acceptance and more. It includes being aware of a player's life off the court. It is knowing the status of the player's academic, family, and personal life. Caring is about more than basketball. It is being there when problems arise for the player or his family and friends. It means visiting the sick, consoling the grieving, encouraging the discouraged, and celebrating joys together. These behaviors are ends in themselves; they are clearly important behaviors to help young people. However, they also end up being means to great relationships in which criticism is understood and "immediate belief" can occur.

Demanding Focus

Coaches and players should always make eye contact when communicating. This is an important life skill that will impact everything from performance in job interviews to family interactions, and it definitely facilitates the understanding of messages between players and coaches. Coaches should not have wandering eyes when addressing a team. Failing to maintain eye contact gives an impression of insecurity, which can decrease credibility. It also hinders the coach from noticing if players are paying attention. Players should expect coaches to make eye contact and vice versa. To make sure focused listening is taking place, a coach should not speak to a team unless all eyes are on him. Starting discussions with "Let me see everyone's eyes" is a good habit for coaches and players. When a player loses eye contact, the coach should immediately recognize it and ask the player to look at him and refocus. This is necessary at times even with mature players. Players who constantly make eye contact and are good listeners learn more and make a great impression on coaches. To make sure listening has taken place, a coach can ask players to repeat key points after they are given or to summarize important points from a practice before dismissal. These "pop quizzes" hold players accountable for listening to and remembering information.

Specificity

The importance of specificity in setting goals was mentioned in chapter 2, but being clear and specific in all communication is important in coaching. The often-used phrase, "Say what you mean and mean what you say" applies here. Messages should have simple, consistent, and deeply meaningful themes.

Many of the messages a coach sends are prescriptive, as in how the team or player should do something to achieve a desired result. This could include how to win a championship, how to be dominant in rebounding, how to get good shots, how to play pressure defense, how to be tough, how to be a productive student and achiever, or how to develop skill or strength. The possibilities are endless. A coach should not just communicate *what* to do (i.e., general messages). The coach should explain *how* to do it (i.e., specific messages).

To do this effectively, the coach must determine in advance what keys are most critical for a particular team or player to be successful. This is another reason why having "team commandments" or "musts" is a good idea. They make communication more focused, and they increase the likelihood that messages will be understood and that more productive actions will be taken. Ideally, many of the most significant prescriptive messages should be presented to players as early as possible (e.g., first team meeting or in recruiting) to immediately create the proper expectations.

Positivity

Though their compelling Cinderella run in the 2006 NCAA tournament brought them into the spotlight, Jim Larranaga and the George Mason Patriots were already a shining example of how positive and functional communication can be beneficial to a basketball program. Larranaga, like

AP Photo/Jacquelyn Martin

Coaches like George Mason's Jim Larranaga know that practices are more fun and productive when the tone is positive, whether providing instructions, conducting drills, or correcting errors.

the best coaches throughout history, focuses his messages on what to do rather than what not to do. The rationale for this might seem apparent, yet it's easy to fall into the negative mode.

A big problem with only warning players against doing the wrong thing is that it often turns their attention to doing exactly what the coach is trying to prevent from happening. The common example to show the problem with negative instructions is, "Don't think of a pink elephant." Well, of course everyone envisions that unusual picture even though told not to think about it. Thus, instructions such as, "Don't lose your poise" are not as helpful as, "We're okay" or "Stay together." Similarly, a coach should tell players how to do things (e.g., "Hit the open man more quickly using two-handed passes instead of one-handed passes") as opposed to giving them overly simplistic and negative instructions (e.g., "Don't turn the ball over").

Even with the positive orientation of communication, George Mason's amazing season wasn't without its setbacks. Larranaga suspended a key player, the team's second-leading scorer, for unacceptable behavior in an incident that occurred during GMU's loss to Hofstra in the Colonial Athletic Association's postseason tournament. The team feared that their failure to win the CAA tourney might deny them an NCAA bid. But on Selection Sunday, George Mason was announced as an 11 seed, matched up against Michigan State at Dayton, Ohio.

Although obviously ecstatic over the bid, Coach Larranaga did not lose sight of his priorities, and he made sure his players didn't either. That was apparent when the coach held fast to his plans to suspend his key player one game for his prior transgression. But Coach Larranaga did not allow his team to focus on the loss, the difficulty in matching up with the Spartans, or the pressure associated with the Big Dance. Instead, Larranaga kept things loose and light, just as he had all season, positively communicating to his players what a great opportunity lay before them. Not every team will earn a Final Four berth like Coach Larranaga's club, but this is a great example of how a team can respond favorably to negative circumstances with effective leadership and communication.

Corrective Messages

Certainly, most people are receptive to positive messages and are resistant to critical messages. Praise is easy to accept; criticism is not. To communicate criticism in a way that can be more easily accepted, a coach must make sure that the problem behavior is the focus (e.g., poor passing fundamentals, poor shot selection, poor work habits) and not personal flaws (i.e., a coach should not call a player stupid, lazy, or stubborn).

A technique called "sandwiching" can make criticism easier to accept. This simply involves beginning with a positive statement (e.g., "You are one of our best defenders"), followed by the criticism (e.g., "But you are shooting a bad percentage, and you cannot continue to take bad shots"). The criticism is then followed by another positive statement (e.g., "Now we need your defense and leadership. Be unselfish and smart on your shots. Get the ball to our best scorers more, and your assists will go up. You will help the team more."). A more concise example would be as follows: "You are so strong you should get 10 rebounds a game, but you have to go after it hard. You are just watching the ball. Now, go be dominant." The sandwich is positive–critical–positive.

John Wooden used the sandwich approach as a critical teaching technique. When a mistake was made, he would stop practice and first show what should have been done (i.e., the correct action). Second, he would show what the mistake was in order to make the mistake clear. Third, he would repeat the demonstration of the correct action to further show how it differs from the mistake and to finish on a positive note.

Here's an example of how a coach might use the sandwich technique in correcting an improper defensive stance. The coach first demonstrates a correct defensive stance. Next, the coach shows the player how standing up too straight led to the player getting beat (by making the player slower). Finally, the coach once again shows the proper defensive stance and how it makes a player quicker.

This approach can be used in any teaching situation. The sandwich approach makes criticism easier to accept by also offering positive messages.

Coach–Player Meetings

Formal communication takes place during scheduled individual and team meetings. Successful coaches may vary widely on the frequency of such communication. Some coaches may hold individual meetings on a daily basis. In these situations, players are required to stop by the coach's office daily to check in. The interchange is often simply a quick hello and a few words to find out how the player is doing that day. However, this system provides the chance to keep communication of feelings and events completely current. If something does need to be discussed, this can be done quickly within the normal structure of the program (i.e., daily check-ins).

Other coaches prefer weekly or biweekly check-ins. These involve a more lengthy discussion of the week academically and personally. Basketball can be discussed, but this is an excellent time to build relationships beyond basketball. This format is also good for planning time management for the week (e.g., when to study for a test, write a paper, meet with a professor, lift weights, or do extra shooting).

Still other coaches dislike creating too many demands on the athlete's time as well as on their own; these coaches will limit formal individual meetings to a preseason meeting and a postseason meeting. In these meetings, the coach and player discuss overall expectations, identify goals, and evaluate academic, personal, and basketball growth. This system does not keep coaches from calling for other individual meetings, which are scheduled only when a situation requires immediate communication. Clearly, whether a coach schedules daily, weekly, or biannual meetings with players will depend on the coach's preference and how much guidance individual players require.

Informal communication can occur anytime and anywhere, such as in the gym after practice, on a bus ride, or at a table at lunch. These opportunities are frequent, and they are probably more important to players than formal meetings. Players who speak of negative relationships with coaches say things such as, "He would just walk right by me. We never talked." Given that these opportunities are important to players and are more convenient than formal meetings between people with busy schedules, a coach should take advantage of them.

With the high number of single-parent homes, many young males have not had a close relationship with or been offered criticism by another adult male. This situation offers great opportunity for a coach to make a difference in someone's life, but it is also a challenge that requires the time to communicate acceptance, caring, and knowledge. This time can often be found in daily informal situations.

Team meetings are one of the most common forms of communication in basketball. Some teams meet before every practice to communicate key points for the day. This can also be done on the court by using a quiet stretching time (after warm-ups and before full-speed practice) to communicate the keys for the day. Once again, short, concise, and powerful meetings are more effective than lengthy ones where attention and enjoyment decrease.

More unique forms for team meetings include team retreats, workshops, and bonding experiences. These forums often provide for powerful communication that creates the kind of cohesion in which all team members buy into the same messages and goals. These forms of communication are discussed in the following chapter on developing team cohesiveness.

"New School" Communication

Because the importance of winning is greater than ever, coaches are demanding more and more of their players. To build a relationship that allows a coach to push a player and to keep players focused on a daily basis, constant communication is necessary. As discussed earlier, this can occur informally in hallways and cafeterias or in any chance meeting. It can also occur formally in scheduled meetings (individual or team meetings).

Technology has introduced another form of communication as well—the text message. Although "texting" should never replace speaking to people, it is convenient and popular among players. Coaches can and should take advantage of texting. Texting an early-morning reminder to do a great job in class is a good thing. Texting congratulations on a good practice is a good thing. Texting a motivational message the night before a game is also a good thing. As discussed earlier, too much talking can become tiresome for players. Thus, quick and simple text messages can maintain communication.

Creative Communication

Some coaches have unique systems to enhance communication on the court. Tom Cooper used colored cards flashed from the bench to signal the next defense; each color represented a different defense. Several combinations of cards could be used to indicate different combinations of presses and half-court defenses. He used a system of multiple defenses to confuse and disrupt opponents, and he changed presses and defenses constantly. The colored cards allowed him to communicate changes quickly and clearly.

Dennis Wolff, the very successful coach at Boston University, has used "false signals" that confuse opponents who are scouting his team. In Wolff's system, many set plays are used, and they are signaled in different ways (e.g., patting the pants, pulling the shirt, raising a fist, twirling the finger, patting the head, and so on). However, the system makes it appear as if different signals are used for the same play, making it difficult to scout the meaning of those signals. After dead balls (e.g., time-outs, free throws), a play is given verbally, and a false (i.e., fake) signal can then be used before the play is executed. This certainly makes scouting Boston University difficult. It also reflects the basketball intelligence of their team—the players must be able to use many different offensive sets with many different and varying signals that allow the team to be unpredictable to opponents.

PLAYER-TO-PLAYER COMMUNICATION

Functional player interaction is a prerequisite to success in team sports. In coach speak, this usually translates to "Talk!"—as in insisting that players communicate more verbally on the court.

The great John Wooden made his centers the verbal directors of the Bruins' defense. His belief was that, with nearly all of the opposition's activities in view, the center had a unique perspective of the court that should be used to the rest of the defenders' advantage. Bill Walton, who conquered significant speech problems, was a maestro in orchestrating the defensive efforts of those great UCLA teams in the early 1970s. More recently, St. Joseph's University had a historic and undefeated season in 2004, but they began the following year with a 3-7 nonconference record. This slow start was quickly reversed with a strong Atlantic 10 record and a postseason NIT bid. When asked what the key to his team's improvement was, Coach Phil Martelli simply said, "We made them talk. We made them constantly communicate on defense."

Defensive Communication

Defensive communication is critical to team success. Before players begin to communicate effectively with each other, they must simply learn to talk on the court and become more verbal. This is a new concept for most players because the beginning player is so focused on the action around him that talking is the last thing on his mind. Learning defensive fundamentals and talking can easily be done simultaneously. Quite simply, players can be required to verbalize their correct defensive position in drills. For example, in a defensive shell drill, every player can call out "ball," "deny," or "help" to communicate what he is doing based on where his man is and where the ball is. Of course, whether players have the "ball," have to "deny," or have to "help" changes every time the ball moves or their man moves. By calling out what they are doing, they are not only learning what to do, but they are also learning to talk.

Once players learn basic defensive positioning and get used to talking on the court, they can then learn to communicate with each other. Every screen the offense sets should be covered with the defenders involved communicating. Some coaches have players identify the screen and simply tell their teammate, "screen coming," "back screen," "screen right," or "screen left." Although this communication certainly increases awareness, it does not tell a teammate how to respond. This is fine if a team always covers screens the same way. In this case, if defenders always go through the screen and don't switch, awareness is all that is needed. However, if a team's defensive rules are more complicated (e.g., players of the same size can switch but others don't), or if a team makes adjustments based on scouting reports, then the communication must indicate *how* to cover the screen.

In telling a teammate what to do, players must use the same language. For example, off-ball screens should be called with instructions for either "through" or "switch," and on-ball screens can be called with "hedge over," "jam under," or "switch" to specify the exact defensive action desired.

Offensive Communication

Offensive communication is also needed to effectively set screens or call out plays and offenses. This can be done verbally, but it often involves body signals that are easier to use in loud gyms. These signals can also keep the defense from knowing what the offense is doing.

In screening, many coaches teach a screener to call his teammate's name or give a signal when setting a screen. Setting a good screen on a defender does not matter if your teammate does not know that you are trying to get him open. Screening signals often include eye contact and showing a fist or waving a teammate toward you to use the screen.

Of course, a very common practice is to use nonverbal signals to communicate offensive plays or patterns in loud gyms (e.g., pat head, show thumbs up, pull shirt, touch chin, raise fist). The coach or the point guard will typically give the signal for everyone else to see and react to.

To liven up practice and also get players to talk more loudly over crowd noise, some coaches play loud music on their public address system during practice. In football, Bill Belichick of the New England Patriots frequently "pumps up the volume" in practice to simulate crowd noise and to get players to talk. This is also a fun and effective technique used by basketball coaches. Players enjoy the music, and the coach can increase the volume to challenge players to communicate more loudly and clearly.

Being a Good Teammate

Communicating appreciation and support for teammates is very important to building unselfish team play. Dean Smith has been credited with teaching several ways players can communicate appreciation. Most well known is pointing to a teammate after a basket to acknowledge or thank the passer for setting up the play. Coach Smith's teams always acknowledged the assist in this way, and it encouraged team play. Players who came out of the game at North Carolina were met by the whole bench rising and clapping to acknowledge the efforts of the returning player. Huddles before free throws were used to let leaders make points or plan for the next possession. In many programs, taking a charge or getting a loose

Affirming teammates' successes is an important way to build positive communication and help players motivate each other.

ball is met with enthusiastic teammates praising the successful player. When a player is on the floor after taking a charge or diving for the ball, teammates will often rush to help him up.

A player should also be aware of his moods, as demonstrated by his body language and tone of voice, in dealing with teammates. Nobody likes being around people who are in a bad mood. The saying, "Moody people make bad teammates" is true. Consistent positivity is something that should be strived for. Coaches who have moody players must show them their blessings and educate them about how everyone has difficulty and encourage them to positively deal with challenges; this helps decrease feelings of self-pity that often go with moodiness. Of course, showing the moody player an example of someone who has far greater difficulty can also put his situation into better perspective. Initially, coaches should not put a player down for being in a bad mood but should try to take him through this educational process. Like any teaching situation, though, if problems persist and the player resists the teaching, a more forceful tone or actions may be necessary.

Off the court, players can also be taught positive communication habits. A popular book years ago, *All I Really Need to Know I Learned in*

Kindergarten, reminded all of us that effectively working with others is an important but simple process. For example, the words *thank you* and *please* are powerful because they immediately convey appreciation and respect. Teaching players to consistently use these words reinforces the right messages and makes them better communicators. Too many young people do not practice these powerful, simple courtesies.

The point is that a coach can teach positive communication on and off the court by encouraging simple courtesies.

Communication With the Opposition

Player-to-player communication also occurs between players on opposing teams. Very little communication between opponents serves the cause of helping one's team. Thus, it should be kept to a minimum, especially in the area of trash talking. How important is it to avoid trash talking? During the 2008 Atlantic 10 season, La Salle University lost a triple overtime game by one point; in this game, the opposition received two extra free throws and points because of a technical foul on La Salle for trash talking. Later in the year, La Salle won a one-point game in which the opposition was called for a technical foul for trash talking. This unnecessary aspect of the game can only hurt one's team.

Fortunately, trash talking is on the decline. In the 1990s, woofing at opponents seemed to be more important to players than their team's own performance. It was ridiculous because it only served to inspire good opponents to focus more and perform better—the exact opposite of its supposed intent.

A few players might gain a very small psychological advantage over an opponent after firing a personal verbal salvo. However, most players will be more distracted and less effective executing their own duties on the court because of the attention they're devoting to creating and delivering the message. Yes, it's OK and perfectly natural in the emotional arena of sport to exchange a barb or two with an opponent in the heat of a game. But problems arise when trash talking becomes part of a player's repertoire and when it spills over to the extent that it penalizes the team.

So put the trash where it belongs and keep it there. Given the common shortcomings in players' functional communication, there's plenty of work to do to improve beneficial interactions on the court and in the locker room.

PLAYER-TO-COACH COMMUNICATION

If a coach is obligated to communicate caring, honesty, and knowledge, the players must likewise communicate loyalty, unselfishness, and honesty toward the coach. The opposite—disloyalty (e.g., "back stabbing"), selfishness, and lying—have undermined many teams and stifled the careers of many young players who were not aware of the importance of these qualities.

The code of loyalty as it pertains to basketball culture is to defend your teammates, coach, and program and to never speak negatively about them. The term "locker room lawyer" is one of disdain that coaches have for players who constantly voice opinions and take sides in team issues, thereby creating dissension among the team. Not only is there no benefit to such negative behavior and not only does it harm the team, but it also forever harms the reputation of the player. Loyal actions include defending others, being a peacemaker, and having the courage to directly address others with concerns instead of doing it secretly and unproductively. Most coaches have an "open-door" policy, and players should take advantage of this to voice concerns.

A player must also be unselfish in voicing concerns. The red flag should be raised when a coach senses that the concerns of anyone in the program are more self-serving than team-serving. Before voicing a concern, a player must think about how this concern affects the team. If the concern has little potential benefit to the team and is selfish in nature, that concern may not be appropriate to address. Player concerns often have to do with their own playing time. However, nearly any concern can be communicated appropriately to a coach as long as the player recognizes that team success is most important. When bringing up personal concerns, the player needs to indicate how they relate to the team.

Finally, honesty from a player strengthens communication and the player–coach relationship. Admitting mistakes on and off the court fosters trust and respect. Having the courage to face a coach with a legitimate but difficult question further fosters respect.

COACHING STAFF INTERACTION

For communication to be effective among coaches, it should be grounded in genuine, caring relationships, just as with players. A head coach facilitates this by showing an interest in helping assistants with their professional goals. Starting a coaching relationship by asking, "What are your goals in coaching?" or "Where do you want to be in five years?" shows interest in helping an assistant. Professional activities, plans, and performance goals can be decided on to help a coach achieve his personal goals. A head coach should take pride in helping coaches advance their careers and in earning the loyalty of his staff.

Assistant coaches should try to understand what the head coach wants in all areas. Their job is to help the team become exactly what the head coach desires. Assistants should voice opinions and provide input, but ultimately, what the head coach decides must be carried out by all involved. For example, some coaches favor practicing jump shots with a hand in the face to teach focus. Other coaches believe this practice is the definition of a bad shot and that players should not practice shooting with a hand in the face (these coaches believe that players should immediately drive the ball when a defender closes out with hands up). Both philosophies have merit, but the assistant must know which of the two the head coach desires. This is only one of many potential examples of how an assistant must learn by listening and asking how the coach wants players taught.

Coaches have different roles on a coaching staff, just as players have different roles on a team. Each coach should know exactly what his role is during each practice as well as his larger role over the long term (the season). Short-term roles in a given practice could be focusing on rebounding, making sure people talk, officiating to reduce fouls, substituting players, leading certain drills, coaching a team in a scrimmage, or watching a particular player. These are only a few possibilities. Roles in practice should be clearly communicated. Each coach should have a clear focus on specific areas throughout a given practice. Long-term roles for the season can be scouting certain opponents, coaching certain skills, coaching certain positions, recruiting certain areas, or completing administrative duties involving scheduling, equipment, or team travel.

The interesting question is how to determine roles. Like players, coaches should have roles geared to their strengths. In areas that the head coach is highly knowledgeable, he should specify exactly how he wants the team to perform and the coaches to teach. When assistants have unique strengths in an area, a head coach may give assistants the freedom to do it their way. This shows confidence in assistants and is motivating for them to use their own ideas. Simply communicating, "This is how we are doing this" or "Do what you like, just let me know" creates a unified staff that gives its players consistent messages.

COMMUNICATION WITH OTHERS

In addition to communication within a team—between players, coaches, and team staff—the team will need to communicate with officials, media, fans, and school personnel. Learning to interact positively and constructively with these groups is important to a good experience for all involved.

Officials A coach should acknowledge the importance of officials and the difficulty of their jobs. Communication is always helped by knowing the officials' names and being as respectful as possible. Most coaches are sure to point out perceived bad calls, but it is sometimes helpful to also acknowledge when officials make a good call, especially a call against your team. When things do get emotional—as they often do—and a coach feels wronged by certain calls, the coach needs to remember who is "boss."

Shooting Straight

Jay Wright—Villanova University

Credibility and communication with players start with honesty. That is the basis for a good player–coach relationship.

Just as the coaching staff doesn't sugarcoat things or lie to players, we expect our student-athletes to do the same in return. If either side compromises that honest and open line of communication, negative things creep in, such as doubts, insecurities, and lack of faith in one another.

Sometimes we lose guys we're recruiting because we are too forthright in our evaluation of them and explanation of where they fit in compared to other players in the program. But the guys we do get are more assured that what we tell them is true and will be able to handle the truth.

Our aim is to develop individuals who will be successful adults and will represent our team and program in a positive, accurate light. So our expectations are consistent. Listen to the coaching staff. Respect and help your teammates. Present yourself in a manner that will be respected and admired by others.

Sometimes even small nonverbal behaviors communicate a great deal about a person and player. Do you open the door for the elderly woman? Do you pick up your teammate who has been knocked down onto the court? Do you smile and nod or say hello when a passerby greets you? All such acts are a statement about what type of person you are, and those acts represent the type of players you have on your team.

In the off-season, we spend more time with players individually. We will join a guy for lunch on campus or have a team breakfast. This helps us keep in touch with what they're thinking and doing, and it helps them know the coaching staff better. It's also an opportunity to encourage communication between teammates or coaches and players who don't know one another well or have not shared the kind of positive and open communication we insist on among the group.

One thing that's more difficult to influence or control is the information received from outside the program. When you hear rumors, receive e-mails, see Internet comments, watch ESPN, and listen to sports talk shows enough, all of that affects your outlook, if not your behavior. So it is important that the coaching staff and the players spend more time communicating with each other than they do with outside influences. That is a key to staying together and keeping on the same page.

During the in-season, about 90 percent of our time together is in team meetings. Before practice, after practice, and traveling to games, we always want to stay connected to ensure there is no confusion or conflict.

Even when we talk about an individual player during the season, we typically talk about the concern as a team. We address the player's problem in a team setting because we want everyone to understand how we are dealing with that problem and to learn from it. We use the term *family*, and not loosely. We talk about family being there to support one of its own when there is a problem. We don't simply dismiss him; we try to work together to help him out.

On the court, the players' job is to listen to what the coaches tell them. It is not the time to discuss players' opinions about what drills we should run or who should be on what team for scrimmage. We have to be efficient in practice, so we tell our players if they have any problems with what is happening on the court, they are free to come to the office after practice to talk. And it's important that they *do* come to us and talk honestly, even if they believe we might not want to hear what they have to say. When they're in our office, we want to hear what is in their hearts. That's the only way we can address and resolve something.

Sometimes a player says what the coach wants to hear, thinking it will make the coach happy. But then he goes on the court and his actions don't represent what he said in the office. That's when we have a problem. And the only way to solve it is to be mature and honest. So if a player believes he isn't getting enough shots or playing enough minutes, he needs to be able to come to me after practice and know he won't be punished for doing so. We'll work it out.

It's not a coincidence that when we have good teams, they are also teams that have great communication. On the court, players on those teams talk constantly on offense and defense, which is how we define playing together. Shouting out screens, helping one another up off the floor, getting bench players' support throughout the game, huddling up at the foul line, running out-of-bounds plays crisply, and making eye contact to get the backdoor play are all indicative of a team's communicating well. We encourage these things repeatedly in our practices in an effort to strengthen that habit.

The other part of communication on the court is respecting a teammate by listening. So whoever calls a switch or whoever makes a call and is attempting to communicate, the other person's job is to listen and respect that call. At that moment, it doesn't matter if the call is right or wrong; just react. If something doesn't work, you can talk about it later.

We show guys game footage of Randy Foye, one of the best guards we've had. When a bad call went against him or he missed a shot or he turned the ball over, Randy remained expressionless and went about his business, clapping his hands and getting ready for the next play. We practice and test players for that. We have coaches make bad calls purposely against certain players in practice to see how they react. That body language, especially on the road, can be interpreted negatively. We also monitor those things during

(continued)

the game, such as how guys look when we substitute for them and when they come off the court. We want them to keep their heads up, maintain a positive posture, and smack all the bench players' hands on their way to an open seat. That's showing respect to teammates, but it's also telling opponents our players are gamers, and the battle isn't over. That's also why we forbid players from bending over and putting their hands on their knees. We never want an opponent to think we're tired. Body language can give either you or your opponent an advantage, and we prefer to gain that mental edge.

In close games, getting a technical foul is costly and rarely helpful. Thus, the coach must learn to read an official and not overstep boundaries. It's okay to get upset with a call, but a coach must keep in mind that every official is different in what he will tolerate before a harmful technical comes.

A popular but incorrect myth is that coaches can intimidate officials. In reality, this does not occur. However, coaches can "manage" officials by encouraging them, letting them focus, and asking them to watch for things the coach is concerned about.

Media   It is never wrong for a coach or team leader to praise players on the team or to praise the opposition, especially after losses. Giving credit is always preferred to assigning blame.

It is also fine, sometimes even helpful, for a coach to have an agenda with the media, using them to share helpful messages to fans, players, and others. In tough situations a coach can emphasize a team's effort, youth, potential, or attitude to give hope for the future.

Be as honest and straightforward as possible with the media (short of publicly criticizing specific people). Michigan State coach Tom Izzo is known for his straight talk, and the media and fans really appreciate him for it.

Coaches should also take responsibility in situations where they may have made a mistake, suggesting what they could have done better. This reflects honesty and maturity. But they should avoid statements made out of frustration, such as, "I can't get through to this team" or "Maybe I'm not the right person here." Coaches have made such statements and never recovered in the court of public opinion. The combination of losing and self-doubt is unacceptable to people who support a program. Strength, confidence, and determination are needed in those "tough" interviews when a coach is explaining poor play.

Another critical but simple courtesy in dealing with the media is to quickly return calls and to do postgame interviews as soon as possible.

Also, taking time to fully explain things, getting to know media people, and giving access to practices will be appreciated. Helping members of the media do their job makes it easier for them to positively portray your program.

A player always does well in interviews by praising opponents and teammates. This is simply the best way to give due credit and avoid harmful controversy. Players must beware of questions looking for controversy (e.g., "Do you think they were overrated?" "Why didn't you play more?"). Players should be well schooled in being positive with the media.

Fans   Positive, supportive fans are absolutely invaluable. Fans give a team a home-court advantage, they personally encourage players, and they help a program through fund-raising and volunteer efforts.

Cultivating that support by communicating with fans is critical. Getting fans excited for future success while managing expectations (i.e., not getting them unrealistically high) is key. This is easier with a winning or rapidly improving program.

At the start of a rebuilding program, a coach must increase aspirations (e.g., "We want to win a championship here") while decreasing expectations (e.g., "It will take time to recruit and develop players"). Distinguishing between aspirations and expectations is important. One athletic director at a very strong program with great fan support (but not a national powerhouse) explained this as follows: "We tell our fans that our goal is to go to the Final Four, and we want to have high aspirations. But it is an unrealistic expectation to do this every year." Thus, this tenuous act of increasing aspirations and controlling expectations is part of the art of coaching and communicating. There are no hard-and-fast scripts that accomplish this balance. Rather, this balancing act requires getting a feel for how to excite fans about what the team can do, what it wants to do, and what it believes it will do—while also explaining how challenging these efforts will be and how the fans' support is needed.

Fans also need to know that a program is about more than winning. Fans see the games, but they do not see the academic success, tough practices, community service, and character development behind the scenes. Talking about values and personal success stories of players can help fans learn more about the program. It can also moderate the fan emphasis on winning and help create pride in a program (i.e., "We have good kids. We do things the right way.").

As previously discussed, acknowledging that fan criticism exists without overreacting to it is necessary to stay positive and focused on the team. Good programs are self-critical enough that applying additional criticism and negativity serves no purpose. A coach should expect criticism. He will never enjoy it, but knowing it exists and expecting it will lead to less frustration. It's part of the job. A coach should politely listen and then move on. When coaches listen to talk radio or read Internet message boards, they end up reacting rather than leading, which is not good.

School Personnel Outside of the players, no one else is more important for a coach to communicate with than athletic directors, principals, presidents, and key supporters. The key is listening. A coach must know the values and resources of an institution, and he must make the program work within the institution's framework.

In any job, the coach must know who he works for. What is most important? Winning? Academic success? Player conduct? Financial responsibility? Of course, every school would like to win championships, have great students, never have a kid get in trouble, and spend little money. Obviously, no program does all of the above, certainly not all the time. Thus, what are the priorities?

The goal is to find a good match between the priorities of the coach and his administration. When there are differences, the coach can advocate for his beliefs and goals. In the end, however, he must simply listen. The coach leads his team and players to accept the roles that he believes are best for the group. Similarly, administrators lead a school, and the coach accepts a role that is best for that particular school.

The coach and the administrators must communicate about priorities and what realistically can be compromised for those priorities. For example, a program may focus on having good kids and students even if that means winning less. Or a program may take some at-risk kids—and do their best to mentor those kids—in order to have championship talent. Or a program may not have the money for a lot of scholarships, recruiting, or top facilities, so the program may just want to be competitive. Or a program may have the resources to win at a high level. One of the biggest mistakes among coaches is to complain that their school is not supported like their competitors are. To help avoid this, a coach must be sure to communicate with administrators regarding budgets, facilities, and priorities before taking a job. If resources change over time, this needs to be discussed.

Dr. Donald Fuhr, professor of education at Clemson University, teaches future school administrators that school maintenance is the underlying foundation for an effective learning environment. A clean and professional environment—and keeping it that way even when unexpected problems arise—is invaluable. For a coach, taking care of and appreciating the maintenance staff ensures clean floors, good lighting, good locker rooms, and working equipment (e.g., scoreboards, rims). Thus, communicating appreciation through words and actions (e.g., giving T-shirts, holiday gifts) keeps motivation high for critically important people behind the scenes. Appreciation for school personnel can be communicated to any group of people who work to help student-athletes in the program.

NONVERBAL COMMUNICATION AND EMOTIONS

Nonverbal communication is just as important as anything said. As discussed earlier, the most common form of nonverbal communication is eye contact. Players should always look at a coach when he is speaking. Eye contact is not only polite, it also shows that a person is listening and giving respect. The opposite—not paying attention to a speaker—shows poor listening skills and a lack of respect. This creates the perception that the message is not important. Coaches should always make sure players are listening by insisting on eye contact. Of course, they should also give players the same courtesy.

Other examples of negative nonverbal behaviors that can be eliminated include the following: players sulking when coming out of a game, players sulking while on the bench, coaches looking disgusted, and players or coaches showing signs of frustration by stomping or facial expressions. These behaviors negatively affect teammates, coaches, and oneself.

Alternatives include always running on and off the court, always supporting teammates, and consciously reacting with a composed response or no response to poor play. Lastly, the great players possess great mental and physical toughness. They do not show signs of fatigue or pain on the court. Many coaches emphasize that players should never let the opposition know they are tired. Nonverbal communication should be used to show enthusiasm, self-control, support, determination, and strength.

Emotions are the underlying cause of people's reactions and nonverbal communication. Different players and coaches may have big differences in the amount of emotion they express. Through the years, coaches such as Louie Carnesecca and Bruce Pearl have shown great passion and emotion. The same is true for players such as Magic Johnson and Joakim Noah. On the opposite end of the emotional spectrum are controlled and measured coaches such as Ralph Miller and Lorenzo Romar and players such as Walt Frazier and Tim Duncan. Basketball is an emotional game played by passionate individuals. The final chapter of this book addresses how to control emotions, deal with frustrations, and stay focused on the task at hand.

Some of the best players and coaches in the game are very passionate and determined but avoid emotional behavior. Generally, NBA coaches are very good at not outwardly responding to poor play with emotionally driven nonverbal behavior. This is wise because of the extremely long season and because experienced, high-profile players do not want to be embarrassed. NBA coaches cannot emotionally push a team for close to 100 straight games, and they cannot publicly question accomplished veteran players (this would be viewed as disrespectful).

Although coaching at lower levels is very different, the coaching demeanor often used in NBA games has clear advantages. Avoiding verbal and nonverbal emotional outbursts during a game reflects a certain amount of self-control, keeps players from being frustrated or flustered, and is usually more acceptable to administrators, fans, and players' family members. This is much easier said than done for emotional coaches, but any attempts at greater self-control are positive.

The ideal model is to emotionally challenge and push players very hard in daily practices so that a certain work ethic is formed. When this occurs, challenging the players is not as necessary in games. It has been said that practice is the coach's time and the game is the player's time. Coach K at Duke University appears to use this model, because his team is clearly accustomed to fiercely competing every day and every game. This allows coaches to trust player effort more in games and stay more positive with nonverbal behavior.

For the majority of NBA coaches and veteran players, when something negative happens, they may instantly want to react negatively, but they choose not to react. After bad plays, they simply move on, understanding that there is no time or benefit to dwell on the negative.

CHAPTER
9

Cohesion

The communication skills and methods presented in the previous chapter are the tools by which individuals and groups interact. As we've seen, the tenuous ties formed by such communication can be torn apart by a lapse in how messages are sent, received, or interpreted.

Given the countless hours that members of a team spend together and the many ups and downs that may be experienced during the course of a season, chances are there will be miscommunications along the way. Therefore, a strong bond—one that will remain intact despite singular incidents of poor interaction—must be established among team members and the coaching staff.

That bond, more formally called cohesion, is founded on a mutual respect for individuals within the program and an appreciation for the team concept. A team is more than a group of people who wear the same uniform; at its most basic level, a team is two or more individuals with shared goals and values. Sounds simple, but the wide range of backgrounds and personalities within a program can create disharmony, and the prevailing "me first" culture of today discourages placing personal pursuits after the greater good of the group.

PLEDGE OF ALLEGIANCE

At key points, especially early season and midseason, the coaching staff should encourage team members to outwardly commit and recommit to the team. This is when leaders tend to emerge, and having a strong subgroup of team leaders greatly improves the chances that each team member will buy into the same goals and values.

A good example of this comes from football and the 1987 University of Notre Dame national championship team. At their first team meeting that year, Coach Lou Holtz asked each player who wanted to win the national championship to stand up. As expected, all the players stood. Coach Holtz then clarified what striving for the national championship meant: superior team discipline, superior execution, and superior conditioning—all formed through superior effort and sacrifice. This requires giving absolutely maximum effort, not being satisfied with marginal performance, and driving until the task is complete and the challenges are conquered.

As all the players remained standing, it was then understood that the coaches would demand their greatest effort and that the players were each committed to giving it. From that point forward, if an individual began to waver, coaches and teammates could challenge the individual to live up to his commitment. The team had made the choice to be the best and was unified by it.

Of course, a team can make such a commitment and not win a national championship. After all, there are a number of unified teams and only one champion. And even the most selfish and disruptive "me first" type of athlete wants to win, if for no other reason than to take credit for it and bask in the adulation afforded champions. That's why the shared goals and values that serve as the bedrock of a truly unified team are not focused only on winning.

However, it is also true that this type of team unity within a program maximizes what a team can accomplish. The sincere, verbal expression of commitment by team members is an effective reminder that the good of the group is the foremost consideration for each athlete on the squad. The coaching staff or leaders on the team should select the most opportune time and manner to do this.

TASK COHESION

Yes, it is preferable that team members like one another on a social basis, because this makes task cohesion easier and increases the enjoyment of being on the team. But I could cite numerous examples of teams that did not hang out socially yet functioned and executed well together on the court.

The point is, a basketball team can demonstrate great chemistry and togetherness in the gym, regardless of whether they are best friends when they leave it. We call this task cohesion. And the two aspects of the game that most reflect a team's level of task cohesion are passing and defense.

Passing Cohesion

The outstanding team play at Princeton University from the late 1960s through the start of this century exemplified great task cohesion—that is, they worked together in very specific, structured ways. The common thread through the highly successful teams of Pete Carril, Bill Carmody, and John Thompson III was their unique, unified style of play. This style has clear philosophies in each aspect of the game, including offense, defense, transition, and rebounding. The trademark of this style is beautiful team execution on offense, with timed cuts and precise, unselfish passing. Players who are normally selfish in passing the ball and executing must be persuaded and taught.

Long-time NBA assistant coach Dick Helm tells a persuasive story about adopting task cohesion on the court. Dick was once visiting and consulting with a very talented professional team overseas that had been underachieving. After observing a lack of cohesion on the court, Coach Helm gathered the team in the locker room and pointed out the obvious: The players took bad shots, they showed their unhappiness with their stats and playing time, and they didn't encourage one another.

So Dick asked them, "Who is willing to give up shots, points, and playing time if it would help the team succeed? Who is willing to appreciate your teammates and encourage them?" Immediately, the team captain

A true desire—not just a willingness—to get the ball to the open teammate is characteristic of good passing, cohesive clubs.

© Human Kinetics

responded positively. Coach Helm said that unfortunately one player isn't enough to make a difference. So he asked the team to think about what would happen if every member was willing to give up shots in order to get the ball to open teammates. The answer is that every time a player passes to an open teammate who makes the shot, he has four other players looking to get him the ball when he is open.

Thus, for every one successful pass made, the player can get fourfold coming back to him, and passing becomes contagious. That's how it works on a cohesive, passing team: Each player actually gets more than he gives. This counterintuitive truth of task cohesion is how teams become special and how players make each other better. It's also how a team becomes greater than the sum of its parts.

The team was persuaded by Coach Helm's argument. The players grasped the fact that to gain more individually, they all first had to give more to the team. That lesson served as a turning point in the season, and the team went on to a championship.

Consistently unselfish, swift passing by all team members is a telltale sign of a squad's task cohesion. Teams that pass freely and willingly in the following ways are fun to watch and even more fun to coach.

• *Get the ball to the teammate who's open.* Coaches can immediately stop practice or use game video to show instances where players miss the opportunity to pass the ball to open teammates—or even better, not just when they fail to pass the ball, but when they fail to deliver the ball. Anyone can make a half-hearted pass to an open teammate when all other options are exhausted, but cohesive teams are full of players who *want* to share the ball with the other members of the team. The team as a whole must agree that a selfish attitude and repeated failures to deliver such passes are unacceptable. And the coaching staff must be consistent in reprimanding players who break this team commandment.

• *Penetrate to create.* Strong defenses provide immediate help to stop dribble penetration. Therefore, against good defensive teams, there will always be a brief moment for the ball handler to pass the ball to an open teammate on every penetration. That's the goal when penetrating—to create a shot for a teammate—not necessarily to get a shot for oneself.

• *Penetrate, kick, and click.* The pass-off penetration is called a kick-out pass, or a kick. Once again, outstanding defenses will quickly rotate to the kick-out pass, but this will often leave another player open because the defense is now in a scramble. Thus, if the shot on the kick-out pass is not open, that player should make a "click" pass immediately to the next open person. The penetrate, kick, and click sequence should be drilled and executed frequently.

• *Post passing.* Any post player with a defender playing behind him can be defined as open and should receive the ball immediately. When the post player is fronted and there is weak-side help, the offensive players must be able to identify where defensive help is coming from. They should quickly skip or reverse the ball to the open teammate while the offensive post player seals the defender who is fronting him. Sealing is similar to boxing out, and the offensive post player should now have the defender on his back and be open to receive a pass. This should result in getting the ball deep into the post. Players should also work on hitting the post player's open hand (i.e., target hand) against fronting defenders when weak-side help is not there.

When post players do receive the ball inside, they should be prepared to kick out against any double team or any collapse by defenders that leaves a teammate open on the perimeter. Players can learn to do this through a low-post two-on-two drill. In this drill, a low-post offensive player has the ball with a defender behind him. Another offensive player is located at the high post or on the opposite wing with a defender on him, too. Once the low-post offensive player begins to make a move, the defender on the perimeter makes a choice to double-team the ball or to stay on his man. The low-post player must read any help defense and learn to kick out or to continue a strong move if no defensive help comes.

• *Trap passing.* Some teams benefit from a three-on-three trap passing drill. The offense is in a triangle with 15-foot (4.5 m) spacing. Two defenders trap the offensive player with the ball. The remaining defender splits the two other offensive players, looking for a steal. The person with the ball must pass out of the trap to an open teammate. The closest defender to the ball then runs to trap the next passer along with the defender who had been splitting and anticipating a steal. The drill continues in this manner until the defense gets a deflection or steal. The teaching points for the offense are to stay low and strong to step through the trap—or use a reverse dribble to create space—and then find an open person. The person being trapped should never turn his back, which is a common mistake. Every ball handler should develop the skill to handle traps and find open people.

• *Pick-and-pop.* Many teams use a good shooter to set ball screens. If the defender guarding the screener hedges to help, as most defenders do, the player with the ball makes an immediate pass back to the open screener popping back for an open jump shot. If the screener can shoot, that is preferred over a pick-and-roll, because it is easier to defensively help on a player rolling to the basket, which requires time and spacing, than on a quick throw-back.

• *Zone passing.* The high-post position in some zone offenses is called a conduit (the person is actually closer to the mid post and is continually slipping in and out of the dead spot, which is a few feet below the free-throw line in the lane). Just as electricity passes through a conduit, the ball often passes through the conduit in zone offense. When the ball reaches this point, all defensive eyes tend to center here, and several defenders instinctively collapse toward the ball—leaving offensive players open. Thus, when offensive players look for the conduit and the conduit finds open teammates, this creates cohesion. Many teams also emphasize the short corner against the 2-3 zone (if a defensive wing covers the offensive wing, the short corner *must* be open). Against a 3-2 zone, many teams will screen the bottom two players. If a bottom defender cheats over a post screen to cover a baseline shooter, the screening post player should be open, or the shooter will be open. An offense should not hold the ball against a zone. The ball should move faster than the defense can make shifts.

• *Passing games, possession games, and screening games.* Passing games reward the offense a point for completed passes and made baskets. Thus, passing is encouraged, and only high-percentage shots are attempted because missed shots reward the ball to the other team (that team will then operate under the same point system). The one-possession game puts a high premium on scoring with the best shot available, which encourages team play. Each team gets one offensive and one defensive possession. To win, a team must get a score and a defensive stop. Losing brings a sprint as a penalty, and another one-possession game quickly follows. Teams will pass with a purpose to get the best shot possible in this situation. Finally, a screening game is one in which a team cannot shoot until a designated offensive player sets a predetermined number of screens. This game requires players without the ball to play cohesively and is an ideal teaching tool for a team running any form of a motion offense.

• *Transition passing.* Transition drills are effective for teaching passing because the offense often has a "numbers" advantage in these drills, which means someone must be open and found. Traditional three-on-two and two-on-one drills are good for this. Another good drill is one in which the offensive team is lined up across the baseline, with a defensive team lined up across the free-throw line facing the offense. A coach passes the ball to the offensive team, and this team begins a fast break while also calling out one or two names of defenders who must run to touch the baseline before sprinting back on defense. This creates a five-on-four or a five-on-three situation. Offensive players must find the open man.

Offensive task cohesion requires good, unselfish passing combined with execution off the ball. This execution will include spacing, screening, and cutting as required by the offense used. As stated earlier, any proven offensive system can be successful if cohesively executed. However, *no* offensive system—even if executed with great spacing, screens, and cuts—can be successful unless teammates willingly share the ball.

Defensive Cohesion

Getting the ball to open teammates is a universal aspect of offensive cohesion. Defensive basketball, on the other hand, has fewer constants because of the extremely wide variety of defenses, strategies, and techniques. However, a few general concepts can be used to define a cohesive defensive unit.

First, any time the ball moves offensively, the defense moves along with it toward proper position (as defined by the system being played). This can be called "air time"—while the ball is in the air, defenders should be moving to new defensive positions. It can also be called "jumping to the ball" because of the principle of quickly shifting toward the ball.

Second, a primary purpose of being in proper defensive position is to be able to provide help. Defensive help is necessary to stop dribble penetration or strong post play. A defining aspect of a great, cohesive defense is that when someone is beat, another defender immediately helps to prevent the easy shot.

© Greg Carroccio/Sideline Photos

Focused, aggressive defense, in which players work hard together to stop opponents consistently, serves to increase a team's cohesion.

Third, whenever help occurs, other players must rotate to help the helper and leave only the offensive player farthest from the basket open. This demands not only quick movement by defenders but also real savvy and awareness on their part to locate open people for rotation.

Fourth, teams must quickly recover, meaning defenders must get back to guard their assigned players in a split second after any help and rotation situation. Recovery requires good court awareness as well as great hustle and determination by the entire defense to close any gap.

That kind of effort, savvy, and teamwork on the defensive end was demonstrated every time the 1999 to 2000 Stanford University men's basketball team took the court. Led by "Mad Dog" Mark Madsen, the squad had very good size with the Collins twins inside, but the team wasn't especially athletic or quick. Still, they scrapped and contested every cut, every pass, and every shot, and they were constant pests to their opponents. This Stanford team was so effectively coordinated and cohesive that they set the all-time record for field-goal defense, holding the opposition to an amazingly anemic 35.2 percent.

Some teams have cohesive, rotating full-court presses. Others use cohesive matchup zones with constant communication. Still others use pure zones with precise, quick, unified shifts on each pass. Pressure defense is also popular, with all players denying immediate passes or pressuring the ball handler tightly. Whatever type of defense is being applied, defenders should understand that it takes only one lapse or error by a single player to result in an opponent's score.

However, if every defender executes together with great quickness, the offense will be hard-pressed to find an uncontested shot. Outstanding defensive stops reflect this kind of cohesive, quick, and well-executed teamwork that attacks the offense rather than sitting back and letting the offense attack. The result is a possession that goes deep into the shot clock and places the pressure on the offense to make an exceptional play or difficult shot in order to score. Even if that happens, the defense has done its job as a cohesive force.

SOCIAL COHESION

As stated earlier, successful basketball teams execute cohesively and unselfishly on the court. However, this sharing and unselfishness come more easily when team members like and care for one another.

Teammates will often share special bonds because they usually have much in common and depend on each other. In some cases, these bonds last a lifetime and transcend the sport itself.

For example, at a memorial service for a former Maine player, Nick Susi, teammates gathered around his uniforms, game pictures, and letter jacket. Stories were told and the school fight song was sung. In this case, basketball clearly led to friends that continued to help each other throughout life. This situation is common and makes our sport special.

There is no single or simple way to build such caring relationships. But before players can care for each other, they must first get to know one another. And, sometimes, because of a player's background or personality, one player may resist getting to know or caring about another teammate.

Some players may come into a program with personal agendas that dominate their thoughts and aspirations. These players are less likely to have the interest in others that is necessary to form any kind of relationships on the team. Similarly, players who have had limited exposure to those of different backgrounds may be resistant to associating with different teammates. A coach needs to make it clear, up front, that if any player finds it impossible to respect and interact with all teammates, then that player should seek to play elsewhere. This type of player can prevent the squad from developing the cohesiveness needed to be successful.

As mentioned, players must get to know each other before they can care for one another. And once players truly start getting to know one another, the process of liking, caring for, and sacrificing for one another takes place quite naturally. Yet a little encouragement always helps, so the following sections identify ways to help players get to know and understand each other.

© Greg Carroccio/Sideline Photos

Players may come from diverse backgrounds and have different priorities, but with the proper team-first mind-set and an environment that encourages camaraderie, the bonds between teammates can become strong through the course of a season and career.

Team Building

Sharon Versyp—Purdue University

At our first meeting each year, I emphasize the need for each of us, players and coaches, to take responsibility for what happens to the team from that point forward. No blaming other teammates, coaches, or anyone. If there's a problem, each of us must first point the finger back at oneself.

Personal accountability and trust in others are the raw materials for team success and cohesion. To develop those resources, we do a lot of team-building activities before we step onto the court. It's a process of getting to know, sacrificing for, being honest with, and helping every other team member that in the end will benefit our basketball performance.

Many of our team-building activities put players in uncomfortable situations or have them perform tasks that they aren't used to doing. Such conditions simulate the new and stressful challenges they will face during the course of the season and will require them to conceive and execute appropriate responses in conjunction with others. Successful performance in such situations not only boosts confidence in oneself and the team but also increases camaraderie. So we work a lot on that before we ever step onto the basketball court.

Team-building activities can be very simple or more involved, depending on the team's experience and cohesiveness. Here are some examples:

1. Hikes and trips. Hiking as a group over challenging terrain is a revealing team task. Don't be surprised if few players have gone hiking before, so try to gauge the appropriate level of this adventure. But dealing with difficult weather conditions and rugged and steep paths in unfamiliar territory takes them out of their comfort zone and exposes much about their character, particularly how they function as part of a group.

More extended team-building trips can create completely different challenges. On one trip, the freshmen had to buy food for dinner, the sophomores had to buy food for breakfast, the juniors were responsible for all the drinks and desserts, and the seniors were responsible for the cookware, napkins, and utensils. So they had to think about others, not just themselves, as they had to feed and provide for a group of 20.

At Maine, after a tough day of mountain hiking at Deer Isle, everyone was hungry when we got back to the house. The freshmen had to cook the meal and were responsible for seeing that everyone received the food that they wanted. Well, it seems the freshmen forgot the chicken, and they started pointing fingers at each other. A few were blaming one particular freshman. So we brought the group together and I said, "Rather than blaming someone for forgetting the chicken, we should be doing whatever is necessary to help out and make the best of the situation." Sure, some of us didn't have the type or amount of food that we preferred, but as one of our players stood up and said, "It's not about the chicken; it's about not failing when others are counting on you. It's about sacrificing; it's about taking care of your teammates and putting them first."

2. Happy notes. We have every student-athlete and coach write a motivational statement, a quote, or simply something they find meaningful at the moment and share it with every player and coach. The notes should be tailored to the individual. So I might write, "Carrie, tonight you are really going to win the battle on the boards. We need you to box out." I will do these specific messages for each coach and player, and they will do the same. In a sense, we are empowering and confirming our faith in one another. So, when the players come into the locker room roughly an hour before the game, they'll read these positive thoughts (as many as 18) before them, and it reinforces their belief that everyone is in the right mind frame to do her best. When I enter the locker room 35 minutes before tip-off for the pregame talk, the whole team has a very strong, positive energy as well as a sense of unity of purpose.

3. The hot seat. A hot seat is where you put someone in the middle of the circle and you tell her something great about herself. So if Jenny is on the hot seat, I might say, "Jenny, you are such a hard worker. You have persevered through so many injuries and have been a blessing for all of us." Then Jenny would turn to the next person, and she would tell her something positive. As many as nine players, coaches, and managers might be selected for the hot seat on a given day. Everyone benefits from sincere, positive feedback since athletes and coaches often receive criticism from themselves and others. Plus, hearing a teammate or coach verbalize the good things one does in front of the rest of the team diminishes the degree of dishonesty and talking behind others' backs.

4. Five positive things. A lot of kids can't voice what they are good at when I ask them. They really don't think they do very many things well. And if they don't feel good about themselves, then it doesn't matter what their teammates say or what I say; they aren't going to perform to their potential or be successful. So, one exercise involves having each team member tell the rest of the team five things she does well. Some are very confident, but others aren't very confident at all. This provides amazing insight into one another, and it's very important both as individuals and as a group.

5. Energy giving. Every team needs energy givers, not energy takers. By that I mean individuals who contribute more to the group's effort than they take away from it. One way to drive this home is to have two people sit back to back and interlock arms with each other. I tell them on the count

(continued)

of three to push together and get up on their feet. You can have the whole team doing this at the same time, perhaps seven pairs, five groups of three, four groups of four, or whatever works out for your team. Coaches can take part, too. It's best to let the team members figure it out. But maybe two or three team members aren't successful. In other words, their failure is draining positive energy from the rest of the team. This contrasts sharply with the positive energy generated when the whole team is able to get up by working together.

6. The human knot. The team stands in a circle. Each member of the team has to cross both arms in front of herself and grab another teammate's hand, but not the hand of a teammate next to her. So this forms a human knot of the whole group, and the task is to try to get out of it. It usually takes an hour or more, and you learn who are the leaders of the team and who aren't, who cares and who doesn't, and who are good communicators.

In terms of team building on the court, it starts with the terminology we use. Nothing is about you or me as individuals; it's about us as a team. It's not me making a free throw; it's about making a free throw for our team. When someone utters the word *I*, I go nuts. We constantly emphasize that what each of them does affects everyone else on the team. If a team member misses a lay-up, each member of the team is doing 10 push-ups. Everything we do is about *we*.

People succeed in basketball not just because they are talented, work hard, and compete tough, but also because they contribute positively to the makeup of their team. Believing in one another, trusting one another, and backing up one another are what make a team a true family, and there is nothing better than that.

Team Retreats

Sometimes it's helpful to get the team away from the basketball setting in order to focus on relationship building. Team retreats provide such opportunities, and one exercise that works well at these gatherings is conducted in the following manner.

First, players are paired together according to who knows each other least well. They interview each other at length. They then report their findings back to the team. The questions can be as follows: What is your full name? What does it mean? Who gave it to you? What is your family like? What do your parents do? Who has influenced you most? What was the best part of your life? What was the toughest part of your life?

The coach should emphasize that no one needs to share anything they are uncomfortable with. Even so, it is amazing how much people can open up and how much can be learned about each other. People quickly find there is much they do not know about each other.

Once, this exercise paired two very different players on a team. One was from an extremely poor family background. This teenager was already a father, not only to his own son, but also to his younger siblings (their father was not present). The other player was from a very wealthy family and seemingly had it all. These two players had little in common, and there was really no relationship or caring between them. After the player from the wealthy family learned of the hardships of his teammate, his respect and caring grew immediately—he learned about the incredible strong will of this player and the tough circumstances he was born into. However, the "well-off" player then, unexpectedly, shared the challenges in his life. He explained how his family immigrated from Europe and worked hard to build a successful restaurant business by working around the clock. He described how people prejudged him for having a nice car or nice clothes. He told how his parents made him work long hours at the family business and how he was torn about whether to work there in the future or risk hurting his parents. His less fortunate teammate came to respect him and his family for what they had earned—and saw him as much more like himself than he imagined. Not surprisingly, these two individuals played better together and had better chemistry after this experience at the retreat.

Team Travel and Social Opportunities

In Division I basketball, team travel is often a big part of the experience, and clubs at other college levels and even high school and AAU teams tend to travel a lot these days. Spending so much time together on the road can strengthen—or strain—relationships.

To help make travel as smooth as possible, plan ahead and raise money through various fund-raising activities before the season. Also, when possible, include a visit to interesting, educational places (e.g., Kennedy Space Center, the Smithsonian, the Alamo) while the team is traveling. Former players often reflect on those trips as important bonding experiences.

Team meals also put teammates together in social situations. In most cultures, breaking bread with people is an act of friendship. Some coaches begin every school year with a "welcome back" picnic, and at the end of the year, they have a cookout for all those who contributed to the program. Some college teams have a daily team breakfast. Many coaches also invite their team over to their home for dinner. And some coaches have lunch individually with each player before the season starts. Other fun bonding activities might include bowling, Wiffle ball, canoeing, hiking, or going to concerts and movies together.

Community Service

Though motives might be questioned (Do they really care or are they doing it for positive attention?) and the positive impact might be doubted (Does a one-time effort really make a difference?), providing a charitable service within a community is a wonderful thing. Community service also draws those who volunteer closer together. Moreover, this service may help teach athletes who are very blessed and gifted physically how to appreciate others who are less capable in some way.

Finding the time to devote to community service can be a challenge with school, homework, practice, and other commitments in a young athlete's life. When time is an issue, one option for providing service is for the team to choose a youth group to mentor. In the preseason and postseason, players can periodically travel to see the youth group. During the season, the youth group can travel to the team. They can come to certain practices and games, and the two groups can shoot baskets and share pizza afterward. In this way, regular contact is possible and is made convenient for players during the season. The players have a chance to be positive role models, and they are once again doing something important as a team to become closer.

Team Pride

Providing the best possible uniforms, gear, locker rooms, and travel is not easy with most budgets. However, these things make players feel like part of something special. So doing some extra fund-raising can make a difference for a program. The coach of a national powerhouse program once said that the most important part of his program is "stuff." He said having the best stuff was important to his players. It made them feel as if they were cared for and were part of a special and elite program. John Calipari took the University of Massachusetts from being one of the losingest programs in America to the 1996 Final Four. His initial premise was that to beat elite programs, they had to look like and feel like an elite program. Thus, he and the school worked to improve the facilities, equipment, and travel. These efforts helped foster pride in the program.

Personal Caring

Birthdays are a great opportunity to show personal caring. A cupcake with a candle and the team singing "Happy Birthday" sounds simple, but it is appreciated.

Another good exercise is to go around the team and have each player say something positive about each teammate. Also, once or twice a year, a coach can teach players to "carry" each other. The team is divided into pairs of players. The first pair lie on their backs head to head. The next pair then lie next to them in the same head-to-head position. This continues until the whole team is lying in pairs head to head. Each person then puts his hands up as if performing a bench press. The first team member stands up, lies across the hands, and is passed to the end of the line. After being passed to the end, he lies down again and waits for his partner to be passed down the line. The partner then lies down again (head to head with his partner), and the group continues to pass teammates down. The exercise is finished when the last player is passed down. The goal is to have fun as a group and encourage trusting in teammates along the way.

Another exercise that may be used at the start of each practice is a team run. In this warm-up run, everyone jogs around the court in a single-file line, and the last person sprints past teammates to the front of the line. The new person at the end of the line then runs to the front of the line, and so on, until everyone has run to the front of the line. To add to the team-building aspect of this activity, the person who is running to the front should give a friendly fist or hand to each teammate he passes, and the teammate must call out his name loudly as the runner passes by. Players will encourage each other, joke with nicknames, and still get loosened up through this simple warm-up activity.

RESPECT FOR TEAMMATES

Ideally, a coach wants a team that does the following: On offense, the team shares the ball unselfishly by identifying open teammates and delivering the ball immediately. As a result, the team gets good, high-percentage shots. On the defensive end, the opponent never seems to get a good shot because even when someone is beat, help is there—with players quickly reacting to ball movement, helping, rotating, and recovering. The players encourage each other, like each other, sacrifice for each other, and trust each other. Realistically, a coach can only demand cohesive play and encourage close relationships. This is an absolute key in helping a team reach whatever potential it has.

Everyone—coaches and players—must treat each other with respect. Disrespect cannot be tolerated. Blaming teammates for problems or not listening to others, especially well-meaning leaders, is unacceptable.

A coach can foster respect by praising team members for doing all of the above and creating pride in being part of a committed team comprised of good people. For example, sharing good news at the start or end of practice, such as good grades on tests or assignments, new personal bests in drills or the weight room, or reports of kind acts all help create the perception that teammates are worthy of respect.

Before a team can become tight knit, team members must value being part of that team. They must have some admiration for teammates and want their approval. They must want to fit in and buy into the team culture. When this occurs—and it isn't always easy—enjoyment and productivity increase. More important, lifelong friendships and memories develop.

CHAPTER
10

Capacity to Lead

Basketball outcomes can be unpredictable, but two results in the sport are as certain as a LeBron James slam dunk. Number one, any coach who wins a championship and has a way with words will be immediately sought after to speak on the banquet circuit as an expert on leadership. Two, a player who is a top scorer or "face" of a title-winning team will be labeled a winner and leader by fans and the media. These scenarios play out each year—a sort of post-tournament version of March Madness.

In reality, demonstrating leadership entails much more than merely having a spectacular season. True leadership comes from the daily demonstration of enduring qualities within oneself, not a temporary taste of stardom or a fancy new ring on one's finger. Leaders are not necessarily blessed with great charisma or the most telegenic appearance. They are not always taking claim of trophies.

Former Temple coach John Chaney was inducted into the Naismith Hall of Fame in 2001. He took a team from an urban campus without big-time facilities and led them to compete annually against the best programs in the country. He went to an amazing 18 straight postseasons and coached a very unique and effective style of play. But there are no magic offenses or defenses (if there were, every coach would use them). Rather, basketball success depends on how well a team executes whatever strategies it chooses. The ability to lead—the ability to get players to play the way you want them to—is the true determinant of great coaching. Coach Chaney had so much success because he was a forceful and remarkable leader.

Coach Chaney didn't hold 6:00 a.m. basketball practices to impress anyone; he did so to encourage his players to adopt good lifestyle habits, develop a stronger work ethic, and use more time in the remainder of the day to pursue educational opportunities. The coach also admitted that his grueling crack-of-dawn practices were a good antidote for players who might otherwise be tempted to engage in late-night social activities.

Originally a junior high school teacher and coach, Chaney rose through the ranks the hard way—the only way for him—so that by the time he was hired as Temple's head coach, he was 50 years old. By then, he was set solidly in the beliefs and priorities developed through personal experiences and the study of great leaders in and outside of sports. His players and teams benefited from his knowledge, his emphasis on personal responsibility, and his insistence that they sacrifice individually for the betterment of the team.

IMPACT ON TEAM CULTURE

True leaders such as John Chaney affect their teams in profound ways. They set the tone, provide the example that others follow, and raise the ability or energy level of those around them. An effective leader changes the culture of a team.

Team culture can be described as the values in a program as reflected in the daily habits and behaviors of the players and coaching staff. Great leaders make teams better by creating a positive team atmosphere that affects how daily business is done and influences the decisions and behaviors of others.

That doesn't mean the leader controls all the thoughts and actions of others. Far from it. A leader senses how much latitude each member of the program needs to function and grow, as well as the point at which that independence becomes detrimental to both the individual and the group. For example, an Academic All-American should receive more freedom and trust with less mandatory study time than an unproven student.

A coach or teammate who is too controlling can stifle the rest of the squad. A player who behaves as if it is "his team"—even though the rest of the squad doesn't consider him a leader—needs to be corrected very quickly. Similarly, a coach who rules with an iron fist and seeks no player input will lose a team's respect and trust very fast. Such domineering behavior is at best met with grudging acceptance—and more often with strong underlying hostility. This creates a divided team, either between a coach and his players or between a player and his teammates, neither of which is beneficial to a team or particularly pleasant for any of the participants.

On the other hand, a team culture that has little or no leadership structure—formal or informal—can be equally as bad for everyone involved. Players might think that they'd thrive if they had complete freedom—that is, until they experienced its consequences. Disorganization, deficient decision making, and, ultimately, deep disappointment are common within programs that have no established leadership.

The best culture for a team is one that maintains a healthy balance on the control–freedom continuum. The often-used analogy is that effective leadership is similar to grasping a wet bar of soap. Squeeze too tightly or hold too loosely and the soap is sure to be dropped. The only way to keep the soap in one's hand is to maintain a sufficient but supple grip. In offensive basketball terms, the analogy is a team that has structure but is also aggressive. They run a great offense and set plays, but they are also aggressive in taking advantage of the first good opportunity the offense gives them to attack. Thus, there is control (we will run this offense) and freedom (if you are open, shoot, and if you have an opening or a mismatch, drive to the basket). Too much control leads to a nonaggressive team and too much aggressiveness leads to nothing but chaotic one-on-one basketball.

AP Photo/Amy Sancetta

Truly great coaches, like Pat Summitt, maintain the right balance between control and flexibility and, by example, inspire their players to become leaders. Candace Parker (3) was both a first team All-American player and an Academic All-American at Tennessee.

Leaders must take into account the experiences, personalities, needs, and skills of each member. Indeed, to understand the culture of a team, the background that each person brings to the team must be understood. Each person has preexisting values and habits. Players have come from previous teams and cultures that may or may not be helping them to grow. Furthermore, popular culture today exerts a powerful influence on all young players.

An athlete from a very successful program with good values and a strong family background will need little time to adjust to a disciplined, demanding team culture. Conversely, players who are used to long summers filled with playground-style games, few focused practice sessions, and no guidelines for off-court behavior can find the transition difficult. Toss in the temptations of the teen culture—such as alcohol, drugs, late-night social activities, and other unhealthy entertainment options—and things can spiral downhill quickly. A coach must identify which individuals need more guidance and provide one-on-one mentoring.

A common thread across all successful team cultures is an appreciation for the importance of practice and improvement. The players have a strong desire to win but an even stronger desire to do things right. They have a clear, shared understanding and acceptance of what on- and off-court behaviors are desirable. The UCLA dynasty of the 1960s and early 1970s, for example, may have had very good athletes, but the program had an even better team culture.

Chapter 6 emphasized that a culture of responsible behavior includes accountability for off-the-court behavior as well as on-court performance. John Wooden's values-based philosophy produced tremendous results. Coach Wooden also authored one of the finest books ever written on leadership. He believed that his teams would succeed if he instilled habits associated with consistent, high-level performance. Those who failed to adhere to those behaviors and attend to details (no details were too small) would simply not be part of the program. But Coach Wooden didn't dismiss players from the team just to prove a point or to show who was boss; he did so because he truly believed that it was in the best interest of the group for that group to consist of individuals who shared a similar approach. That approach was founded on these five principles:

- Industriousness (work ethic)
- Enthusiasm
- Conditioning (mental, moral, physical)
- Fundamentals
- Team spirit

Yes, Coach Wooden's UCLA teams benefited from having a number of superb athletes, but the program benefited even more from the culture that was instilled by the coach and the players who took on leadership roles. They set the bar high, bought into the same set of principles, and excelled.

As the standards for behavior have relaxed and the consequences for irresponsibility have been reduced in the broader culture through the years, the effect has been apparent on the basketball court. The decline of U.S. basketball teams from being the dominant worldwide leader to struggling to medal in international competition is perhaps the most glaring example of this falloff. Wooden and others have cited this cultural demise in leadership and teamwork as a reason for the disappointing performance of the 2004 Olympic team and other U.S. clubs during the past decade.

In recent years, USA Basketball—under the direction of Jerry Colangelo and Coach Mike Krzyzewski—has tried to stem the downward slide by gaining a greater commitment from the nation's best players and adopting a more team-oriented style of play. But in the end, a resurgence to the top will require consistent and strong leadership on future U.S. squads to enforce a more positive team culture.

College and high school programs can more easily instill and retain such a culture because there is more continuity in the coaching staff and player roster. The University of Pittsburgh is an example of a college program that has emerged over the past decade to become a perennial power. One reason, of course, is that team coaches—previously Ben Howland and now Jamie Dixon—have provided strong, positive direction. Their approach created a culture that encouraged upperclassmen to take leading roles, and season after season those junior and senior classes have stepped up to ensure that the winning environment is kept in place. Sometimes even the Pitt coaching staff has been a bit stunned by the players who emerge as leaders within the system. For instance, Coach Dixon remarked during the 2007 to 2008 season how pleasantly surprised he was that junior Sam Young—previously a very talented but quiet contributor to the club—had become an effective, vocal mentor to other team members.

If nothing else, one point concerning leadership and team culture should be apparent: Positive cultural change and continuity come about only if coaches and players share and adhere to the same standards. Also, leaders must emerge from both the staff and roster to provide proper examples and to insist that the standards remain high.

COACH LEADERSHIP

Almost every coach—from the high school level on—is under pressure to win. Parents, fans, administrators, and the media want and often demand winning seasons, if not title-winning seasons. Coaches who fail to get their clubs into contention for the conference crown often come under much criticism and receive a cold shoulder from members of their community.

As a result, coaches feel a sense of urgency to win. So what do they do? They play the best players in order to give their team the best chance of winning. This, in itself, isn't necessarily harmful. However, if the team culture has not developed a desired level of effort and discipline, the starters can become complacent and lazy, and they will underachieve. In addition, the reserves may lose their drive and become negative and apathetic.

In the short term, a coach might get by with this "win now" approach. But avoiding any move that might reduce the chance for victory—such as giving more playing time to deserving athletes who may be inexperienced or slightly less skilled—will hurt the team over the long haul. In other words, by focusing solely on the result of a current battle, a coach often undermines a team's chance of winning the bigger war waged over the course of the season.

A coach who truly wants to demonstrate leadership and create a team culture that can potentially achieve greatness must, ironically, be willing to incur losses that otherwise might have been avoided if coaching solely for immediate success. At times, this might require denying playing time to an athlete who is talented but is also undisciplined or negligent. This is not an easy thing to do, especially if the kid has double-double potential every time out on the court. But the standards must be set and enforced in order to instill a culture of high achievement for all.

This is a very challenging and bold path for a coach to take, knowing how difficult it is to win. However, this is also the nature of true leadership—standing for ideals. A major task for this leader is to help his supervisors (e.g., athletic director, president, superintendent, principal) understand the need and priority for building a positive culture. With support "from above," one can make the correct choices even though they are difficult.

Although Phil Jackson and Pat Riley are similar in having had excellent relationships with their best players and team leaders, these coaches are different types of leaders. Phil Jackson is known for promoting unselfishness, team harmony, and binding relationships while being sensitive to the long season and peaking at the right time. Pat Riley is known for task focus, intensity, and driving toward excellence, thereby creating expectations of consistency and dominance. Leadership researchers have referred to these two leadership styles as relationship-oriented and task-oriented, respectively. The labels largely speak for themselves. The relationship-oriented style is focused on fostering interpersonal respect and liking, and the task-oriented style involves being very organized and demanding in accomplishing daily tasks.

Chapter 8 discusses building relationships to improve communication, and chapter 9 discusses building relationships to strengthen team cohesion. Both discussions capture the type of efforts needed to build respect and liking in relationships. Similarly, chapter 2 discusses setting specific goals and forming team missions to accomplish important tasks.

Regarding the relationship- and task-oriented styles, coaches also need to know how to emphasize one or both of these orientations in providing leadership.

One suggestion by leadership researchers is that a task orientation is most effective in either unfavorable or favorable situations. An unfavorable situation can be thought of as a dysfunctional situation that needs direction, or, in basketball terms, a program that is in disarray and needs fixing. The culture is likely one that involves few expectations, and the focus needs to be on the tasks that can lead to improvement. This approach reflects the idea that "there is a new sheriff in town" and the old way is no longer acceptable. Relationships are secondary to having individuals prove that they are up to the task. However, coaches should be aware that this may not be the best approach when dealing with *extremely* unfavorable conditions—such as a program that doesn't have its own gym or is extremely limited in what can be provided to players. In very poor circumstances and in working with young players, only positive relationships can keep motivation high.

A task orientation is also preferable in favorable conditions. A favorable situation is one in which the program and the talent are in place and success is imminent. The culture is geared toward achievement, and focus cannot be lost. In this case, a coach may need to adjust the approach used when dealing with elite or more mature players. Elite players desire a strong relationship with their coach, and the coach must make efforts

Mitchell Layton/Getty Images Sport

John Thompson III provides his Georgetown team with an effective blend of relationship-oriented and task-oriented leadership to bring out the best in each player and the team as a whole.

to build trust. In this situation, much of the relationship can be based on sharing how the coach and player will work together to achieve the important goals of the elite player. Research also indicates that female athletes generally prefer a more relationship-oriented leader.

Professional and high-level college programs often go through a cycle of alternately hiring task-oriented and relationship-oriented coaches. For example, a struggling team often selects a task-oriented coach to instill discipline and a culture of achievement. After experiencing success, the consistent pushing and discipline of the task-oriented coach—who may be very demanding and authoritative—can become tiresome for veteran players and coworkers, especially at the professional level. They start to desire a more positive, personable, and understanding coach as morale and performance start to slip. Thus, the next coach is often more relationship-oriented, and morale and performance will likely increase. However, over time most programs slip, and a renewed task focus will be called for. This is how the cycle of leadership changes can occur.

Although different situations may call for leadership that is focused more on tasks or focused more on relationships, the ideal leader may be one who is strong in both areas. A leadership concept promoted by the Harvard Business School is called "primal leadership." Primal feelings that are desirable are those of pleasure and excitement. The premise of primal leadership is that highly effective leaders make the task of pursuing success enjoyable and exciting. This reflects a combined focus on tasks and relationships, along with enthusiasm and creativity.

ADDITIONAL LEADERSHIP ATTRIBUTES OF COACHES

As mentioned in chapter 8, to be a good communicator and therefore a good leader, a coach must be knowledgeable and organized. Coaches gain a certain level of credibility when they have demonstrated their knowledge and convinced others that this knowledge can benefit them. But few coaches can be experts on each and every aspect of the game.

Indeed, the truth is that few successful coaches teach a wide variety of strategies. The saying, "Know what you teach and teach what you know" is especially true in coaching. The most successful coaches in the sport have been those who are excellent at teaching certain strategies for which they are well known. Once again, if there were a magic offense or defense, every coach would use it. Rather, any proven system of basketball will work as long as it suits a team's personnel and is well understood, well taught, and well executed.

Look at Butler's success over the past decade. Here's a school that garners far less national attention than its in-state counterparts, Notre Dame, Indiana, and Purdue. Yet, the Bulldogs have participated in 10 postseason tournaments in 12 years (1997 to 2008), including 7 NCAA bids. The program has accomplished this by teaching and adhering to a certain style of play, focusing on the fundamentals of the game, and recruiting athletes who will fit into its system and culture.

Good organization is also essential. A study by Ronald Smith and Frank Smoll of the University of Washington looked at which coaching behaviors led to more positive experiences for athletes. The results showed that one of the key factors was organized coaching behaviors. Players appreciated well-planned and effectively executed practices, and coaches who conducted such workouts were perceived as better leaders.

A second key behavior was "mistake-contingent instruction." This refers to giving athletes positive, technical instruction to help them improve on mistakes. Interestingly, coaches who were only positive and encouraging after mistakes were not viewed as favorably as coaches who gave specific technical instruction (i.e., how to correct the mistake). In short, effective

© Greg Carroccio/Sideline Photos

During the course of a game, instructions need to be stated in a specific, clear, succinct manner that holds players' attention and helps them transfer the input onto the court.

coaching leadership requires good instruction and organization. That's true for young athletes, like those in Smith and Smoll's study, as well as high school and college players.

Consistency is another key in leadership. Effective leaders are consistent in their expectations, discipline, and behavior. Successful people are the same every day—through good and bad circumstances. Athletes know what to expect from a good coach. Similarly, athletes who are leaders are consistent every day and are not subject to the mood swings common among some young people. As stated previously, moody players make bad teammates. Conversely, emotionally consistent, focused players make good teammates and leaders.

As a leader, the coach *must* be a role model for personal behavior. Just as coaches try to teach athletes to learn from the mistakes of others, coaches must do the same. It is not necessary to recount public coaching scandals that have caused far-reaching harm. However, coaches must understand the constant public scrutiny of their profession and that it extends into personal lives. For young athletes to have "immediate belief" in a coach, that coach must not give them reasons for doubt.

Finally, as the leader of a program, the coach must accept responsibility for all of the program's shortcomings. A true test of leadership is being able to acknowledge those areas that need improvement and accepting the challenge to coach and lead better each season. A coach must be objective and humble enough to see the weaknesses, yet confident enough to believe she can correct and strengthen those weaknesses. This type of program and self-evaluation provides a good model for players who are asked to honestly examine their own pluses and minuses. Remember, when problems arise, the first place leaders look is in the mirror.

PLAYER LEADERSHIP

What percentage of basketball players in high school and college think they are (or want to be) leaders of their teams? Probably a pretty high percentage—certainly far higher than would be apparent to their coaches or fans.

Many players want to be leaders of their team simply because of the positive perception others have of athletes who are ascribed that designation. But the label of "leader" is earned, not wished for or won by popular vote. Leadership behaviors, just like a positive team culture, must be nurtured and reflected each day.

Effective leaders on high school or college teams understand and accept the responsibilities of their role. They know that their teammates depend on them. They also know that they represent the program and the school—as well as the larger community in which they live.

True leaders model and enforce proper actions on and off the court. They are highly attuned to their teammates' behaviors in the gym, in the locker room, and in social settings. And, as an example for their teammates, leaders must "walk the walk" when it comes to exhibiting the dedication, conduct, and loyalty expected by school administrators and their coach. They must lead by example.

To a leader, the team comes first. Individual acclaim is not a priority. Sacrificing time, energy, and perhaps public attention for the betterment of the program, the team as a whole, and each individual squad member is part and parcel of player leadership. In a nutshell, a leader is a person who is already a hard worker and role model and now worries about getting others to share those values. He does not just worry about himself. A hard worker who does not try to get others to work hard is not a leader. Leaders take care of themselves *and* others.

At Maine, one of the most positive changes to the program was the addition of Andy Bedard. Andy was a fine player, but he was a far better leader. Andy's presence and example were vital in transforming the team culture into one that centered on hard work, improvement, and winning.

Andy practically lived in the gym and weight room, and he made sure that teammates came with him. He had a positive way of teasing teammates who were not working hard or playing well to gently shame them into stepping it up. He would come in at 5:30 a.m. to shoot before 6:30 a.m. weightlifting. He told all recruits and teammates that he came to Maine to win. He made others understand key values, and the team culture became one in which practice, toughness, and winning were all important. Consequently, the team did a good job in those areas.

Perhaps the most important actions in leadership take place in dorm rooms, locker rooms, training rooms, and buses. Leaders cannot allow negativity toward coaches or teammates. For example, two college teammates were also roommates and best friends. One of these players was having a difficult time because his playing time was being cut back. He wanted a shoulder to cry on, and he started complaining to his friend, expecting his support. The response was one strong in leadership. The player looking for sympathy was told, "Actually, you are not playing better than anyone else. If you want to play more, you have to play better." This realistic response surprised the struggling player, but it also helped him take more responsibility for his play and his role. This is an example of good leadership with teammates.

In mentoring players to be leaders, coaches also need to prepare them for resistance. Many players have tried to lead but then stopped trying when teammates didn't listen to them. When encouraging a potential leader to speak up, a coach often hears this common response: "Coach, I tried, but they don't listen, so I am not going to try anymore." Leaders should not stop trying to lead just because it is challenging. They should expect it to be challenging and should not get overly frustrated when desired results don't come quickly. They must be persistent, using different times and methods to affect their teammates. Although it is sometimes

Leadership Values

Tony Bennett—Washington State University

Leadership starts with loyalty. A coach must be loyal to players and the program. Players must be loyal to the program and their teammates. Demonstrated loyalty breeds great trust and indicates that you're concerned about what's best for the team and the program, not just your own success.

Great leaders sell their approach to success—that is, paint a picture—that others can envision and buy into. Leaders are visionaries who share and gain others' support for what they want done. Players who achieve strong leadership roles have an almost contagious ability to get their teammates to see something special and then strive to achieve it.

Leaders are true to who they are. When I became a head coach, I knew I couldn't be and shouldn't try to be a replica of my father. He was a great example, but in the end it was my personality, beliefs, knowledge, and actions that determined whether I could lead a team. Yes, for certain things you have to step out of your comfort zone, but never to the point of becoming something you are not. Players and others will realize that your actions aren't genuine, and you'll lack the credibility to lead or be trusted.

Leadership must be earned. You don't get crowned a leader as a young player when you step onto the court. A leadership position is attained through performance and behavior on and off the court. A great leader has those special qualities that gain the immediate respect, attention, and support of others.

Actions speak louder than words. Many can talk a good game, but what's important is who will be there when things get tough. Leaders step up when adversity is present. It's okay to be a quiet leader, but there will be certain times to speak up. A leader doesn't have to be a cheerleader-type guy, but selective and effective words of encouragement and direction can really motivate a team.

At the first press conference after my father had accepted the Washington State job, he said that he had to recruit guys whom he could lose with first before his team would win. At first I didn't fully understand that, but after being part of the rebuilding process, I thought it was an extremely important statement. He meant that when you rebuild a program, you will experience many hard losses. When this occurs, you need the type of players who won't fracture and abandon ship because the results aren't there. Instead, they will continue to grow and learn from the losses and eventually be a better team because of the valuable lessons learned through adversity. This usually occurs when they become upperclassmen. That is why character and toughness, especially in your leaders, are essential in rebuilding a team.

Here at WSU, we don't have a ton of rules, just five core values that must be demonstrated on and off the court: humility, passion, unity, servanthood, and thankfulness. These intangible qualities, based on biblical principles, are what any leader in our program must consistently demonstrate. My father instilled these values in his program when he was coaching at the University of Wisconsin at Green Bay over 20 years ago. They have been a significant part of his program and mine ever since. Many other college programs have adopted these for their teams as well. Each value has a specific meaning for us:

- *Humility* is knowing who you are—not thinking too highly of yourself, but also not thinking too little of yourself. Simply put, it means having sober judgment. Do you know who you are as a player on the floor?

- *Passion* is all about being vibrant and eager to put forth the effort. Are you hungry to compete and excel and enthusiastic about the opportunity to do so? Will you be passionate when you don't feel like it?

- *Unity* is best illustrated in this adage: The whole is greater than the sum of its parts. Basketball, more than any other sport, is one in which a team can come together and achieve greatness without having the greatest individual talents.

- *Servanthood* is knowing your role and sacrificing as needed to make your teammates better. It's a key element of team unity and greatness. It involves having a true servant's mentality when it comes to your team. Will you truly give of yourself to make your team better?

- *Thankfulness* involves being truly grateful when things go well. But equally or perhaps more important is to be thankful for what you learn in the hard times and have the wisdom to grow from them.

These values are the cornerstone for our program, but they are present as well in most of the great leaders I've observed who are coaches or players. I also don't think these characteristics are specific to basketball or sports in general; they apply to most professions and to anyone in a leadership role.

difficult to take criticism from coaches, it is far more difficult to take criticism from peers. Thus, a leader needs to use friendly persuasion, positivity, humor, directness, subtle messages, and occasional criticism to make points. In other words, a leader should keep trying different ways to spread the message of hard work, focus, and unselfishness.

Good leadership is most needed when things are going badly and doubt creeps into a team. This is especially true during times when the team is losing. Team leaders must stay positive, offer encouragement to others, and work to turn it around on the court. The key is belief. As others doubt the coach or team, the leader believes. If the leader has a doubt, it must be removed by addressing it with the coach. The coach and the leader must be of the same mind, and both are responsible for ensuring that they are on the same page. Belief is trusting that persistence will be rewarded, which is a realistic expectation. It is not false hope. It is knowing that improvement is not a matter of if, but when.

CAPTAINS

In all sports, the title of captain has special meaning. This person is the formal and recognized leader of the team. And it's no coincidence that strong teams have strong captains and leadership.

Moreover, a key for any program is that the best, most talented players totally buy into the team culture. If this happens, great things occur. If not, success can occur, but it will always be below what would otherwise be possible. Exceptional leadership must then come from other players to compensate for the lack of a great player who is also a great leader (the type of leader that usually defines a great team). Thus, coaches should cultivate as many leaders on a team as possible, with special focus on individuals who are especially talented.

As mentioned earlier, two NBA championship coaches who have clearly had special relationships with great players are Phil Jackson and Pat Riley. Phil Jackson had a very obvious bond with Michael Jordan and Scottie Pippen with the Chicago Bulls. Their belief in and loyalty to each other were so strong that they told management that they wished to be together—and that if one left, they would all leave. With the Lakers, other players have also stated that Phil Jackson was the only coach they wanted to play for. This is fascinating in that Phil Jackson does not cater to his star players. In fact, the purpose of his triangle offense is to make sure that all players are involved in the offense and that all are threats (thus, all players are able to develop). His message of team harmony is embraced by his best players. As stated, when the best players "buy in," everything becomes much easier.

With the Los Angeles Lakers, Pat Riley's teams dominated in the regular season and postseason with the leadership of Kareem Abdul-Jabbar and Magic Johnson. The drive to be the best was so clearly the primary goal that even the leading scorer in basketball history, Kareem, would be open to criticism and accept responsibility when the team lost.

Riley speaks in terms of "voluntary cooperation" when finding leaders. Much like Coach K's concept of "immediate belief" (see chapter 8), Coach

Riley had great players voluntarily give whatever the team needed on a daily basis. With the New York Knicks, he had the same relationship with Patrick Ewing. Coach Riley was known for being very demanding in training camp, practices, and the regular season. He required very intense effort from his players. Kareem, Magic, and Patrick bought in. They could be called warriors who were willingly molded according to the philosophy of their coach, and they made teammates follow their lead to build a culture of daily excellence.

A captain must merit respect and serve as a role model for all others to follow. This individual should be strong in five areas: personal behavior, academic performance, playing ability, unselfishness, and courage. A captain with shortcomings in any of these areas can prevent the development of a positive team culture.

A captain must have a history of responsible personal behavior. If mistakes were made, they must be put in the past, and the player's recent history must be highly positive. Sometimes this situation makes for a very effective leader because the person has clearly learned from his mistakes. In the present, the captain must be perceived as a trustworthy, mature decision maker in his personal life. The captain must be a person who lives by the rules and values of the program.

As a student, the captain should have a record of academic achievement. Although having a captain who is a great student is preferred, this is not necessary. However, the captain needs to be a responsible student who does solid work in building a future beyond basketball.

As a player, the captain does not have to be great, although this is preferred. The captain does need to be a "winner"—that is, a player who is totally committed to improvement, to winning, and to playing as a team. Coaches and teams need players who lead by example. These players "voluntarily cooperate" and have "immediate belief." They do not question or doubt. They know that the team's philosophy (with key commandments and teaching points) will work if it is executed. When a player embodies these characteristics and continually works hard to improve individually, he is prepared to be a captain. Improving personal play is critical to being a captain because other players respect those who can play. Respect must be earned on the court by being a good player.

After proving that he can play, the person must also prove that he is unselfish. Many outstanding players have a chance to be very good leaders, but they foster negative feelings by not being good passers or by placing their own scoring and playing time above the team.

The final step in becoming a true captain—after proving oneself off the court, in the classroom, and on the court—is to have courage. A captain shows courage by speaking out when he sees wrong and by standing up for what is best for the team during difficult times. It takes courage to take a view that is opposite from that of peers and friends. This may mean trying to change a "locker room lawyer" or taking a stand against partying during the season. It could also mean telling a teammate that his effort is not good enough or agreeing with the coach when team members do not. In such situations, courage is not bravery; rather, it is choosing not to conform.

Competitiveness

Michael Jordan, Candace Parker, Larry Bird, and Bill Russell aren't just among the best basketball players of all time; they're also among the game's greatest winners of all time. Winners such as these special athletes thrive in competition. They relish the chance to outwork, outthink, and outperform their opponent. They'll do whatever is necessary to win championships, whether that means rebounding, defending, passing, scoring, or making a key play. We can learn a great deal about the defining qualities of top competitors by studying such special players.

The flip side of the coin is the athlete who finds strong, direct competition unsettling. Through previous disappointing or disconcerting experiences, these players have developed a tendency to become anxious and perform poorly in games. Sport psychologists label this personality disposition as A-trait, or anxiety trait. This is differentiated from A-state, which refers to the situational discomposure or lapses that competitors may demonstrate in a particular contest.

In basketball, A-trait individuals have no place to hide. When they are required to engage and confront opponents, their inhibitions become apparent, resulting in unforced turnovers, repeated missed free throws, lost defensive assignments, and so on.

Most players' desire for and response to competition lies somewhere between the extremes of the highly competitive "winner" and the athlete who crumples in competition. The aim for coaches is to get as many players on the high end of the competitive spectrum as possible, either by good fortune, effective recruiting, or reinforcing learning. Coaches can also create positive gamelike practice situations that build confidence for the competitive setting.

Even the greatest competitors lose now and then. But their reaction to losing is often what sets them apart from their peers and further establishes their high level of competitiveness. Rather than complain, sulk, or give in, high-level competitors simply become more determined and diligent in their efforts to get back on top of the competition.

Truly great players seek out top competition and take the outcomes personally. They take great pride in victory, and they are highly disappointed in losing. But losing only motivates them to apply even more effort in the next practice and game. The great ones persevere long after most others have thrown in the towel.

Stanford women's coach Tara VanDerveer had such a player, Candice Wiggins. As VanDerveer explained at the time, "Candice does what we need. She gives whatever she can give. She leads by example. She's the most competitive person in this room by far. Coaching her, the only other people I think are in her league are people I've coached on the Olympic team who'll knock you down for just a nickel." Wiggins, by the way, led her team to the 2008 NCAA championship game with 25 points and 11 rebounds in an upset over top-seeded Connecticut in the semifinals. As said in a summary of the game on ESPN.com, "Candice Wiggins refused to let Stanford lose. . . ."

Sport psychologists who study and write about these things use the term *high achievers* to describe such athletes. These athletes' drive is instilled in their personality—it's who they are and what they do. But just the same, individuals with and without this personality trait can be influenced by extrinsic factors and conditions that make them more or less effective in competition.

SETTING THE COMPETITIVE STAGE

The University of Florida basketball program has used the following slogan: "Winning is only important if you want to be elite." This describes the mind-set of great competitors. They seek to prove their superiority through victories. They enjoy successes but are never fully satisfied, and they are always looking forward to the next challenge. They have a deep, constant drive to succeed. Players who are less naturally oriented to compete can benefit from verbal and visual reminders of what it takes to consistently defeat opponents.

Not surprisingly, highly competitive players aren't just that way in games; they're also the most competitive players in practice. They believe in the motto, "Being good means proving it every day." There is no cutting corners; true competitors have great respect for the process of becoming elite.

Respect for Practice John Wooden said, "Failing to prepare is preparing to fail." The great competitor wants to prove himself to be superior every day in practice. He also wants to prepare with the proper levels of intensity and execution needed to win on game night. Practice is preparation to win. Anything less than maximum effort in practice is not acceptable. Numerous stories have been told of Michael Jordan taking a loss in a practice drill or scrimmage very hard and becoming even more determined not to let it happen again.

To build competitive pride, Coach Tom Cooper developed a method called the Competitive Motivation System. In this system, each practice drill or scrimmage is scored in order to produce clear winners and losers. This includes shooting, rebounding, and defensive drills. Thus, players not only learn physical skills through repetition, but they also learn to constantly strive to outperform others.

This system gives constant feedback on how a player or group compares to competitors. It helps players develop knowledge of how to consistently compete hard and how to handle defeat. After a defeat (which happens for someone in each drill during practice), the players must analytically explain why they lost (e.g., fumbled passes, poor conditioning, not contesting shots, not boxing out, not containing the dribble). Thus, they learn from their mistakes, learn how to constantly compete, and learn how to emotionally control themselves and remain focused. The great competitor does these things, but a coach can help teach this competitiveness through competitive practices.

A note of caution: Emphasis on competitive situations can be too stressful for younger players who are just learning the fundamentals of the game. The first task for a coach of very young players is to help them develop a love for playing the game. Competitive consequences should be minimized to avoid burnout and frustration. However, competitive consequences definitely help teach competitive pride and lessons about winning that are necessary for highly motivated players who want to be elite.

To teach a respect for the value of practice, coaches can use a strategy employed by the Northwestern University football team that won two Big Ten championships in 1995 and 1996 (shared with Ohio State). The starting point for the team is to recognize that each practice has two goals: (1) to outwork their upcoming opponents and (2) to outwork those who are competing for starting positions and playing time. Before their first contest of the 1995 season, which was against Notre Dame, the Northwestern coaches told their players to assume that the Fighting Irish maximized their efforts in practice every day.

They used a legal scale (i.e., scale of justice) and placed a token on Notre Dame's side of the scale before every practice, giving the opponent credit in advance for a strong day. After practice, they would decide if their team deserved credit (i.e., a token) for their efforts. The scale enabled the team to see whether they were keeping pace with their competition or falling behind. Thus, the team was constantly aware of making daily progress to keep up. If they did not practice well, they did more or came back later to "earn" their credit for the day. After the last practice before the opener, the coaches said, "Guys, there is no way Notre Dame was good every day. We definitely outworked them." They then gave themselves the last token to tip the scale in their favor. This preparation and confidence led to a stunning upset and began a two-year championship run.

This same approach can be applied to basketball. A team can use a scale with their logo on one side and a key opponent's logo on the other side. When the team falls short of deserving full credit for a day's work (which will happen), the coaches and captains must determine how to make up for the lost time (it will usually be an extra workout). The strategy increases respect for practice, and it helps players develop appreciation for preparation and daily competition. This is a good way to ensure consistent effort through the preseason.

Respect for Each Possession Respect for each possession is a critical, defining quality of the great basketball competitor. The success of each season will hinge on several very close games that often come down to the last play of the game. However, common sense dictates that every play in the game is equally important—every point scored counts the same in the game, whether it happens immediately after the tip-off or with one second left to go. The last play does not decide the game any more than the many plays before it.

Every possession is critical and should receive maximum effort and focus. Each possession (i.e., each rebound, loose ball, defensive stop) should be considered the play that can make or break not only the game, but also the season. This creates a sense of urgency. *Urgency* describes the feeling held by great competitors that the current stop, rebound, or loose ball is critical.

Great competitors don't have letdowns. They may commit overaggressive mistakes (e.g., commit a foul on a steal attempt), make poor decisions (e.g., force passes or shots), or miss shots, but they do not have lapses in intensity or focus.

To increase respect for each possession, players can compete in one-possession games in practice. As described in chapter 9, each team receives one offensive and one defensive possession. In other words, it is a scrimmage with one trip up and down the court. To "win" the scrimmage, a team must get a score and a stop. A team "loses" the scrimmage if it fails to score or fails to stop the opponent. Thus, both teams can lose, but only one can win. Immediately after the game, the losing team or teams run a timed sprint (usually a sprint up and down the court in 10 seconds), and another one-possession game can immediately begin.

This drill shortens the game to a couple of possessions, creating great urgency. Players also learn the most basic premise of winning basketball— a team must consistently get stops and scores in order to win.

Players must place great value on ball possession and do their best to claim every rebound and loose ball.

© Greg Carroccio/Sideline Photos

Respect for Each Game   For the great competitor, every game is a big game. Each game is a chance to demonstrate superiority, or what some call dominance. This player has a constant need to be the best and pursues victory through effort and execution every game. This player also understands that every game counts the same in the standings. A win against a lesser opponent counts the same as a win against a great opponent, so each game should be pursued with the same urgency. Thus, the great competitor rarely suffers a surprising loss or an upset.

Coaches can use a very simple idea to teach respect for each game: counting team wins. Before the first game, the team should talk about getting number 1. After the first win, they should then talk about getting number 2, and so on throughout the season. With a potentially very good team, the coach can set the number 20 as the goal at the start of the year (or the number 15 to ensure a winning season). Players respond to this and take pride in winning, in their record, and in comparing well with other teams. Thus, the immediate goal is always to win the next game, and each game (and win) is equally valued.

No Tangible Rewards Needed Competitors don't require incentives. More money or extra attention doesn't add to a real competitor's effort or intensity. In fact, trying to encourage competitiveness through rewards often backfires. For the majority of athletes, these rewards tend to make them more satisfied and less driven in upcoming competitions.

Great competitors are very sensitive to this, and they guard against feeling content no matter how great their achievement. Even in situations where their superiority is unquestioned, they might seek or make up a challenge—such as interpreting an upcoming opponent's comments as disrespectful—just to give them that extra mental edge entering the next contest. With young players, providing tangible rewards can be perceived as bribes. They are led to believe that if they do well, they will get whatever they want (e.g., new gear). The message is that they are playing to get something rather than for the love of the game and the desire for success.

Coaches and parents of young players should be very cautious about using extrinsic rewards. Consider the following cautionary tale:

Imagine an unpleasant, old sport psychologist who lived by a playground and was disturbed every morning by noisy, fun-loving kids dribbling and playing nearby. Understanding motivation, he set out to solve his problem. One morning he visited the enthusiastic players and said, "Kids, I love to hear you play every morning. It brings back good memories for me. I'll give you each a couple dollars every morning you play." The sport psychologist even gave them a raise after a couple weeks, up to five dollars each, because he "enjoyed" them so much. Finally, after a few more weeks, the sport psychologist explained to the kids that he was low on money and could no longer pay them. After a few days without their money, the kids said, "Let's not play here anymore. It's not as much fun when we can't go eat afterward."

Obviously, playing for money and lunch had undermined their motivation of playing simply for enjoyment and love of the game. To develop a young player into a great competitor, the game itself needs to be the reward.

Outside the famed Palestra in Philadelphia is a plaque which reads, "To win the game is great. To play the game is greater. But to love the game is the greatest of all."

In summary, the great competitor loves both preparing to win in practice and outworking and outexecuting the opponent on game night. This player has a constant and highly intense sense of urgency. Satisfaction only lasts until it is time to prepare for the next game. No one can be this highly motivated without loving what he is doing.

HEALTHY COMPETITION?

Is it healthy for a player to have this constant intensity and the extremely demanding mind-set of never being satisfied? It is only healthy under two conditions. First, the player must have goals in life outside of basketball (see chapter 6). It is fine to practice and play as if the next loose ball is a matter of life and death on the court, as long as the player realizes that there are more important off-the-court priorities (i.e., school, personal behavior, character, family, friends). Second, as mentioned, an obsession with winning and competition may not be age appropriate. Being an elite player is the final phase of a process and is not a realistic goal for players until the high school varsity level.

It is inappropriate to call someone an "elite" player at the grade school, junior high, freshman, or junior varsity level. The best players at these young ages are not always the best players as high school seniors. Players progress differently based on how they physically mature and grow as well as their motivation to practice and improve. And yet, more and more Division I coaches are starting to recruit kids down in the seventh grade. Outstanding young players would be wise not to be concerned with where they rank on some Internet recruiting site. Whether a player is ranked by a so-called "expert" who probably hasn't even seen him or her play should not matter at all. Still, such early acclaim often distracts and sometimes consumes players.

The focus for the young player should be on developing skill and a love for the game. These are critical first steps in becoming an elite player in later years. Although important, winning and losing should be secondary. When players reach the level at which they can compete with elite high school competition, this is when the competitive drive to win begins to separate the best players from others.

COMPETITIVE TOUGHNESS

In basketball, the competitive nature of a player is often most apparent in defensive play and ball toughness. *Ball toughness* refers to getting the ball and keeping the ball. Again, personal pride is a factor here, because it translates into taking responsibility for getting in position and grabbing rebounds, gaining possession of loose balls, and not allowing the ball to be turned over against defensive pressure. Highly competitive players believe that the ball is theirs to claim and no one else's. They attack rebounds by exploding to the ball and snatching it. A loose ball means diving on the floor with reckless abandon to get the ball before anyone else does. There is no picking up the ball or trying to dribble it as it bounces around. The ball is snatched or dived on. When a competitive player handles the ball against defensive pressure, the ball handler is "strong" with the ball and minimizes turnovers.

During time-outs before an opponent's offensive possession, top defenders on a team encourage teammates with words such as, "This is personal. Don't let your man score." Although team defensive concepts such as helping are critical, no defense can be successful if individuals regularly get beat one on one. Great competitors take pride in shutting their man down. After the game, they want to see the stat sheet—not to find out how many points they scored, but to find out how many their opponent scored.

A key ingredient to a strong team is having a defensive stopper—someone to guard the best scorer on the other team. The role of defensive stopper is a proud role that is critical to team success. Even when playing zone defense, coaches can talk about each player taking pride in no open shots coming from his side or area of the zone.

The highly competitive player takes great pride in stopping people defensively, getting rebounds and loose balls, and being strong with the ball (i.e., no turnovers). This is a player who will successfully outcompete opponents through superior effort and toughness. This is a "winner." To help players develop ball toughness, coaches can do several things.

First, a loose ball drill can be done in a way that does not increase the risk of injuries. Players line up along the baseline, and the coach rolls a ball out onto the court. When called, a player must sprint to the ball, dive onto it, and pass it to a coach (or manager) while on the floor (to avoid traveling). The player then quickly gets up and sprints down the court to receive a pass back from the coach for a layup. To reduce the risk of injury, this drill is done with a single player at a time, as opposed to having two players fight for the ball. However, players must pursue and dive on the ball with gamelike intensity.

Competitive toughness is also developed in a lot of rebounding drills. A good one for ball toughness is to start with three or four players on the three-point arc and have them all crash to attack a missed shot. The successful rebounder will then attempt to score on the offensive rebound while the others try to stop him. The ball is played live until someone scores on a rebound. After going through the net, the ball is immediately returned to a coach who will attempt (and try to miss) another shot. The players must sprint to touch the three-point arc and then crash again. This teaches great aggressiveness in going for and getting the ball.

To teach a defensive stopper mentality, a coach can ask for a volunteer (players must want to be a stopper). The whole team will watch this individual defend a good offensive player starting under the basket. Screeners can be set up at the free-throw line and on each block (i.e., three or more screeners with no defense on the screeners) so the offensive player can use multiple screens and go anywhere. When the offensive player comes off a screen and receives the ball, the screeners move off the court and let the "stopper" defend the man with the ball. Thus, the stopper must get through screens and stop a good player one on one with the whole gym watching. This simulates the abilities, toughness, pride, and attention that go with being a stopper and guarding the other team's best player. The defender should continue until he gets a stop, and then continue to see how many stops in a row he can get.

Do More Than Talk Tough

Highly competitive players are critical of themselves and may sometimes be critical of teammates. Two conditions are necessary for criticism of teammates to be accepted. First, the critical player must be a great competitor who consistently practices what he is preaching; otherwise, he will not have the credibility or respect to be taken seriously. Second, the critical player must be short with criticism, making his point and then continuing to encourage and lead by example.

Constant criticism by a teammate is not positive—no matter how talented or competitive that teammate is. In fact, some people believed that Michael Jordan was too hard on certain teammates and hurt their confidence. Even the greatest player, coach, or person in life will have faults, and excessive criticism can be a fault. Yet, some criticism is necessary to point out and correct mistakes or lack of effort. The highly competitive player lets his play do his talking, and when he needs to challenge teammates, he does so by being direct and to the point. Most important, being competitive means backing up what you say.

Want the Ball

Competitive players want the ball in their hands, not because they are selfish, but because they are confident in their abilities to make positive things happen. This is a good thing.

For example, the best ball handlers have to come to the ball hard against the press. Even if the pass is denied by the defense, the ball handler must find a way to get open. The ball handler must be proud of his role, because the team relies on him to break the press. A dominant post player must seal the defender on his back to get open. An excellent scorer must set his man up and come hard off screens to get open. A competitor must want the ball.

Michael Jordan typically demanded the ball at the end of big games, as in his memorable top-of-the-key floater over Craig Ehlo in Chicago's win over Cleveland in the 1989 NBA playoffs. But in the 1993 NBA finals, Jordan gave up the ball to teammate Scottie Pippen, who in turn bounce passed it to Horace Grant about five feet from the hoop. Rather than shooting the ball or passing it to Jordan, Grant kicked the ball out to a wide-open John Paxson, who nailed the game winner from just beyond the three-point arc. Four years later, at the end of game 1 of the Bulls' memorable NBA finals matchup versus the Utah Jazz, Chicago's strategy was simply to "get the ball to Michael and get out of the way" (as forward Scottie Williams said). They did, and Jordan's crossover dribble freed him from defender Byron Russell for the game-winning shot just inside the arc. Five games later, as the Bulls were breaking from a huddle in which Coach Phil Jackson had drawn up a play that could well decide the game, Jordan turned to a teammate. Here's how Jordan later described what happened: "Everybody in the gym, everybody on TV knew the ball was coming to me. I looked at Steve Kerr and said, 'This is your chance,' because I knew [Utah's John] Stockton was going to come over and help." As Kerr described it, "He [Jordan] said, 'You be ready, Stockton is going to come off you.' I said, 'I'll be ready, I'll knock it down.' He's so good that he draws so much attention. And his excellence gave me the chance to hit the game-winning shot in the NBA finals. What a thrill. I owe him everything."

Layne Murdoch/NBAE/Getty Images

Chris Paul wants the ball in his hands when his team needs to score, because even when he doesn't make a basket himself, he's very adept at getting the ball to open teammates who have a better shot.

To Michael Jordan and anyone else who strives to be a competitor, the lesson is clear: Want the ball, get the ball, and then take what the defense gives you. This may be a shot or an assist. The right decision must be made.

When a player does not want the ball, this can result in a costly turnover because the passer does not have any options (i.e., an open teammate). Not wanting the ball also reflects a lack of confidence. The competitive player wants the ball, is confident, works to get open, and then makes the smart play (i.e., what the defense gives him). Thus, one of the most overlooked skills of the great competitor is the desire and ability to get open (i.e., move without the ball). Great competitors read and use screens, along with hard cuts (e.g., V-cuts, L-cuts, backdoor cuts, breaking to the ball hard), so they can get the ball and use their scoring and passing skills at critical times.

Denial defensive drills can be used to help players learn to move without the ball. In these drills, offensive players must learn to cut and use screens to get open. Coaches can also emphasize moving without the ball by not allowing the offense to dribble, which makes passing and catching more difficult. Another option is to play games in which the offensive team receives a point for each completed pass. This increases defensive denial (the only way for the defense to get the ball back is to steal it) and further teaches players to get open and get the ball against a tough defense. Wanting and getting the ball against a defense designed to stop a player from doing so shows true competitiveness.

Do Whatever It Takes

Highly competitive players do whatever it takes to win. At elite levels, they have played hurt (e.g., the dramatic performance by an injured Willis Reed in game 7 of the 1970 NBA finals) and sick (e.g., Michael Jordan in the 1997 finals). They will set screens, take charges, get loose balls, deny the ball to a key opponent, or sacrifice their own scoring to set up teammates. Statistics and personal glory are not the goal. The goal in competition is to win, pure and simple.

As stated earlier, the competitive player understands the game and what it takes to win. Thus, he fills whatever role is necessary. For example, Magic Johnson was moved from his usual point-guard position to fill in at center for an injured Kareem Abdul-Jabbar in the deciding game of the 1980 NBA championship series versus the Philadelphia 76ers. The team needed low-post scoring and rebounding. Magic responded with 42 points and 15 rebounds, even scoring with a beautiful hook shot on occasion. This is an example of an incredibly versatile player being able to truly do whatever is necessary for his team. Coaches refer to such outstanding players as "complete." They can score, but they can also defend, rebound, handle the ball, pass, and screen.

A player starts to become complete through the type of self-evaluation, goal setting, and practice habits discussed in chapters 1 through 3. Competitiveness has much to do with the motivation to develop a complete game. Once again, the "whatever it takes" attitude is necessary to become a complete player. This may include hundreds of practice shots daily, hours of ballhandling drills, high-intensity strength training, or tough conditioning drills. Competitiveness is a desire to be the best and is based on outworking opponents *before* the game as well as during it. Many wars are won before the first battle is fought by being more prepared than the opponent. One must be willing to do whatever it takes—even sacrificing personal scoring stats or working on fundamentals that fans don't notice—both during the game and in preparation. Less competitive players are not as motivated to practice hard, are less prepared, play more selfishly, and do not do as many things to help their team win.

Respect the Game

The great competitor is highly motivated out of a love for basketball and a great desire to be the best possible player through team success. Love for basketball and respect for the game go together. The great competitor respects how the game should be played.

Coach Larry Brown in particular speaks of the rewards of trying to play the right way. This involves understanding the importance of fundamentals (i.e., execution), effort, and unselfishness. All players want to win, but the ones with the greatest desire to win not only give the greatest effort, they also study the game. They know the importance of staying in a low defensive stance, using both hands for passing and catching, jump stopping, not fouling carelessly, boxing out and pursuing rebounds, diving for loose balls, and setting good screens. Many other key fundamentals for winning could be listed, but the point is that great competitors understand the importance of fundamentals. Many games have been lost because of a missed box-out, a sloppy pass, or an uncontested shot. The competitor knows this and respects the fundamentals of the game. He has a clear idea of how the game should be played correctly.

Many coaches use individually edited videotapes (or DVDs) to help players develop respect for fundamentals. Each game tape is initially coded possession by possession. A note is made for each possession in which an individual player clearly demonstrates successful execution of a fundamental or a clear error. Plays that lead to clear outcomes (e.g., scores, stops, turnovers) are then selected so the players can clearly see the impact of fundamental play. A coach may then create individual teaching tapes for each player by copying the possessions identified on the game tape onto the player's personal tape (this is extremely time consuming, but very worth it if the time is available). Successful plays can be copied two or three times in a row so the good play is ingrained.

Negative plays may be copied only once. This should be a positive, habit-forming, confidence-building tape, but showing periodic errors is also instructional. Plays from each game are copied onto the same tape so that a player can have a fundamental highlight tape at the end of the year. This could include fundamental passes resulting in assists, physical box-outs leading to defensive rebounds, or offensive rebounds for baskets. It could also include good defensive position resulting in charges, well-contested shots ending in stops, ball pressure forcing turnovers, and sprinting the floor for transition baskets. The player can repeatedly see effort and fundamentals leading to success. This creates a respect for playing the game the right way.

MENTAL TOUGHNESS AND MISTAKES

The shot misses the rim, and the crowd chants, "Air ball, air ball, air ball." A defender gets beaten off the drive and gets dunked on. Critical rebounds are missed; passes get stolen. These things have happened to all players, even to the greatest players in the world.

Even Jerry West—whose likeness serves as the logo for the NBA and who was widely known as "Mr. Clutch" (because he was so cool and productive at key moments in a game)—made his share of errors at crunch time. But those miscues never stopped him from taking the next game-deciding shot, and they never caused him to fret over potential failure.

Mentally tough players such as West acknowledge that they're human and that errors are inevitable a certain percentage of the time. They also acknowledge that sometimes an opponent can come out on top. So when they fail or when errors occur, tough-minded players admit it, learn from the experience, and then forget about it. They move on, even more eager to get back on top.

Admitting a mistake has two components. The first component is the acceptance of responsibility. The second is the realization that such mistakes are part of the game. Then the player can move from the emotional part of the reaction to the cognitive part, which involves analyzing how to do better the next time. For example, a guard who got beat on a driving layup to the basket might say, "That guy was quick, so next time I'll allow a little more room and stop penetration." A player must forget the mistake and must remember what was learned.

The 2002 to 2003 University of Kansas basketball team started the season with a 3-3 record, which was highly disappointing for them. Then KU head coach Roy Williams had developed the best winning percentage in the nation at Kansas, and his team was expected to succeed, even against the country's best competition. Media and fan reaction varied from concern to panic. Things only got worse at midseason, as starting forward Wayne Simien went out of the lineup with an injury. Kansas, however, had great leadership from captain Nick Collison and point guard Kirk Hinrich, plus Coach Williams' inspiration from the bench. The Jayhawks went on to compile a 30-8 record, win yet another Big 12 championship, and come within three points of winning the national championship game. Collison, reflecting back on the season, said the team's turnaround and performance could be credited to the fact that the players did not blame their teammates or coaches when the going got rough early in the season. Rather, they rose to the challenge of playing better basketball. With good leadership and competitors throughout the roster, teams manage to overcome the mistakes and criticisms that all players and teams are subject to at some point.

Basketball is a paradoxical game of striving for perfection and yet accepting mistakes at the same time. The successful, competitive player must do both of these things. Accepting mistakes without concern creates an apathetic, noncaring attitude. Striving for perfection while not accepting mistakes creates frustration, distraction, and tension that harms play. The successful player is always demanding of himself, but he understands that mistakes happen and simply moves on to the next play.

Types of Competitive Miscues

Errors should elicit an appropriate response. Some errors are acceptable, while others are unacceptable. Different types of mistakes are covered in the following sections, and each type requires a different attitude and reaction.

Effort Mistakes

Players have little or no control over some of the factors that determine the outcome of a game. These factors could include the bounce of the ball, normal variations in shooting percentages, the strength of the opponent, and officials' calls. The one thing the player can always control is effort. Maximum effort is a nonnegotiable aspect of being a successful player, and all good coaches demand it. Not making an effort for loose balls and rebounds, not sprinting the floor or quickly getting to the correct defensive spot, and not fighting for position in the post are all examples of a lack of physical and mental toughness. Mental toughness involves constant intensity and effort. Any mistake caused by a lack of effort should be unacceptable to player and coach alike. There is no harm in being fearful of letting intensity drop. Always be on guard against this, especially when a game lacks great atmosphere or involves a clearly favored team. The great players do not accept mistakes that result from lack of effort. When such a mistake does occur—which is rare—the great player admits it, learns, and moves on.

Skill Mistakes

A player's skill level is determined before the game by the amount of repetition done in practice. For example, no one tries to miss shots. Many times, trying harder creates tension that interferes with the skill of shooting. A player should have no fear of missing shots. As long as the shot is an open shot and an unselfish play, the player should have no concern about the outcome of the shot. Taking open shots within one's shooting range is good basketball. Players and coaches must learn to live with good and bad shooting nights and simply focus on confidently taking good shots. Missed shots should not even be considered mistakes. The mentally tough player takes every shot with complete confidence, especially after some misses. Improving shooting skill is done in practice.

Ballhandling and passing skills are also based on repetitive practice and will involve some unavoidable mistakes. Mishandling the dribble, inappropriately handling a pass, or getting a pass stolen because of exceptional defense are things that are going to happen occasionally. When a mistake results from an error in skill, the player must admit it, learn from it (address it in practice), and play on. Some of these mistakes must be accepted as unavoidable. Obviously, if too many mistakes occur because of a lack of skill, the player needs a great deal of repetition to develop increased skill. Until the player increases his skill level in the area where mistakes are occurring, he may need to limit himself in that area and let more skilled teammates do more of the ballhandling or shooting.

In summary, missed shots and turnovers occur in every game. When mistakes happen in these skill areas, it is important to accept them and not overreact, which could lead to worse problems. If, on the other hand, missed shots or turnovers are happening because of a failure to execute fundamentals or strategies that have been well taught, a more critical approach can reduce these errors.

Execution Mistakes

Mistakes that result from a lack of execution may be acceptable or unacceptable depending on the philosophy of the coach. For example, whether a player gets beat defensively to the baseline (acceptable) or middle (unacceptable) has different consequences in some systems. Not boxing out on defense or not crashing the boards on offense may be unacceptable in one program, while forgetting a play may be unacceptable in another. Players must fully understand the philosophy and system of the coach to understand what mistakes must be avoided.

Some mistakes that seem to be related to skill (i.e., turnovers, bad shots) are actually execution mistakes. For example, a well-intended, fundamentally sound pass that is stolen because of good defensive anticipation is different from a sloppy, one-handed, no-look pass that sails out of bounds. Both are passing mistakes, but the latter is usually unacceptable in our philosophy because it is poor execution of key passing fundamentals. Similarly, missing a wide-open shot happens to all players and is acceptable, whereas taking a selfish, forced shot with two defenders contesting the shot would be unacceptable to most coaches. Mentally tough players understand the importance of their team philosophy, and they execute the key fundamentals very consistently. When execution mistakes are made, they admit it, learn, and move on.

Outstanding Opponent Play

Sometimes what seems like a rash of mistakes is actually the result of the outstanding play of a strong opponent. This reflects the nature of basketball. Each team will have "runs" or streaks of strong play during a game. This is where mentally tough players shine. They learn and adjust to stop the run. They demonstrate great composure. They accept that the other team has shot well and made good plays. Now, they focus, stop the run, and soon start a run of their own. Strong leaders are always great in the huddle during time-outs when the opposition is on a run. They do not get frustrated with mistakes or with the opponent's success. They say things such as, "We'll be okay. Lots of time left. They made a run. We will make one too." The mentally tough player understands that a run must be handled with composure, learning, continued effort, and execution of the team's system.

Most coaches call a time-out to stop the opponent's momentum. It is interesting that Bob Knight, the winningest coach of all time, did not call time-outs when opponents made runs. One of the messages behind not calling a time-out is that the opponent's run is not a reason to panic. Not calling a time-out also teaches players to solve problems and to not rely on the coach. This practice was successful for Coach Knight because he did this consistently and, as a result, the intended messages were well learned. Most coaches do call time-outs when their team is losing momentum.

Aggressive Mistakes Versus Foolish Mistakes

Aggressive players will understandably make some aggressive mistakes. Aggressive mistakes may include the following: an over-the-back call when going for a rebound, a blocking call when trying to draw a charge, an offensive foul on a post player trying to get deep position, a travel call when making a strong drive, a turnover on a long pass to an open teammate up the floor, or getting beaten on defense after unsuccessfully trying to steal a pass. Players should be aggressive and can expect some of these errors to occur. Of course, they should also learn from them and not make the same mistake repeatedly in a game. Not learning would lead to foolish mistakes.

Other foolish mistakes involve time and score, foul situations, and bad gambles. Foolish mistakes related to time and score usually occur when a team with a safe lead late in the game does something to make that lead unsafe, such as shooting too quickly or playing overaggressive defense (too much fouling, stopping the clock, and gambling for steals). Foolish fouls are those that occur when foul trouble or a late lead calls for less aggressiveness. Bad gambles are overaggressive, unlikely defensive plays. The most common examples are reaching in on the dribbler for steals and trying to steal the ball from the rebounder instead of sprinting back on defense. Mentally tough players make aggressive mistakes, but they rarely make foolish mistakes.

To eliminate overaggressive mistakes late in the game, the call "solid" can be used. "Solid" is a call that signals an adjustment in defensive mentality. When "solid" is called, it means the following: (1) Do not pressure the ball tightly; emphasize containing the ball and contesting the shot. (2) Do not gamble for a steal by attempting to run through a passing lane or reaching. (3) Do not trap the ball. (4) Stay vertical when contesting shots and do not foul. Basically, "solid" is less aggressive, but it is the best insurance against giving up an easy shot or fouling when only one or two more stops are needed to win the game. "Solid" can also be called in the last few seconds of the shot clock to help avoid bailing out the offensive team with a foul or breakdown after playing great defense throughout a possession.

To eliminate quick, unnecessary shots when protecting a lead late in a game, the call "zero" can be used. "Zero" signals for a spread offense that is difficult to pressure or trap (e.g., four corners, no post motion, high motion), and it indicates that no shots other than layups should be taken until the end of the shot clock. This call helps players understand that they are in a special situation requiring patience in shot selection.

Conquering Competitive Frustrations

Some players never accept responsibility for or learn from a mistake— thus, they never improve. Other players take every mistake too hard and are devastated by each one. These players are typically the highly motivated players who want desperately to do well. They may curse themselves, slam the ball, shake their head, or talk to themselves after mistakes. If they are not outwardly frustrated, they may internalize their frustration. This is the beginning of "choking."

Frustration that leads to choking involves a process. It starts with negative thoughts (e.g., *That was horrible, I stink today,* or *I am losing the game*), which create muscular tension and mental distractions. Muscular tension slows reactions and interferes with shooting skills. The negative thoughts cause other problems as well. First, they make a person more emotional and more frustrated. Researchers have observed that a person's focus of attention gets more narrow as the person gets more emotional. When people are mentally calm, their attention is more wide or broad. They see better. For example, a mentally calm player can see the whole court more easily. The emotionally frustrated player is more likely to get tunnel vision and fail to see the whole court. This results in more turnovers, not finding open teammates, and not seeing defenders in position for steals. It could also mean more charging calls that result from not seeing defenders stepping into help position.

Developing Competitors

Tom Crean—Indiana University

Competitive basketball players have both a mental and a physical toughness. We have had success in developing those two dimensions in players through a variety of methods, but it is a challenge.

Fewer modern athletes are equipped with mental toughness when they start their basketball career. In our entitlement culture today, young athletes grow up assuming they deserve things without having to work and compete for them. Then, when they enter the competitive arena and things don't go their way, they blame someone else for their shortcomings. Such players give a team no chance to succeed.

One thing we emphasize more than anything else is team. Wins and losses are team wins and team losses. Everyone must understand that there is a lot of room for improvement, win or lose. We must keep striving for that.

We ask players and coaches to do three things every day: Come mentally prepared and focused on the practice session, bring a high level of energy to the practice court and weight room, and be ready to compete. If they don't come to compete that day, they are going to stand out in a big way, and not positively. That is why we introduce a competitive element at the very first part of practice. Oftentimes we'll do a shooting drill before we stretch and run our break. This gets players' minds right into a competitive mode and sets the standard by which the whole practice will be performed. Under such competitive conditions, leaders emerge.

Michigan State has proven the effectiveness of practice competition through the years. Mateen Cleaves, one of the most strong-minded individuals I have ever been around, thrived in that system, and his presence on the practice floor made each of his teammates better, more competitive athletes. Yet that wasn't always the case. During his freshman year, after a car accident on a recruiting trip to the University of Michigan, Mateen had trouble getting mentally focused. But to his credit, he looked at himself critically and honestly, worked diligently to get into great shape, became a tremendous leader for the Spartans the rest of his career, and led the team to the 2000 NCAA Championship.

The second dimension of competitiveness is physical in nature. Basketball is a quick-moving contact sport. The game's best competitors willingly embrace physical play and accept that contact will occur hundreds of times in a contest. That does not involve competing in a dirty way. Cheapshot guys aren't competitors; they're punks. But it does mean being fully prepared to use the body effectively to gain an advantageous position to perform necessary and desired skills and tactics.

Players must have the physical strength to withstand contact and initiate it when needed, whether it's at the point of contact of a screen, in defensive rebounding, or whatever. To develop that strength, our players compete inside the weight room. They compete against time, their previous records, and each other. We also do some fun things to keep their interest and energy levels high. For example, our strength and conditioning staff holds a midnight lift for the team in the summer. Guys come in wearing all kinds of getups and paint their faces in an effort to look like the toughest dude in the room. They compete in the bench press, curls, and a variety of lifts to see who measures up.

The coaching staff should spend time with the players in the weight room because the physical conditioning is a huge part of the mental toughness required for competition. Athletes who push their bodies to the highest possible level and encourage teammates to do the same are often the mentally toughest on the court.

We also introduce competition into our conditioning activities in the basketball gym. The ladder conditioning drill involves climbing up and down a "ladder" (lines) on the court in a specified time. A first group sprints for 5 seconds. Then the next group goes for 5 seconds. Then there are three lines, and players have to get those done in 16 to 18 seconds, and the only break is the 16 to 18 seconds for the other team to run their numbers. They go all the way up the ladder: 1, 3, 5, 7, 9, 11. Then, however far they go up, they come back down. It's an incredibly tough, mentally draining drill, and players have to be mentally ready to do it. But through it they learn that, just as on the basketball court, they can't do it alone; they have to have their teammates.

Roughly 75 percent of our basketball drills have time and score elements to make them more competitive. The war rebound drill is a no-holds-barred, go-at-each-other type of drill in which five people are in the lane and five people are outside the three-point line, except for one player who moves to the foul line. That person becomes the horse, so to speak. One guy is at the foul line, one defender is next to him, and the other defenders have to run out and get to the other people who started out at the three-point line on the shot. You can do it for three trips, or you can do it for five trips, but it should be really competitive at the point of contact.

You can also do a two-on-two block-out drill that, if you aren't careful, can turn into a wrestling drill. Players are divided into two teams. Two players from one team start on both blocks; two opposing players start at the elbow. Teammates line up behind the block players, and teammates line up behind the elbow players; they keep rotating so players are always going against a different color (opponent). Play that game to a predetermined

(continued)

number for 5 minutes. Run up and block out; whoever gets the ball is the one who is on offense. If you score right away in the lane or a couple feet outside the lane, you do it again or you kick it out to the coach on the side and turn it into some aspect of two-on-two that you want to work on that day defensively and offensively. There are a lot of things in the form of scrimmaging and in the form of three-on-three and four-on-four to make it really competitive.

Bubble drills can be effective in building toughness, especially concerning missed shots. One of my favorite drills is from Jerry Wainwright. The team on offense is up by 17 with 8 minutes to go. This team has to go against the bubble. The other team has no bubble on the other end. The only way the team with the bubble can score is to get offensive rebounds and to run the clock. So they get no points. They are up 17 points no matter what, and they have to hold on in order to win the game. They get a new possession on an offensive rebound and they have to run a clear offense. They have to run it down, take a shot, and get the offensive rebound. If they don't get it, the other team runs down to play and they are playing to win. This is an incredibly competitive game because both teams have to execute. One team has to execute their offense under pressure and get rebounds. The other team has to execute in a hurry and score in a hurry so they can get back in the game.

Another thing we do is the war drill with the bubble, where a defensive rebound counts as 1 and an offensive rebound counts as 2. Play to 10, 12, or 15 depending on the time frame of the scrimmage.

Defensively we do a lot of two-on-two or three-on-three help-and-recover drills in which there is no one guarding the ball. Defenders have to step up to stunt at the ball. Then as the ball is passed, they have to get back quickly. The offensive players are allowed two or three dribbles and no more than three passes. My favorite is to play one-on-one to 5 and then two-on-two to 10. So if it's you against me, you have two dribbles to score and I've got to stop you. If you score, you are up 1-0; if I score, my team is up 1-0. We play until someone gets to 5. Once a side gets to 5, we go two-on-two, with the coach passing to either side off a help-and-recover. This continues until one side reaches 10. This drill can get extremely competitive.

Practice competition is great, but like anything, too much of it can be harmful. When you practice hard for 90 minutes, including several competitive drills, players' energy levels and attention spans run low.

You can shoot for 30 minutes and then review an opponent's offense and defense, but players aren't likely to be at their sharpest. Keep this in mind over the course of the season; you really need to guard against wearing down the troops. As the saying goes, fatigue makes cowards of us all. And I'd much rather have a team full of competitors.

Frustration spawns negative thoughts, which become distractions and cause the player's mind to be sidetracked from the game. Following are several strategies to help players deal with mistakes better and increase their mental toughness.

Cognitive Restructuring

Cognition means thought, and *restructuring* means change. Cognitive restructuring is a process of changing the negative thoughts that create frustration and lead to choking. The first step is to identify the problem situation. In this case, the problem involves making mistakes (e.g., turnovers, missed shots, poor defense) in games. The second step is to identify negative thoughts that the player has in this situation—for example, *I must not do that, That's terrible,* or *I am going to get taken out.* The third step is to come up with a more appropriate thought—for example, *Learn and forget, Focus on the next play,* or *Relax, it's a part of it.* The fourth step is to actually use the positive thought in the problem situation. This can be done using mental imagery and must be done in practices and games.

Replacing negative thoughts with a simple positive thought can stop the process that leads to choking. The result is mental toughness following mistakes. The key is to identify the problem situation and the problem thoughts—and then to create a positive change using new beneficial thoughts. The player must keep playing hard, focused, confident basketball. Coaches should also use positive words to encourage positive thoughts that will prevent choking. The goal is for specific, positive thoughts to become a habit, especially following mistakes.

Centering

Centering is a quick, simple relaxation technique that is done as follows: Take a deep breath in through the nose, completely filling the lungs and expanding the chest. Now, momentarily hold that deep breath (a few seconds) and tighten up the fists, arms, and shoulders. Then release the breath slowly through the lips, and at the same time, release the muscular tension. Concentrate on the sensation of air passing out of the mouth and the looseness of the muscles. (A player may even want to shake his arms some to further loosen up.) Finish the technique by thinking, *Play on.* This technique is quick and effective, and it goes unnoticed. It takes just a few seconds during a dead-ball situation or a time-out. The technique has two purposes. The first is to actually take a relaxing breath and to relax tense muscles. The second is to focus attention on the technique as opposed to the last mistake or any negative thought. Centering is a technique that needs to be used often to be effective. It can be used periodically throughout practices and games. The more it is used, the more effective it will be in helping the player stay calm and focused.

Desensitization

Being sensitive to feelings, especially the feelings of others, is important in life. However, on the basketball court, a more warrior-like approach to battling and fighting throughout the game is the trademark of great players. The feelings they experience are those of the joy of competition—intense desire, high energy, and excitement. Worry is not one of those feelings.

Basketball warriors are not overly sensitive to mistakes. They don't change their entire approach if they make a few bad plays. They are always intense, confident, and focused. If a player gets upset or frustrated following mistakes, he must become less sensitive to those situations. To become less sensitive, a player can use mental imagery. All basketball players think about their games and often think with mental pictures. They imagine how a game will be or how they will play. Confident players imagine positive things, which is good mental preparation.

Imagery can desensitize players who are burdened by their mistakes. To do this, the player incorporates some negative imagery (mistakes) and follows that up with a positive thought and positive imagery (successful plays). Players must mentally prepare to play well and must be mentally tough after mistakes. The end goal is being less sensitive to mistakes or criticism (i.e., being tougher!) in practice and games.

Eliminating Fear of Failure

A little fear in life is a good thing. Fear usually stops people from speeding in their cars or cheating on tests. No one wants to be caught in a negative behavior. This fear helps prevent people from making poor decisions. A little fear on the basketball court is a good thing too. A fear that getting beat too much on defense or on rebounds can lose a game is a realistic fear, and it can make players work harder. However, too much fear or too much focus on what can go wrong is a debilitating thing. Fear of failure can become harmful to a player's efforts to play well.

Consider this: People usually do not like to do things that they are not good at. If a person is not good at something, he is likely to avoid it. The reason for this is that no one likes to look bad or fail. Failure and shame go together. On the basketball court, players who worry about making mistakes even before they happen have a strong fear of failure. They often experience anxiety, and this anxiety gets worse following mistakes. The players think those mistakes are failures. They think that they look bad, and they feel ashamed. Once again, fear of failure is brought about by high motivation. The player wants to play well desperately, but he has a negative focus. Instead of focusing on his desire for success, which leads to aggressive play, he tries to avoid failure, which leads to tentative play and less success. Following are ideas to reduce the fear of failure.

Players who have an opportunity to win a game from the foul line at the end of a contest must approach the task with a focused routine that eliminates worry about making or missing the shot.

© Greg Carroccio/Sideline Photos

Focusing on Success

Players should focus on their desire for success, and they should be completely aggressive in pursuing success. Mistakes or bad games are not failures. They are just obstacles to overcome. Players should not expect to play poorly, but they should expect obstacles to success because everyone has them. Chapter 10 fully discusses overcoming obstacles through mental toughness. Mistakes and poor play should be seen as challenges to play better, not as failures. A player should fear nothing and always play aggressively. When mistakes happen, the player should keep being aggressive and focus on playing well. He needs to eliminate fear and eliminate failure. There are no lasting failures in basketball because the next play or game always presents a new opportunity.

For some players, a fear of failure or mistakes can lead to a loss of playing time (as discussed in chapter 7). In this situation, a player may be confused because he gets taken out of the game for making a mistake, while teammates who make the same mistake are allowed to stay in the game. This may happen for two reasons. First, coaches can see when a player reacts poorly to mistakes (e.g., gets frustrated) or when the player is playing tentatively because of a fear of failure. When this occurs, the coach loses confidence in the player, because the player is losing confidence in himself. As a player increases his mental toughness, the coach sees this and is less likely to take the player out after a mistake. Second, a coach may take a player out more quickly because the player's abilities are simply not developed enough to play at a high level consistently. The challenge for this player is to desire success, further commit himself, build his ability, and improve his play. By doing this, the player will earn greater confidence from the coach.

Building Confidence

Greater confidence decreases fear of failure. The topic of building confidence is covered in detail in chapter 3. One useful method is for the player to write a descriptive self-statement of how he intends to play (see page 63). The statement should be positive and aggressive, describing a specific role for the player to focus on (e.g., animal rebounder, defensive stopper, efficient passer, low-post beast). This statement can help the player be more focused on success and less on potential failure. However, the best way to boost confidence and reduce fear of failure is for the player to reduce poor play by building his ability. For example, if a player misses a certain shot in a game, the player needs to make that shot repeatedly in skill work the next day. Whatever the problem area is, the player should focus on it until his performance is at a higher level. With higher performance and ability, the likelihood of failure and the fear of failure are reduced. This is the "old school" approach in which weaknesses, mistakes, and fears are met head on and overcome through work on the court.

RISING TO THE COMPETITIVE CHALLENGE

The toughest and most successful people in life are the same every day whether they experience great success or are confronted with great difficulty. They stay focused and never become discouraged or frustrated.

Great basketball players are the same way. Watch certain outstanding players after they have made a mistake. Their facial expressions remain exactly the same. They look poised. As mentioned earlier, younger players usually show more frustration and less mental toughness. Following a mistake, a player may be seen slamming the ball, arguing with others, tightening up, or talking to himself. Instead, players need to be mentally tough by showing confidence, poise, and focus after mistakes. Great players do not show frustration. They admit, learn from, and forget mistakes.

Mistakes are often accompanied by criticism. This is an important topic because criticism is a part of being an athlete. A player cannot fear criticism. As mentioned, a fear of being taken out of a game for mistakes can increase a player's fear of failure. A fear of criticism can do the same thing. The purpose of a coach's criticism should be to help a player learn about a mistake.

Listening to the coach in order to learn from him is part of being coachable (which is covered in chapter 7). Mental toughness includes being able to take coaching criticism and use it to improve effort, execution, and decisions. Accepting and not fearing coaching criticism becomes easier when the player understands the proper relationship between player and coach. This should be a special but demanding relationship based on working together for continual improvement. A coach's criticism should be designed to teach and should be welcomed by the player.

Players should understand that even criticism that seems harsh is not directed at them personally, but rather at behaviors that harm the team. By accepting criticism, an athlete can quickly become a better player and have far less fear.

Team members need to understand that they will make mistakes. They must also understand that if the coach is a good teacher, he will identify and correct those mistakes. To be good players, team members must be good students—listening, learning, and internalizing the coach's lessons. At times these lessons will sound critical. However, if a player learns quickly, his play will improve, and he will usually receive praise from the coach. Thus, the coach must be a critical teacher, and players must be willing students. Individuals become better basketball players by becoming better students on the court. Players respond to this analogy, realizing that the purpose of criticism is to create improvement as opposed to hurt feelings. Furthermore, this concept is easily extended to being a better student academically and to handling criticism throughout life.

Accepting criticism from others who are clearly not trying to help is far more difficult. No one learns to like this type of criticism, not even great players, celebrities, or our national leaders. Such criticism can come from fans, media, or anonymous posters on Internet message boards.

Many professional athletes and coaches who get a lot of outside criticism have learned the following valuable lesson: You cannot please everyone, and the only way to avoid criticism is to do nothing. Most high-profile players and coaches choose not to read newspapers or visit the Internet when struggling, because they know and accept that there will be criticism. This criticism would make anyone feel worse, so the best strategy is to not read it or listen to it. This keeps team members focused on the opinions of the people who matter most—the coaching staff and teammates. Their criticism is informed, knowledgeable, and helpful.

In the book *The Road Less Traveled,* Scott Peck makes a profound statement about mental toughness in life. He begins by stating, "Life is suffering." Many people operate under a false sense of reality, believing that life should be good, fair, easy, and full of success. Life is not this way. Life presents a mixture of joy and pain. The suffering is what makes people stronger and allows them to truly appreciate life's successes and joys. When a person stops seeing adversity as unfair and unnecessary and begins to understand that life is difficult, life becomes easier. What a paradox! It is so powerful that it is worth repeating: When a person understands that life is difficult, life becomes easier.

The mentally tough individual knows that adversity will come. Lou Holtz, former football coach at Notre Dame and South Carolina, emphasizes that how a person handles adversity is one of the most important factors in winning. This is not just because it helps a person perform better. Holtz reasons that every person and team that we compete with has adversity; we just don't always know about it. If everyone has adversity, then the people who respond best to it will clearly have the competitive edge needed for winning. This is why mental toughness—the ability to do tough things—is a critical factor in success.

As a basketball player, one will likely encounter great adversity at some point. This adversity is a chance to grow stronger as a person and as an athlete. In the face of adversity, players can choose mental toughness, or they can choose quitting, self-pity, and depression. The correct choice is obvious. Perhaps the greatest lesson that basketball teaches is how to deal with disappointment.

Coaches also face many difficulties, including player injuries, close losses, disciplinary problems, harmful transfers, difficult player attitudes, and outside criticism. By understanding that adversity does indeed visit every team, coaches should experience less frustration with the problems that strike their team. Players clearly sense when coaches think injuries or problems are serious. By staying focused on the task at hand and moving past the emotions that come with problem situations, a coach can help his team do the same.

Adversity must be expected and overcome. Many outstanding coaches have a policy of never using personnel losses as an excuse for losing, no matter how significant those personnel losses are. This mentality may reduce public sympathy, but it also sends a message to team members that the coach fully expects competitiveness from each and every player in the program.

12

Concentration

With his team trailing 73-71 and only 19 seconds remaining in the 1993 NCAA championship game, Michigan's Chris Webber rebounded a missed North Carolina free-throw attempt. As the other players ran downcourt, Webber pivoted and appeared to travel before dribbling up the sideline while being hounded by UNC's Derrick Phelps and George Lynch. Finally forced to pick up his dribble—and with precious seconds ticking off the clock—Webber signaled for a time-out. The only problem was, Michigan had no time-outs left. The Tar Heels' Donald Williams sank both technical free throws, clinching the game and the NCAA title for Dean Smith's squad.

How does one explain a mistake like this by a consensus All-American player? Webber's coach, Steve Fisher, didn't seem to know: "How did it happen? Sometimes you get in the heat of the moment and things happen that you just say, 'It can't happen.'"

To many observers, Webber's faux pas was simply a case of a player choking under pressure. A more analytical and useful way to view the incident is as a lapse in concentration.

ATTENTION CONTROL AND CONCENTRATION

In this chapter I'll strive to keep your attention, but that's getting to be more and more difficult these days. Although players and coaches have always faced distractions, the distractions have never been so intrusive or abundant as they are in today's age of technology, information, and media saturation. Disruption and prevention of creative thought, strategic planning, mental and physical task performance, and reflective analysis have undermined the quality of play on the court as well as the sharpness of decision making on the sidelines.

Yet, it doesn't have to be that way. Players and coaches can still take control of what they choose to attend to and how intently they do so. They simply need to make concentration on the matters and tasks of basketball a bigger priority than other things vying for their attention.

If you've ever witnessed a child who is completely captivated by a novel item or toy, then you know that humans are wired with the capacity to concentrate. And, as with kids, that potential is maximized when focused on something specific that is intrinsically interesting to the person.

Most players and coaches love basketball and are willing to devote a great deal of time and effort to it. But that general attraction of interest must be sharpened and targeted in order to resist distractions and significantly improve performance.

No one in recent memory has demonstrated better concentration on the court than Tyler Hansbrough of the University of North Carolina. Although certainly a very talented and hardworking player, what sets Tyler apart from his opponents and teammates is his unwavering focus on the task at hand, along with the energy that he directs fully to that task. As a coach, I think it is great for basketball that the 2007 to 2008 Division I Player of the Year is such a superb model of concentration—something sorely lacking at the college and high school levels today. The following sections describe some attributes and disciplines that can help players increase their ability to concentrate.

One reason Steve Smith, one of La Salle's greatest all-time players, was so effective was his ability to focus and not get rattled, no matter what type of pressure applied by an opponent.

© Greg Carroccio/Sideline Photos

High Motivation

Bob McEwan is a very successful business person who started his own construction company over 20 years ago. Over those years, every time he was asked, "How are you doing?" he would reply, "Diligently pursuing my goals!"

This idea of "diligently pursuing my goals" is a mantra for him, something that he focuses on every day. His goals are business success and long-term financial security for his family. As a result, he has daily focus on all aspects of his business, and he performs at a high level. He makes good decisions, works hard and fast, builds honest and strong relationships with employees and customers, and produces high-quality products. In addition, he is constantly finding new opportunities for growth, and he is always looking to learn.

The basketball player who is highly motivated also diligently pursues his goals daily. He has daily workout goals, consistently evaluates his strengths and weaknesses, always seeks out competition, and takes great pride in his performance. He wants to win, and he seeks to learn from coaches. This is a focused basketball player. Less motivated players rarely have this daily focus.

Positive Character

Chapter 6 discussed being a responsible student and person off the court. When school and life are going well for a player, it is easy for that player to focus when on the court. When school and life are troublesome, those troubles will often come onto the court with the player. This player is distracted by his problems, and he plays with poor reactions and drained energy levels. Players who are committed to academics and positive choices in life will have far fewer negative distractions to bring with them to the court. These players will have a better quality of life. A commitment to becoming an outstanding basketball player requires several hours per day. How a player spends the rest of his day will affect him as a person, and it will influence his ability to totally focus on basketball for those several hours each day.

Sometimes difficulties in life cannot be avoided. All coaches have had young players who have experienced a personal or family tragedy. These life events are more important than basketball. Once the player is able to resume play after a personal tragedy, a sharp focus on the court can give the player a healthy, temporary break from life's difficulties. The emotional support of teammates and coaches can help a person through life's difficulties.

Successful Routines

Regular routines for practice and game preparation give players a consistent way to focus attention. In short, a coach should try to create a predictable, controlled environment that eliminates as many distractions as possible. On game days, most college teams have consistent wake-up times, meal times, menus, practice times, departure times, arrival times at the game site, meeting times, and warm-up times. Most teams conduct all these functions in a consistent way game to game.

Many people ask how to prepare for "big" games. Coach Lou Henson led the University of Illinois to the 1989 Final Four. He was a coach who knew the importance of routine. Coach Henson prepared for the NCAA tournament and the Final Four the same way he prepared for the first game of the season and every other game. Consistency in preparation leads to consistency in focus. Every game is considered a big game. This philosophy has led to regular-season and postseason success for many teams.

Of course, the coach cannot script everything a player does leading up to a game. Therefore, young players need to develop their own pregame routine beginning the night before the game. Times to sleep, eat, relax, attend classes, leave for the game, and arrive for the game should be part of a plan to be fully focused. Choices of music, food, and dress should be consistent to eliminate trivial decisions, which will help focus attention on resting and on mental preparation. A player needs to find out what works best and then be consistent in his preparation.

A common concern is that a team will have letdowns against lesser opponents and put too much focus on stronger opponents. This is a natural problem. A very effective team strategy is to have one all-important goal during the season—to play well and win the next game. A complete focus on the next opponent, regardless of who that opponent is, maximizes performance and is the key to the process of building a successful season game by game.

Having a team mission (see chapter 2) to motivate players throughout the year is very important. However, during the season, a simple focus on the next opponent is key to reaching any team's ultimate mission. No opponent should be overlooked, because every poor loss during a season neutralizes every great win. Great players are highly motivated regardless of the opponent. They are always focused and consistent. They have a maturity that enables them to take every game seriously. The way to build a successful season is to respect each opponent, focus, and try to win the next game. In the locker room immediately following a game—win or lose—many successful coaches close with a brief discussion of the next opponent. This starts to create a new focus on the next challenge.

Early Preparation

Players who rush into practice at the last moment tend to begin practice unfocused. As a result, they play poorly. They are often just leaving friends, schoolwork, or problems behind and are not focused on basketball. Part of a practice routine should be to arrive in adequate time to change, tape, warm up, and do extra individual work without rushing. This will enable the player to be relaxed and to prepare physically and mentally to play well. Late players are not focused on playing well. Their focus is on whatever they just finished doing—and on not getting in trouble for being late.

Positive Self-Talk

As discussed in chapter 11, a positive self-statement can be used to help a player's confidence. This type of statement can also enhance mental preparation and concentration. The player should write out a vivid description of the ideal way for him to play. Here's an example: "I am a strong guard. Nobody takes the ball from me. I attack pressure and go by anyone who tries to get in my face. I always hit my teammates whenever they are open. I get them easy shots. I am unselfish, and I am a good teammate. When I am open, I stroke the ball into the basket. My shot feels good and has good arc, rotation, and follow-through. Every shot feels like it is going in. On defense, my man never gets by me, and I have a hand in his face on every shot he takes. When he is away from the ball, I am always ready to help my teammates. I take a lot of charges."

A self-statement such as this can be regularly changed and can be used with imagery. As a player reads his statement, he can stop and use imagery to see himself making the plays described. This form of mental preparation is short, but it is also an effective way to make a transition from thinking about daily events (classes, friends, problems) to starting to focus on basketball performance. This self-statement can be taped onto the player's locker and can be required prepractice reading.

Routines in Games

Many different routines can be used in games to help create proper focus. These could include always sprinting on and off the court (for time-outs, substitutions, halftime), slapping the floor to get into a defensive stance, using a consistent free-throw routine, and using positive self-talk. For example, a consistent free-throw routine is critical to eliminate distractions. Focusing on the routine (e.g., number of dribbles, the same positive thought, or a deep breath) takes the focus off the score or a taunting crowd. Every excellent free-throw shooter has a consistent routine to focus on and never lets distractions in.

Self-talk can also be shortened to simple cue words: "be a stopper," "animal rebounder," "see everything," or "hit open people." Cue words such as "move on" or "next play" can also be used as an aid in concentration after mistakes (see chapter 11). Once again, the key is consistency. A player should consistently use the same positive words and actions to eliminate distractions.

Certain pregame and in-game rituals can help players focus their minds on the mission and reconfirm their identity as part of the team.

TYPES OF FOCUS

In football, the quarterback must have a very broad field of focus. The quarterback must see all of the receivers, the defensive backs, and the rushers before making a decision about when and where to throw the ball. Defensive linemen must have a narrow focus to attack the ball; offensive linemen must also have a narrow focus to block a specific person. In football, different positions require different types of concentration.

In basketball, different skills require different types of attention. Passing, ballhandling, and off-the-ball defense require very broad concentration. This is the ability to see the whole court or all players at the same time. Shooting, rebounding, and on-the-ball defense require a very narrow focus on the middle of the basket (shooting), the ball itself (rebounding), or the person being guarded (on-the-ball defense). The ability to shift focus from broad to narrow is critical to becoming a good player.

Some highly motivated, intense players are poor passers under pressure. The reason is that high emotional arousal (i.e., being "pumped up") creates a sharp, narrow focus. This is why the defensive football player can get emotional and charged up to attack the ball, but the quarterback must stay relaxed to help him see the whole field. Thus, the basketball player with the ball must be relaxed to see the whole court. The player who plays very hard must learn to relax with the ball.

Players can learn how to relax and have a broad field of concentration in highly stressful basketball situations. One helpful drill begins with an offensive player having the ball and closing his eyes. Two defenders then go to the player with the ball, ready to trap him as soon as he opens his eyes. The other offensive players are in the proper spots for a press attack. Simple math indicates that there are only three defenders left guarding the four other offensive players. Someone must be open. The three defenders can go wherever they wish. When the ball handler opens his eyes, he must immediately see the whole court and find the open man before being trapped. This is a critical basketball skill requiring a broad field of vision. This drill teaches the right type of concentration for this skill.

Another simple exercise can help players learn to shift their focus. This exercise is done as follows: Start by picking a very small point in a room to focus on (e.g., a thumbtack, a spot on the wall). Stare at that object without blinking. Notice every detail about it. Strain to keep the focus totally on the small object, not seeing anything else. Now take a deep breath, relax, and without moving the head or eyes, widen the focus. Peripherally, see everything in the room. Note every object visible in the room with a broad focus (i.e., using peripheral vision). Then repeat the process of straining to stare at a specific point and then relaxing to see the whole room. By doing this exercise, a player is learning to change focus, as must be done during a basketball game.

The opposite scenario is another common problem for certain players. Instead of having a difficult time relaxing with the ball and seeing the whole floor, some players have a problem getting highly intense to focus on the ball and aggressively attack rebounds. Loose balls also require great intensity and an aggressive focus. Great players such as Jason Kidd and Lebron James are great passers (mentally relaxed, broad focus) *and* great rebounders (mentally intense, narrow focus). Great players must be able to continually change their focus.

One key to being a great rebounder, especially on the offensive end, is to focus on the flight of the shot and to be able to anticipate where the ball is going to hit the rim and bounce to. Players can practice this form of narrow focus in shooting drills. The rebounders in shooting drills should focus on not letting a rebound hit the floor. This is easy when missed shots fall to the rebounder's area. However, long rebounds or short shots hitting the front of the rim require great quickness to the ball. Anyone can get a rebound in his area, but great rebounders are quick to get the ball no matter where it goes. This requires a sharp focus on the flight of the ball and the direction of the rebound. Over time, a player learns to anticipate where the ball is going and develops the habit of pursuing it with great quickness and ferocity. This is another example of matching the right type of concentration with a specific skill.

COMPOSURE

As we saw in the Chris Webber example, concentration and composure often go hand in hand. The mind and body are closely connected and constantly interacting. If a player concentrates on negative or worrisome thoughts, the muscles become tight, and focus becomes more narrow and more inward on personal concerns. If a player is focused on inward thoughts and not on the game itself, the body is not prepared to react with quickness or intensity. On the other hand, if a player is focused on the challenge at hand and on positive, confident thoughts, the player will be physically primed to quickly respond and to give great effort.

Low levels of arousal produce low levels of performance. For example, sleep and boredom reflect two extremely low levels of arousal. Clearly, no one can play outstanding, highly competitive basketball while bored or not focused. After a game, coaches and players are sometimes heard saying things such as, "We just weren't up for tonight's game," "We were not into it," "We had no emotion or energy," "We looked lethargic out there," or "We lacked intensity." These are examples of poor performance resulting from low arousal. Skills that suffer because of low arousal are those that require an intense effort and narrow focus, such as rebounding, individual defense, and transition.

Similarly, but on the opposite end of the continuum, very high levels of arousal will produce poor performance. Very high levels of arousal reflect an extremely excited state with high heart rate, muscular tension, rapid breathing, and heavy sweating. Imagine an elite boxer before a championship fight. The body is highly activated with sweat pouring off it, fast breathing, and constant movements (e.g., bouncing, punching, head movements). This is appropriate preparation for a sharp focus on an individual opponent and explosive, powerful movements, but not to play basketball.

In basketball, it is possible to be too psyched up. Overarousal tends to restrict a player's attentional field, which interferes with the broad focus needed to see the floor for passing and off-the-ball defense. It also creates too much tension in the muscles for smooth and quick ballhandling, shooting, and passing. So, yes, there is some validity to the following types of statements after a game: "We were too pumped up tonight," "We never relaxed," "We were too tight," "We rushed everything," or "We played too fast." All are examples of poor performance resulting from very high arousal.

According to what sport psychologists call the inverted-U hypothesis, moderate levels of arousal lead to the best performance (see figure 12.1). A moderate level of arousal could be described as excited but under control and not tense. It is a level of arousal greater than disinterest and boredom, but less than anxiety, tension, and hyperactivity. With moderate arousal, the athlete can be excited to give great effort and react quickly without

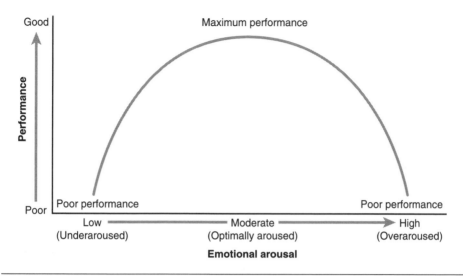

Figure 12.1 Inverted-U hypothesis: relationship between arousal and performance.

Reprinted, by permission, from J.M. Williams, D.M. Landers, and S.H. Boutcher, 1993, Arousal-performance relationships. In *Applied sport psychology: Personal growth to peak performance,* 2nd ed., edited by J.M. Williams (Palo Alto, CA: Mayfield Publishing), 170-184. Reproduced with permission of The McGraw Hill Companies.

excess tension; he can also easily shift focus from broad to narrow. Players and coaches may call this "the zone" or "in the flow." It is a state of peak performance that leads to quotes such as, "I was pumped up, but I was relaxed too," "Everything came together," "We played hard and smart tonight," and "We were totally prepared and totally focused."

Optimum Level of Arousal

Obviously, people have different personalities and preferences. Some people are highly energetic and perform their best when they are emotional and excited. They may still perform poorly because of arousal that is too low or too high, but this is compared to their usual level of arousal or what they are used to.

Some players, such as former Duke standout Steve Wojciechowski, play well with a high level of arousal. These tend to be excitable and emotional individuals who are used to operating at a highly stimulated state. Other athletes who are more relaxed, laid-back types tend to perform better at lower levels of arousal—although they too can suffer if they get too relaxed or too aroused.

Harold Katz, former owner of the Philadelphia 76ers, once admitted a mistake involving not drafting former North Carolina star Brad Daugherty. Daugherty was an All-American seven-foot center destined to be a high NBA draft choice, but some people, including Katz, believed Daugherty was too laid back in his demeanor. Without having known Daugherty or coached him, these people misunderstood a relaxed personality for lack of desire. Daugherty did not have to be highly aroused to give high effort and play well. Many teams, including the 76ers, passed on him on draft night. He ended up being an outstanding pro and played in three NBA all-star games.

Sam Perkins was another great North Carolina player known for performing well at lower arousal levels. Perkins was so laid back that at times he appeared sleepy. His nickname, "Big Smooth," fittingly described the seemingly effortless way in which he excelled at carrying out tasks requiring intensity, such as defense and rebounding. In fact, Perkins still holds the all-time records for blocked shots and rebounds at North Carolina. Sometimes coaches misread such players' demeanors. There is a big difference between lazy, underachieving players and highly productive players with quiet personalities.

The point is that players have different personalities; therefore, the ideal level of arousal is different for different people (see figure 12.2). The key is to find "the zone" of arousal where one plays best. To do this, players need to develop the psychological skill to control arousal. In addition, two simple guidelines can be used to help a player find his "zone." These guidelines are (1) to make practice more intense than games and (2) to control emotional displays.

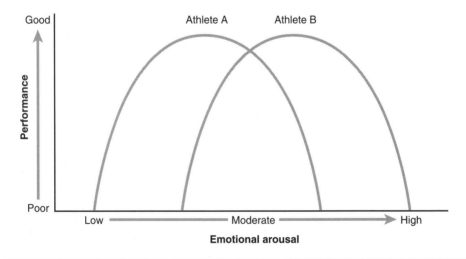

Figure 12.2 Inverted-U hypothesis: athlete-specific ideal arousal for performance.

Reprinted, by permission, from J.M. Williams, D.M. Landers, and S.H. Boutcher, 1993, Arousal-performance relationships. In *Applied sport psychology: Personal growth to peak performance,* 2nd ed., edited by J.M. Williams (Palo Alto, CA: Mayfield Publishing), 170-184. Reproduced with permission of The McGraw Hill Companies.

Practice Intensity

A player should not have to get "pumped up" to play a game. A player should play hard because he always plays hard. If the player always plays with maximum intensity, he will never be too low in arousal because he is aroused to play well every day. Being aroused to play hard is a daily habit which will carry over to games. This player will also never be too aroused or tense, because he only needs to play the way he does every day. He does not have to get pumped up or get "jacked" since playing hard is a normal thing.

"You play the way you practice" is a coaching cliche that has a lot of truth to it. In fact, many coaches pride themselves on making practice more demanding than games. When John Calipari led UMass to the 1996 Final Four, he noted that 40-minute games were easy for his team because the players were required to put forth maximum effort and concentration for 2 hours of scrimmage competition every day in practice.

Most great coaches and players work under much greater physical and mental demands in practice than they do in games. These practices are intense and critical. Coaches must prepare teams by being harder on them in practice than their competition will be in games. This is the most common way to prepare players to defeat talented, motivated, and dedicated opponents. Thus, players must strive to develop a daily work ethic for competitive excellence. This is accomplished by sticking to team commandments, rules, goals, and standards each and every day.

Trying to motivate others does not work as well as teaching others to work with winning habits. A player who tries to get motivated every day will often end up being too low on some days and too high on other days. A strong work ethic will lead to emotional consistency and regular high levels of effort. In other words, the player should try to find the "zone" every day—not too relaxed and not too tense.

Controlling Emotions

Although a strong work ethic will likely prevent the disinterest, boredom, and low arousal that leads to low performance, it does not guarantee that players will not get too aroused and excited on game night. Even though players with a strong work ethic always compete hard, they can get extra excited when playing in big games.

Under Coach John Chaney, Temple University was one of the most consistent teams in the country, because they played hard without getting too emotional. Some other teams believe in trying to get motivated by doing dances, chants, and chest bumps. Temple, on the other hand, always refrained from using emotion for spectacle or show. They emphasized using emotion only for playing hard.

Showing emotion does not score points or get rebounds. In fact, showing emotion often leads to more emotion. At that point, players and teams can get too pumped up, play too fast, make quick (and poor) decisions, or lose emotional control. A common mistake of younger, inexperienced players is to get carried away with emotion, displaying and expending emotion instead of saving it, controlling it, and using it to play harder. If a player is always displaying emotion, the player will find it difficult to

Upperclassmen Focus

Jamie Dixon—University of Pittsburgh

During the first two of the four years I served as associate head coach and recruiting coordinator for Ben Howland, we really struggled. Even though we thought we were getting it done and taking steps forward, something was holding us back. Then, that third season, we broke through and went to the Sweet 16 in the NCAA Tournament for three straight years.

Pitt basketball got to that next level because of a combination of things. One factor was that several freshmen and sophomores played a lot of minutes those first two years. And though they took some lumps, they also gained valuable experience and confidence that they could compete with anyone. They were able to grow from their trial by fire. Perhaps most important, they learned the high intensity required for competing at the major college level.

We also had some upperclassmen and a junior college transfer who stepped up. It was a good group, and it helped immensely to have a tremendous point guard in Brandin Knight. Brandin had struggled to become a leader in his freshman and sophomore years. But in his last two seasons as a Panther, his toughness, focus, competitiveness, and leadership elevated everyone's level of play.

Since then we have always had a leader or multiple leaders in our junior and senior classes who made a difference. Those upperclassmen served as models for younger players to emulate. They set and maintained a high standard of effort, dedication, and teamwork. They kept us centered on our objectives, refusing to be distracted or denied because of the strong sense of purpose with which they played.

Our upperclassmen take great pride in being leaders for their younger, less experienced teammates. It has become an important tradition in our program. Each year we have two or three seniors who pass along to the younger players the work ethic, mental toughness, discipline, and attitude it takes to be successful. Achieving the right balance among the four classes is a critical factor in ensuring that continuity.

It can be a challenge, however, when senior leaders go into a prolonged slump or suffer a significant injury that eliminates their on-court contributions. Just this past year, two of our most experienced players had to sit out the whole season with injuries. That meant we had to find other ways to stay on course.

Despite the personnel losses, we never considered putting things on cruise control. We have high expectations within our team and weren't about to let the injury setbacks derail our aspirations. Though we don't talk much about winning a national championship, we have very high aspirations and try to let our accomplishments speak for us. So with the setbacks to our seniors, we simply became more focused and worked even harder and smarter.

When people see our practices and are asked what's different or special about them, they usually say how intense, physical, and competitive the practices are. Everything we do in practice has a competitive component to it to maintain players' full attention and effort throughout the session. I believe that if kids are playing for something—they have something at stake pending the outcome—it increases their focus and intensity.

In terms of games, we consider every opponent equally important. We do the same amount of preparation for an exhibition game that we do for a Big East championship game. So our players know what they're going to face when they take the court, and they see that the coaching staff has the same enthusiasm and attention to detail for every game. That consistency is reassuring to players; it helps them find an effective comfort level and keeps them from panicking under pressure.

When we recruit, we seek the type of kids who have been in successful programs, played for championships, and delivered for their teams in stressful situations. Although high school and college competitions differ dramatically, the perception of pressure at both levels is similar, and it's better if they've experienced and conquered that before they arrive on campus. They're more likely to keep their poise when the heat is on. That's because almost every one of our games is a sellout. Our players have to be prepared mentally and emotionally, and not just for the crowd. In many cases our opponents look at us as their biggest opponent of the year, the one they'd like to beat the most because of what it would mean to their program.

So, every time out, players must be ready not just for a large and rowdy audience but also an extremely motivated opponent. They need to be consistent in their emotion and energy level for competition. It's fine if their passion is displayed physically, just so they don't overdo it. It shows that they care and have great enthusiasm for the game and being successful together. But they also know we won't accept individual demonstrations or heated exchanges with opponents that show disrespect for—and fire up—the team we're competing against.

Ideally, our players will perform with the perfect blend of high energy and full concentration. Often, it takes experience and maturity gained through a season or two before they exhibit both consistently. And that's one reason why having upperclassmen leadership on the team is a real plus.

control his emotion and use it to play better. Players must have a strong work ethic to prevent poor performance resulting from low arousal, and they must control emotions to prevent poor performance resulting from overexcitement.

INDIVIDUAL ATTENTIONAL DIFFERENCES

At Parkland Junior College in Champaign, Illinois, Coach Tom Cooper won the 1986 NCJAA Division II championship and had many other outstanding teams. Coach Cooper understood the need for every player to be mentally ready to play. However, he also knew that everyone was different. Some players found their "zone" by getting pumped up, and others found their zone by relaxing. Thus, 10 minutes before the final pregame meeting with the team, Coach Cooper had the team split into two groups. Each group went to mentally prepare based on whether they required more arousal or more relaxation to play well. One group did progressive muscle relaxation according to the following steps:

1. Breathe in fully through the nose until the lungs are completely full.
2. Now hold the breath and tense the neck and shoulders as hard as possible (by shrugging the shoulders tightly).
3. After holding the tension, "let go." Exhale slowly through the lips. Let the tension out of the neck and shoulders.
4. Breathe comfortably. Let the neck and shoulders feel loose. Concentrate on the head, neck, and shoulders feeling heavy and loose.
5. Repeat steps 1 to 4, tensing and relaxing the arms.
6. Repeat steps 1 to 4, tensing and relaxing the legs.
7. Imagine successful plays using mental imagery.

The other group performed preparatory arousal exercises. They focused on a small point on the wall until their eyes seemed to burn. Then they closed their eyes and were led through aggressive imagery using aggressive language (e.g., "box out physically," "rip the rebound with animal force," "deny on defense like a crazed animal, all over your man," "post with force"). At times, relaxing music or high-energy music was also used with the groups. As a result, each player prepared according to what was best for him. Each player must find out how he can find his zone most easily.

Finally, relaxation, preparatory arousal, imagery, self-talk, and centering are all psychological techniques to help a player get in a personal zone that is not too high or too low in arousal. Those techniques can help, but a strong work ethic and a conscious effort to control and use emotion are first and foremost in building true composure.

INDEX

ABOUT THE AUTHOR

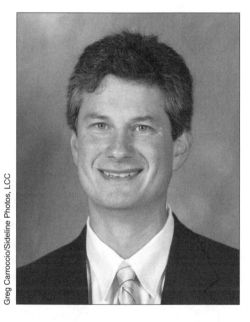

Greg Carroccio/Sideline Photos, LCC

John Giannini, PhD, is the head men's basketball coach at La Salle University, which competes at the Division I level in the Atlantic 10 Conference. He has led La Salle to its best Atlantic 10 record in school history. Giannini accepted the job at the Philadelphia-based school in 2004 after a successful eight-year stint at the University of Maine, where he became the winningest men's basketball coach in the school's history and turned the Black Bears into a perennial force in the America East Conference. Prior to that, Giannini amassed a remarkable 168-38 record in seven seasons as head coach at Rowan University. He also brought a Division III national championship to the Glassboro, New Jersey, school and was named Coach of the Year.

Giannini's collegiate basketball career began as a player at North Central College in Naperville, Illinois. He continued his education through graduate school and in 1992 earned a doctorate in kinesiology with a specialization in sport psychology from the University of Illinois at Urbana-Champaign. While at Illinois he served as a graduate assistant coach for two years, including the 1989 season when the Fighting Illini made it all the way to the Final Four.

Coach Giannini applies many innovative motivational, communication, and instructional techniques with his players. As a result, his teams have been known for their effort, teamwork, and attention to the fundamentals.

Giannini, his wife, Donna, and their two daughters reside in Mullica Hill, New Jersey.